D1490215

Web Development with TIBCO General Interface

Developer's Library

ESSENTIAL REFERENCES FOR PROGRAMMING PROFESSIONALS

Developer's Library books are designed to provide practicing programmers with unique, high-quality references and tutorials on the programming languages and technologies they use in their daily work.

All books in the *Developer's Library* are written by expert technology practitioners who are especially skilled at organizing and presenting information in a way that's useful for other programmers.

Key titles include some of the best, most widely acclaimed books within their topic areas:

PHP & MySQL Web Development
Luke Welling & Laura Thomson
ISBN 978-0-672-32916-6

Python Essential Reference
David Beazley
ISBN-13: 978-0-672-32862-6

MySQL
Paul DuBois
ISBN-13: 978-0-672-32938-8

Programming in Objective-C
Stephen G. Kochan
ISBN-13: 978-0-321-56615-7

Linux Kernel Development
Robert Love
ISBN-13: 978-0-672-32946-3

PostgreSQL
Korry Douglas
ISBN-13: 978-0-672-33015-5

Developer's Library books are available at most retail and online bookstores, as well as by subscription from Safari Books Online at **safari.informit.com**

**Developer's
Library**
informit.com/devlibrary

Web Development with TIBCO General Interface

Building AJAX Clients for Enterprise SOA

Anil Gurnani

✦✦Addison-Wesley

Upper Saddle River, NJ • Boston • Indianapolis • San Francisco
New York • Toronto • Montreal • London • Munich • Paris • Madrid
Cape Town • Sydney • Tokyo • Singapore • Mexico City

The publisher offers excellent discounts on this book when ordered in quantity for bulk purchases or special sales, which may include electronic versions and/or custom covers and content particular to your business, training goals, marketing focus, and branding interests. For more information, please contact:

U.S. Corporate and Government Sales
(800) 382-3419
corpsales@pearsontechgroup.com

For sales outside the United States please contact:
International Sales
international@pearson.com

Visit us on the Web: informit.com/aw

Library of Congress Cataloging-in-Publication Data:
Gurnani, Anil.

Web development with TIBCO General interface : building Ajax clients for enterprise SOA / Anil Gurnani.

p. cm.

Includes index.

ISBN-13: 978-0-321-56329-3 (pbk.)

ISBN-10: 0-321-56329-8 (pbk.)

1. Web services. 2. Ajax (Web site development technology) 3. Service-oriented architecture (Computer science) 4. Business[md]Computer networks. I. Title.

TK5105.8885.A52G87 2009

006.7'8—dc22

2008053100

Web Development with TIBCO General Interface

ISBN-13: 978-0-321-56329-3
ISBN-10: 0-321-56329-8

TIBCO, General Interface, and ActiveMatrix are either registered trademark or trademarks of TIBCO Software Inc. in the United States of America and/or other countries. Other product and company names mentioned herein may be the trademarks of their respective owners.

THIS PUBLICATION IS NOT ENDORSED OR SPONSORED BY TIBCO SOFTWARE INC.

Text printed in the United States on recycled paper at RR Donnelley, Crawfordsville, Indiana. First printing February 2009

Editor-in-Chief
Mark Taub

Acquisitions Editor
Trina MacDonald

Development Editor
Michael Thurston

Managing Editor
Patrick Kanouse

Senior Project Editor
Tonya Simpson

Copy Editor
Barbara Hacha

Indexer
Erika Millen

Proofreader
Paula Lowel

Publishing Coordinator
Olivia Basegio

Book Designer
Gary Adair

Compositor
Mark Shirar

❖

Dedicated to my family.

❖

Contents at a Glance

Table of Contents

Foreword by Michael Peachey

Building rich interactive web-based applications without proper tools is a daunting task. Web application developers face numerous challenges when building large, world-class client applications that run in the browser—including but not limited to a lack of standards around Internet browsers. For example, a piece of JavaScript code that works well in Internet Explorer may not work at all in Mozilla Firefox or on Safari. Additionally, while good tools existed for easing the burden of building web pages, there were no similar tools for web applications. There were no web equivalents for the standard UI controls or widgets found in software design—objects such as dialog boxes, tables and grids, tabbed panes, etc. had to be designed and built by hand as one-off implementations. There was no interactive visual environment to develop rich client interfaces using JavaScript. And to make matters worse, JavaScript interpreters were slow and caused performance issues with the current browsers.

In 2001, a small team of web developers and interaction designers set out to solve two challenges: first, to dramatically improve the level of interactivity available in web-based applications, and second, to dramatically reduce the effort required to build these applications.

I was part of the original team that developed TIBCO General Interface from a concept to a modern, feature-rich, rapid application development tool to build rich Internet applications that could be at least as good as, if not better than, their desktop counterparts. General Interface is a mature product, and over the years, we have packed a lot of features and functionality into the platform and the development tools. Even with the reference materials, online help, product manuals, developer guides, and the examples that ship with the product and are available in the online developer community, developers frequently come to me looking for the best way to get started.

Anil Gurnani's book greatly augments the available information for developers learning and using TIBCO's General Interface. If the product documentation is data, then the content of Anil's book is *information*. If the online developer community resources are knowledge, then the real-world, step-by-step examples in this book are true developer *power*. The chapters in this book will help you build powerful rich Internet applications using General Interface and show you how to integrate them with your backend infrastructure and services: databases, portals, JMS, and ESB. Anil has shared his real-life experiences in building complex systems with a web-based user interface, which make this book really valuable for anyone trying to build web-based applications with or even without a platform like General Interface.

It is refreshing to see that this book includes examples of using General Interface applications with TIBCO applications including TIBCO ActiveMatrix®, popular .NET technologies such as Microsoft SQL Server 2005, Visual Studio 2005, as well as Java/J2EE classics such as JBoss Portal, JMS (Apache ActiveMQ), and Eclipse platform.

I highly recommend this book to anyone who wants to fully leverage the power of General Interface to build enterprise-class applications that can challenge those built using other popular technologies such as Flex, Google Web Toolkit, WinForms, WebForms, Java Server Faces, Java Swing, and others.

Michael Peachey
Co-Founder of General Interface and Director of User Experience, TIBCO Software

Foreword by Luke Birdeau

When we first conceptualized TIBCO General Interface back in 2001, a critical piece of our strategy was to improve the user experience on the Web. We felt that if we could make the browser "smarter" we could use it to deliver desktop-like applications. Instead of treating a browser like a simple terminal, used only to render HTML, we felt it could truly become a platform, upon which one could build any range of application complexity.

But like all new technologies, adoption is key. It is true that most developers are interested in delivering a quality user experience, but it is neither the only nor the primary driver. In fact, the developer needs to understand how a prospective tool solves their real-world problems and what the total cost of ownership will be over the lifespan of the given application. In other words, what is the true cost of choosing this tool over another?

Ultimately we determined that a visual development environment was key to reducing the true cost of adoption and released our first version of the GI Builder development tool in 2002. Over time, in our quest to deliver more and more developer tools, we ultimately hit a wall of diminishing returns. For every new tool we provide, the choices increase, and the developer is potentially left more confused, not less.

What's needed in such situations is not just documentation, but relatable, concrete examples that cut through the myriad choices and present a clearer understanding of how a particular tool solves a problem. Anil's book delivers this by detailing very specific integration points between General Interface and various server-side technologies, including .NET and Java. Particular attention has been paid to those areas where the existing product documentation ends; namely, server- and implementation-specific details. If you are familiar with Java or .NET technologies and want to better understand how TIBCO General Interface fits into an overall solution, this book provides many relevant examples.

Luke Birdeau,
Sr. Architect, TIBCO Software, Inc

Acknowledgments

I would like to thank the entire team at Addison-Wesley for all the hard work they put into helping me with reviews and styling and numerous suggestions for improvements. I am sure I could never have done it without their help.

I also want to thank the TIBCO General Interface engineering teams who took the time to provide excellent reviews and corrections despite their extremely busy schedules at work. They have created an excellent tool for building the new wave of web-based applications.

I also want to thank my family for being very supportive throughout the effort and missing out on family outings so I could stay home to work on the book. Special thanks to my good friend Bob Lyons, who taught me a lot about XML and XSLT and a host of other technologies and helped me with ideas and suggestions.

About the Author

Anil Gurnani has written extensively for prestigious computer magazines and online forums on various topics including web development, enterprise portals, building financial systems with J2EE, Allaire ColdFusion, payment systems using CyberCash, multiprocessing technology, and artifical intelligence. He has more than 20 years of experience in the area of software development and has been working with web technologies for many years. Anil runs his enterprise software company CNI Systems (http://www.cnisystems.com), and is also an adjunct at New York University, where he teaches advanced courses focused on web and enterprise technologies including Core Java, JEE, and .NET.

Anil is an expert at managing large, global, multifunctional teams to architect and build complex distributed systems with a portfolio of front-end applications and back-end services. He recently built a complex system for managing trades and settlement exceptions using TIBCO General Interface, Java Portal, and Web Services technologies for a major global bank. This application is one of the most successful implementations of TIBCO General Interface in the enterprise.

Introduction

The primary focus of this book is an award-winning product—TIBCO General Interface. Because TIBCO provides excellent documents and tutorials on building client applications using TIBCO General Interface, much of this book focuses on how to integrate those client applications to various back-end technologies. The first part of the book discusses the basics of building General Interface clients. The second part dives into specific back-end technologies and provides complete end-to-end examples with each major server-side technology. For example, Chapter 12, "Integrating with Messaging Systems," includes complete details about how to set up a message queue, send messages to it, and build a simple middle-tier application using the CometProcessor interface that receives messages. It also includes how to use TIBCO General Interface to build an AJAX client that receives those messages asynchronously and displays them in the browser. The third part discusses advanced topics such as optimizing performance of General Interface–based client applications.

This introduction provides an overview of tools and technologies available today to build browser-based client-side applications. Then it takes a closer look at TIBCO General Interface and discusses its unique advantages. Finally, it provides a list of all the sample applications that are included in this book and on the companion CD-ROM.

The Web 2.0 Wave

The Internet has changed much more than the way business was done. It changed the way we live. The World Wide Web was a major 10X force for many businesses in the early to middle '90s. Business and technology changed very rapidly. Many brick-and-mortar businesses could not survive the tsunami of the Internet wave and were replaced by Internet-based businesses. Traditional technology giants like Microsoft were threatened by new entrants like Netscape. Internet startups were springing up everywhere like weeds. New standards and technologies evolved that dramatically changed the application development landscape from client-server tools like PowerBuilder to web-building tools like Dreamweaver and FrontPage.

New standards are evolving yet again to redefine the World Wide Web. Web 2.0 has taken shape as the next tsunami to hit the Internet world. This one is many times the size of the first wave. The power of the individual is recognized everywhere now. Time magazine's 2006 person of the year was "you." Whereas the traditional media model was one to many—for example, newspapers, television, and radio—Web 2.0 offers many-to-many communication with blogs and Wikis that allow anyone anywhere to reach out to a number of people. Sites like YouTube, MySpace, Facebook, and Digg have become the favorite destinations of many. People are now connected even more by instant messaging, live meetings, and desktop sharing.

The music and publishing industries have also been transformed. Napster introduced the concept of Peer to Peer (P2P) computing and threatened to take the power from big record companies. Music albums and songs are released for digital downloads now instead of being sold in stores. Sales of digital books have been rising, and sites such as Safari Digital Bookshelf (www.safaribooksonline.com/) are giving readers an alternative to printed books. Modern eBook readers are introducing a new concept in how books and the news are delivered and consumed.

Zoho, ThinkFree, and Google are threatening the software giant Microsoft's dominance in the office applications market by providing office tools online for little or no licensing cost. Software as a service has now become a reality. Most common software applications such as accounting, time management, project management, and many others are available online for anyone to use and pay per use.

Client-Side Technologies

Technologies such as AJAX, Flex, and web services are commonly used by developers to create Web 2.0 applications. New standards such as WSRP, Portlet (JSR 168), WS (Web Services), and JEE5 are again changing the application development landscape. Applications or services that are built using these standards can collaborate much more effectively and easily.

Rich Internet applications use the Internet as the platform and are capable of running inside any browser, regardless of what machine or platform it is running on. TIBCO General Interface helps build such rich Internet applications for Web 2.0, and it does so remarkably well. Its unique model and approach to design gives it an enormous performance edge that is hard to beat today and will continue to remain difficult to surpass.

AJAX is the underlying technology for several new frameworks that have appeared in the marketplace. Simply put, AJAX is no different from an HTTP request from the browser to the web server, except that in reply to an AJAX call, a server does not have to return the complete HTML for the entire browser page. Instead, response to an AJAX call can be a fragment of HTML or merely data that the caller can then embed into the browser page. JavaScript code embedded in an HTML page can make an AJAX call and can update a small part of the browser window from the response. A typical application for this type of AJAX call is a table displaying the stock price of several securities at once, which is updated automatically in place as the price changes.

Although it is possible to build such user interfaces by making individual AJAX calls, it can be very time consuming, and the resulting code can become quite difficult to maintain. Several frameworks based on AJAX have evolved in the past several years to address this issue. Following is not a comprehensive but a brief overview of some tools and technologies similar to TIBCO General Interface and how their targets and uses differ from those of TIBCO General Interface.

Google Web Toolkit

Google Web Toolkit (GWT) (http://code.google.com/webtoolkit/) is a framework that allows developers to write GUI code in Java and then use a compiler to convert their Java code into JavaScript code that runs in the browser. It comes as a set of Java libraries with some ready-to-use widgets that can be used to build GUI applications in Java. GWT allows developers to build AJAX applications using Java with embedded JavaScript code in some cases.

GWT is in the open-source domain, available with source code under the Apache 2.0 license. Google uses it on its own website in its popular email web interface of Gmail and other Google websites such as Google Docs.

Using GWT, developers can write Serializable Java objects to communicate with server-side Java components. These Serializable classes are converted appropriately to communicate with the server-side components using AJAX calls. GWT is a great tool for server-side web developers who are comfortable with Java IDEs like Eclipse, NetBeans, or IDEA, or any other Java development IDE. However, it has little to offer a front-end developer who is very adept at JavaScript and knows CSS and browser DOM very well.

Google Mail and Google Maps are both built using GWT and are excellent examples of AJAX-enabled web applications. Because of the Java backbone, GWT supports a number of features, including the capability to do debugging in the IDE, integration with JUnit for unit testing, internationalization, and others. JavaScript as a language is not 100% compatible across all browsers; therefore, a developer must include code to detect the type of browser and the appropriate code for each. However, GWT compiler generates browser-agnostic JavaScript; therefore, code that is generated by GWT compiler works in all major browsers, including IE, Firefox, Mozilla, Safari, and Opera, without any special effort on the part of the developer.

A GWT developer must be thoroughly familiar with the Java programming model, as well as know enough JavaScript and CSS to be able to embed them directly as needed. It supports an event model that is similar to that of Java Swing. On the client side, GWT relies solely on JavaScript for both rendering as well as for performing AJAX interactions with the back end.

A JRE Emulation library includes a number of Java classes that can be converted by GWT into JavaScript to run in the browser. It includes JavaScript Native Interface (JSNI), which allows developers to embed handwritten JavaScript code in the Java code to access browser functionality. It also includes integration with JUnit with a base test class `GWTTestCase`, which can be used to build unit tests automated regression testing.

Also included in GWT is a mechanism to pass Java objects to and from server-side components over HTTP using AJAX calls—known as Remote Procedure Calls—which is implemented as a collection of Java interfaces and classes. Developers can use it in the GUI code to communicate with the back-end server-side components as needed. TIBCO General Interface, on the other hand, allows developers to directly consume the output of a web services call, pass it through an XSLT style sheet, and display it in a Grid

Control on the web page. TIBCO General Interface programs are built using the technologies that web developers are already very familiar with: JavaScript, XML/XSL, CSS, and DHTML. This makes it easy for web GUI developers to learn and use General Interface.

Adobe Flex

Adobe's Flash player is the most popular browser plug-in available for most browsers on most platforms. It is almost an integral part of all web browsers and has an installed base that is almost equal to that of Internet browsers. Initial versions of Flash used a downloadable file that could be played back similar to media files like audio or video. Adobe has since extended that model to include streaming media and a number of controls and widgets that can be used to program dynamic web applications with a rich user experience. Although the primary target of Adobe Flex is media-rich applications such as games and videos, it is possible to build applications using the Adobe Flex framework that run inside the browser using the Flash player software.

The latest version of Flex is Flex 2, which is available from Adobe to build applications for Flash. Adobe's model allows users of Flash Player software to download it for free; however, technologies and tools required to "build" on that platform are not free.

Adobe's Flex technology includes a Flex Builder, which is based on the popular Java IDE Eclipse. If you already use Eclipse, Adobe provides a plug-in that can be downloaded and installed to use with Eclipse. To build applications, developers use the IDE to create a Macromedia XML (MXML) file that defines the screen canvas and the controls and widgets in it. The MXML format is XML constrained by tags defined by Adobe. Because Flex was originally developed by Macromedia, hence the name—MXML.

Component gallery in Flex 2 Builder includes a number of ready-to-use controls and components such as widgets. Visual components like Button, CheckBox, ComboBox, DataGrid, DateChooser, and others can be combined with Navigators like Accordion, Menubar, and TabBar in layouts including Panel. Tiles can be dragged and dropped onto the Canvas to build the GUI for the application. Flex 2 also includes various Chart components to create charts for the web.

Flex 2 Builder supports "source code" and "design view" similar to tools like Dreamweaver. In the source code view, developers can manually insert components by typing the corresponding MXML tags that define the controls. In the design view, developers are able to drag and drop components onto the canvas and set the appropriate properties in the Property Sheets on the right. Program coding is done in Macromedia's Action Script files, which can contain logic to update screen components. To prepare the application to run in the browser, you must "build" it into a "swf" file, which is Adobe's proprietary format for files that are run by the Flash player plug-in in the browser.

Although Adobe Flex follows a very similar concept as TIBCO General Interface, its primary target is media-rich applications that require animation and need to have embedded movies or video content in them. Running a TIBCO General Interface does not require any plug-in software, whereas Flex applications will not run without the Flash plug-in.

Dojo

Dojo is an open source framework. Its design is very similar to that of TIBCO General Interface. It comprises classes and programs written completely in JavaScript.

Dojo's widget library, Dijit, is the collection of GUI controls including accordions, combo boxes, date picker, and more. These controls are template driven and highly extensible so that developers can build their own widgets using Dojo. DojoX extends this widget library further and adds Grid and Chart components to the Dojo Framework.

JavaScript code in Dojo uses a prototype model of JavaScript to provide an object-oriented foundation to build other JavaScript code. Similar to General Interface, all JavaScript for Dojo applications is written manually in JavaScript using a library of numerous built-in JavaScript functions and modules. However, Dojo lacks a design-time builder tool like GI Builder, and it does not make heavy use of XML/XSL like General Interface does.

Dojo is available under the Academic Free License, which is extremely liberal and allows commercial distribution and sublicensing of the software for works derived from Dojo. Dojo can also be used under the BSD License, which is also quite liberal and does not impose any restrictions on use and distribution of the software. Dojo's intellectual property rights are owned by Dojo Foundation, which is a nonprofit organization created to distribute the Dojo code in a vendor-neutral way.

Direct Web Remoting

Direct Web Remoting (DWR) provides the basic interfaces and mechanisms for communicating using HTTP from JavaScript directly to the back-end classes written in Java. It's a small framework that consists of a Java Servlet that runs on the server under any Servlet container such as Tomcat or WebLogic and a set of JavaScript functions that are used to make calls to Java Objects on the server using AJAX. DWR handles the marshaling of the parameters and return values back to JavaScript callers. It is available under Apache Software License.

DWR complements TIBCO General Interface very nicely and provides a framework for TIBCO General Interface classes and widgets to make direct calls to custom Java components on the server side. General Interface provides the framework and base classes, and DWR provides the marshaling and unmarshaling to make it easy to develop applications that need to communicate back and forth between browser and server. This can enhance the already rich library of GUI widgets that TIBCO General Interface has.

Backbase

Backbase Enterprise AJAX is the closest to TIBCO General Interface in design and concept. It includes more than 200 ready-to-use widgets that use AJAX and can be used in web applications. Backbase developers build application code in JavaScript and can use XML APIs as well as JavaScript utility functions provided by Backbase libraries.

Development tools for Backbase are based on Eclipse and offer many capabilities similar to those offered by TIBCO General Interface. It includes a JavaScript-based runtime component that runs in the browser similar to the one included with TIBCO General Interface. It includes a set of foundation classes in JavaScript and a layer of abstraction that is also similar to the JavaScript APIs offered by TIBCO General Interface. Backbase's UI Management layer includes various services such as Visualization Services (animation, themes, skins), Data Services (Formatting, Validation, Transformation), Communication Services (XML, JSON, SOAP, Portal), and others. At the top of these layers is a collection of widgets and the capability to create custom widgets.

Backbase provides early access to a custom Integrated Development Environment (IDE) similar to TIBCO GI Builder for building Enterprise AJAX applications using Backbase.

Laszlo

Laszlo is a relatively new entrant in the market of rich Internet application tools compared to the others listed previously. OpenLaszlo 4 was released in 2006 as an abstraction layer over multiple runtime formats. Applications created with OpenLaszlo 4 can be translated into Flash or into DHTML (mostly a combination of JavaScript, CSS, and HTML) so they can run in any browser with or without the Flash plug-in. OpenLaszlo is also an open source project with the ambitious goal of providing translations into many target platforms, including Flash 9, Java ME, Firefox, and other browsers. Laszlo distribution includes J2EE Servlets that serve as the back end for OpenLaszlo front-end JavaScript code. Its client-side components, built with OpenLaszlo, communicate with its back end server-side components, which in turn execute custom Java components in an architecture that is very similar to that of DWR, or Direct Web Remoting.

OpenLaszlo does not include a visual IDE to build applications. Developers must build applications by coding the `main.lzx` file with XML syntax to include components that are predefined by the OpenLaszlo framework. The server component then interacts with the user and supplies the appropriate runtime to the user depending on the client browser.

Miscellaneous Toolkits

Proliferation of AJAX frameworks and toolkits in the last few years points to the importance of AJAX technology in shaping the future of the Web. Among other similar frameworks are

- **Atlas**—A free framework for building AJAX-enabled .NET applications
- **Prototype**—A framework for building object-oriented JavaScript code that includes a library of AJAX and other JavaScript functions that can be used in web applications
- **CGI::Ajax**—A Perl module that can be used to generate JavaScript to call a CGI written in Perl

- **ZK**—A collection of widgets that can work with a variety of back-end technologies including Java and Ruby
- **AjaxAC**—A framework written in PHP to create AJAX-enabled web applications

There are many more. TIBCO's General Interface is one of the earliest entrants in the AJAX world since 2001. Backbase started in 2003, and most others started afterward. The rest of this book is focused on TIBCO General Interface.

Overview of Sample Applications

This book explores various features and aspects of TIBCO General Interface and provides examples of how to build fully integrated rich Internet applications using TIBCO General Interface tools. Following is an overview of the sample applications that are available on the companion CD-ROM and are discussed in the following chapters:

Chapter 3:

dow30 client application: A simple General Interface application that displays the 30 component stocks of the Dow Jones Index.

dow30 war file project: A complete project for deploying General Interface applications under Tomcat.

Chapter 4:

dow30 client application: The dow30 application from Chapter 3 built using XML Mapping Utility.

dow30 client application: The dow30 application from Chapter 3 built using XML Transformers.

Chapter 5:

GI Component Gallery: Simple General Interface application showing built-in General Interface components and widgets.

GI Menus and Toolbars: Simple General Interface application to demonstrate menus and toolbars and other useful General Interface elements.

Chapter 6:

Online Banking example: A simple General Interface application showing menus and some sample content for a retail banking application.

Online Investing example: A simple General Interface application showing menus and some sample content for a retail online investment management site.

Chapter 7:

Multi Select Menu example: A simple General Interface application using a custom menu component. The application also demonstrates the powerful event mechanism available with General Interface.

Chapter 8:

Oilconsumption example: A General Interface application that shows world oil consumption for the past several decades. This application demonstrates the use of value templates to control the styles in the Matrix component in General Interface.

Watchlist example: A General Interface application that demonstrates how to dynamically update the contents of a Matrix cell in General Interface.

Chapter 9:

MiTunes Service in .NET: A .NET web service built in Visual Studio 2005 that returns a list of songs.

MiTunes Service in Java: A Java web service built using Apache Axis 2 that returns a list of songs.

MiTunes client application in General Interface: A General Interface application that communicates with the web service to retrieve and display a list of songs.

Chapter 10:

GI Portlets Page: A JBoss portal application consisting of two JSR 168 portlets, each of which has a General Interface application embedded in it, and both portlets are embedded into a single Portal page.

Chapter 11:

GISQL in .NET: A .NET database application that returns Customer Orders and Order Details from the Adventure Works database on SQL Server 2005.

GISQL in Java: A Java database application that returns Customer Orders and Order Details from the Adventure Works database on SQL Server 2005.

Master Detail example: A complete application including General Interface and the Java components to display orders and details from the Adventure Works database using SQL Server 2005.

Paginated Grid example: A complete application that uses server-side pagination to display a list of Customers from the Adventure Works database.

Chapter 12:

JMS Publish and Subscribe example: A General Interface application that communicates with middle-tier components to publish JMS messages and displays messages received via JMS Topic.

Rolling Grid example: A General Interface application that uses CometProcessor to asynchronously receive data and display it in a scrolling grid.

Chapter 13:

Active Matrix Booklist service example: An Active Matrix service to get a list of books.

Active Matrix client in General Interface: A General Interface client application that displays the list of books returned from the Active Matrix service.

Chapter 14:

StockPrice example web application: A complete web application that uses General Interface to display Charts of stock prices.

Chapter 15:

StockPrice example web application: A General Interface Application with four parts—one publishes stock prices, and the other three components display the prices using different views and communicate using TIBCO PageBus.

Chapter 16:

StockPrice sample application: General Interface Application from Chapter 15 modified to load components asynchronously.

StockPrice sample application: General Interface Application from Chapter 15 modified to demonstrate instrumentation and optimization in General Interface applications.

1

What Is TIBCO General Interface?

This chapter provides an introduction to the vast set of tools and technologies of TIBCO General Interface and provides an overview of the architecture of TIBCO General Interface applications.

TIBCO General Interface is a collection of tools and more than 100 ready-to-use widgets and controls you can use to create interactive applications that use the Internet browser as the platform. It includes an Integrated Development Environment (IDE) similar to Microsoft Visual Studio (or Eclipse), which you can use to design and create rich Internet applications. There is a collection of JavaScript Framework classes developed using a pattern similar to the Prototype framework. TIBCO General Interface framework features many utility classes similar to the ones available in Java. API documentation included with the product is in a similar format as Java API documentation. JavaScript code for General Interface applications follows the principles of object-oriented development. Figure 1.1 shows typical high-level interaction between a General Interface application and web services and other server-side applications.

TIBCO General Interface applications can be deployed to any back-end server, including simple web servers such as Apache or IIS. The GI Builder tool includes a utility that you can use to create an HTML file that can bootstrap the full General Interface application. When users type the URL of the HTML page containing the General Interface application in the browser, General Interface's application loader is first delivered to the client browser, which in turn begins to load the application canvas and other components as needed. General Interface applications can directly communicate with a web service and consume XML that is returned and then renders HTML elements such as lists, grids, and trees based on the response.

TIBCO General Interface is available as open source with a BSD license, which means it is free to use in your applications. Not only that, it is also free to distribute with your software applications, and you do not have to include any copyright when you include TIBCO General Interface in your application. You can download the latest version from www.tibco.com/devnet/gi/. The download package is a zip file that contains the GI

Builder tool and several utilities, as well as the JavaScript files that make up the components necessary to build and deploy TIBCO General Interface–based applications.

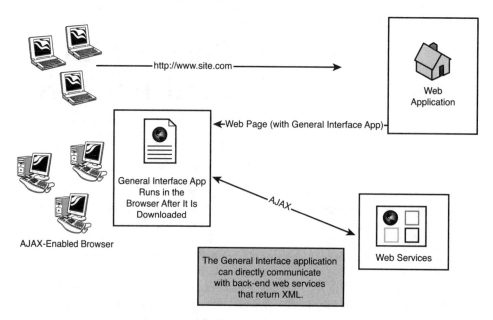

Figure 1.1   High-level interactions between General Interface application and web services and server-side applications.

Tools and Utilities

TIBCO includes several utilities and tools with TIBCO General Interface that can help in building complex applications for the browser. Following is a brief description of major tools and utilities included with TIBCO General Interface distribution (more detailed coverage of these tools is included later in this book):

- **GI Builder**—The fact that GI Builder is written using General Interface is a testament to the capabilities of the framework and is a great example of how General Interface can be used to build complex graphical user interfaces (GUIs). If you are a developer, you will find the GI Builder development environment very familiar and comfortable to work in. It is an IDE very similar to Microsoft Visual Studio, Eclipse, or NetBeans Studio, and it consists of panels and quadrants similar to those found in other IDEs.

- **JavaScript Debugger**—A built-in debugger that can be used to step through JavaScript code line by line is definitely a very useful tool that the JavaScript developer community has been requesting for many years now. Additionally, the framework API includes a function that may be called (conditionally or unconditionally) from any application code to enter the debugger.

- **JavaScript Test Utility**—A simple tool that helps quickly test any JavaScript code is included with General Interface as a development aid. JavaScript code can be typed in a pop-up window and executed by clicking a button to see the results visually.

- **Test Automation Kit**—Included with General Interface is an adaptation of the popular Selenium framework to build functional and regression tests for General Interface–based applications. Also included with the General Interface source code is a modified version of JsUnit (in test directory), which is very similar to the jUnit testing framework for Java language applications. When used together, these two frameworks can greatly simplify and speed up the task of testing TIBCO General Interface–based applications.

- **Color Picker tool**—A simple color picker is available on a menu in GI Builder. This is a very handy tool for converting colors to their RGB and hexadecimal values to be used in web development.

- **XML Mapping Utility**—Included with the GI Builder is a nifty tool that allows developers to create mappings from an XML file to the elements on an HTML page. This is a versatile tool that can accept URLs that return an XML file or the URL of a WSDL. The URL is called, and the resulting XML is available to be mapped to various elements of General Interface components.

- **Deployment Utility**—GI Builder includes a tool that can be used to package General Interface applications for deployment to a web server. Several modes are available for packaging. The application may be placed inside a `<div>` or `<span>` tag in an HTML page, or an HTML page may be created containing the application. The former is used to include a General Interface application in a small part of a larger HTML page with other elements on the page, and the latter is used when the entire page is the General Interface application.

- **XML/XSL Merge tool**—A simple tool is included that can be used to process XML/XSL merges as they will be performed. General Interface applications make heavy use of XSL style sheets, and this tool makes it very convenient to test them. If you are used to building your XSL style sheets in a Linux/UNIX environment, you might be familiar with the command `xsltproc`, which can be used to merge XML and XSL style sheets. The tool included with TIBCO General Interface is a visual tool that lets you do exactly that so you can view the results of the merge and debug your XSL style sheet.

- **General Interface Runtime Optimization tool**—TIBCO General Interface includes a tool to customize the deployment footprint of the resulting web application, depending on the components that are being used. Not all applications will use all the widgets/controls that are available in the library. TIBCO's tools make it possible to customize the files and widgets that are downloaded by the client in re-

sponse to their HTTP request for the application, resulting in faster download
times compared to other toolkits.

- **General Interface Performance Profiler**—A performance profiler is invaluable
  when trying to improve the performance of a web application. Users are ever more
  demanding and want better, faster applications. In a typical web application, hundreds (if not thousands) of lines of JavaScript code exist. It is very difficult to figure
  out what parts are taking a long time to execute and causing a less than optimal
  user experience. General Interface includes several useful tools to help in this regard. The debug build of TIBCO General Interface can detect and report multiple
  paints of the canvas in addition to displaying time taken to perform each major
  JavaScript function call. General Interface Performance Profiler, or GIPP, is an additional tool you can use to profile certain parts of the application that are slow to
  run or render and includes capabilities to log time spent in making and waiting for
  server-side calls to return.

Web Application Model

Web protocol (HTTP) is completely stateless. Each request for a page is considered a
"new" request with no relationship to the one the user made before from the same
browser. HTML also is a very flat and static model for presenting content. Some
JavaScript can be used to spruce up the presentation a little, but only to a limited extent.
Traditionally, the model for building web applications has been to have a server-side component generate the entire HTML and send it back to the browser. Figure 1.2 shows the
typical architecture for a server-side web application.

The user clicks a button or types in a URL in the browser's address bar, and the server
invokes a component (in a typical Model-View-Controller pattern this component
would be the controller) and passes it the input provided by the user. The controller may
then access some back-end service, such as a database, a messaging service, or a web service, and update the data object in memory that corresponds to the elements on the web
page (in MVC pattern, this would be the "model" component). This model then regener-
ates or updates the view component, which will send out new HTML to the browser.
Upon receiving the HTML, the browser renders it onscreen, and the user sees the updated content. Thus, for every user action, a round trip to the server is required. In the
traditional web application model, each call to the server returns a completely new
HTML document to be displayed on the web page, even if only a single cell in the grid
was changed.

AJAX makes it possible to use a more efficient model for web applications. TIBCO
General Interface supplies a controller and takes the view and model components over to
the client side, so now the model, view, and controller all are in the browser (backed by a
controller on the server side). Figure 1.3 shows how TIBCO General Interface enables
MVC on the client browser.

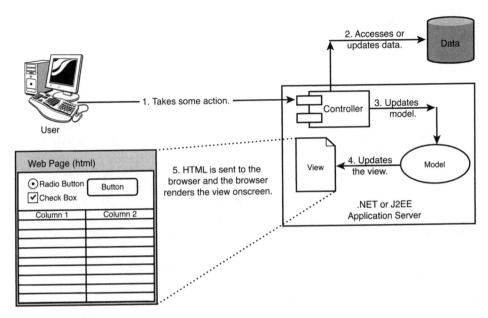

Figure 1.2   A typical server-side web application.

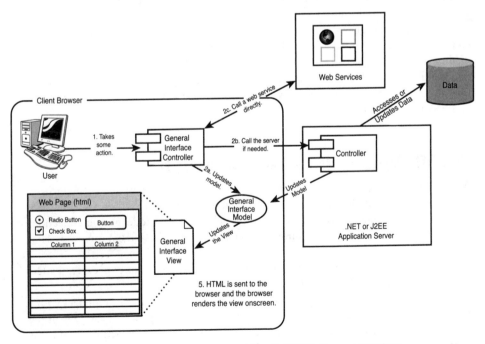

Figure 1.3   MVC on the client side with TIBCO General Interface.

With TIBCO General Interface, the user's actions are picked up by the controller running inside the user's browser. If the local controller can handle the event and update the model, it does so, which in turn updates the view. Only in cases where the controller needs to communicate with a back-end server, it makes an AJAX call to the server. The General Interface controller can also directly make calls to a web service and then update the model based on the response.

This model makes the application more responsive in handling user events for a couple of reasons: First, because not all the actions are being sent back to the server, simple actions that can be served locally are handled by the General Interface controller and are processed locally. Second, the server does not need to send a new HTML document for every request; instead, it sends only the updated model, which is merely the data required to rebuild the view and therefore is much smaller in size.

General Interface builds on the familiar technologies of the web to create a powerful model for defining, rendering, and running dynamic screens, controls, and their interactions. An XML file on the server defines the design of the canvas to be displayed in the browser. Developers use GI Builder to put together components visually on a canvas, which is saved in an XML format that is interpreted by General Interface's runtime components. When the user brings up a General Interface application, an XML file is first downloaded from the server; it points to other resources on the server that need to be downloaded to render the screen and begin user interaction.

The extensive library of controls and widgets composes a collection of XML, JavaScript, and CSS files and XSL style sheets. Developers build General Interface applications by assembling user interface components on a canvas writing minimal JavaScript code to handle events generated by the user and/or the system. General Interface provides major building blocks and the capability to extend the built-in classes to build custom controls/widgets for the application. General Interface's deployment utility can be used to create code snippets to put a General Interface application inside a `<div>` or a `<span>` or a complete HTML file.

TIBCO General Interface Application

A TIBCO General Interface application does not necessarily take up the entire browser window. In fact, multiple General Interface applications may exist within a single browser window. Each General Interface application is a self-contained, independent collection of GUI controls that work together through a single instance of a General Interface controller.

All General Interface applications may use the facilities and features provided by General Interface's common utilities. For example, in a portal, each portlet may contain a different General Interface application, and each portlet may allow users to interact with it. For example, a Stock Quote portlet might have a text box where a user can type in the security symbol and click the Go button to display stock price information within that portlet, without affecting any other part of the screen.

An application built using GI Builder runs in a browser. It can take up the entire browser window, or it can run inside a smaller section of the web page known as a `<div>` or a `<span>` in HTML terms. Each application built with General Interface has at least one XML file that defines the components to be displayed on the screen. The simplest application built using General Interface will need only the one file that defines the screen. Although developers can change the name of this file, by default it is named `appCanvas.xml`.

The Deployment utility generates a small piece of JavaScript code that is used to bootstrap the General Interface application. The JavaScript snippet embedded in the HTML page begins by downloading the `config.xml` file and then goes on to load other components as identified by `config.xml`.

In its simplest form, a TIBCO General Interface application requires absolutely no coding. Many common interactions can be built using the tools provided in the GI Builder. More complex interactions may require additional coding in JavaScript.

Standard CSS files can be used with General Interface applications to provide a common look and feel across your entire web application. Additionally, a gallery of custom components may be built to provide a common set of behaviors and look and feel across your entire application or a set of applications built using TIBCO General Interface.

General Interface's Performance Edge

All data consuming controls in TIBCO General Interface use the XSL processor that's included with the browsers. Traditional methods of handling presentation logic in the browser were based on JavaScript, browser DOM, and CSS. Dynamic HTML implied using JavaScript to change the rendered HTML or the CSS styles associated with elements upon user interaction.

Browsers also have the capability to use a high-performance XSL Transformation engine that runs natively. General Interface uses it to render HTML from XML data. General Interface includes numerous predefined XSL style sheets that can render controls such as grids and menus from XML data. This unique strategy makes General Interface screens render significantly faster than the ones rendered using traditional methods such as DHTML.

JavaScript is an interpreted language, which means the browser reads each line of JavaScript code and compiles it each time it reads it and then executes it. This process continues until the end of the JavaScript file. This makes JavaScript very inefficient.

Compiler in the Browser

Web developers have been asking for a compiler in the browser for several years to make their code run faster in the browser. Even as personal computers become more powerful, JavaScript execution performance is unacceptable for any reasonable-size application.

XML/XSL processors run as compiled processes in the browser. XSLT merge is provided by precompiled binary extensions (DLLs or Shared Objects), which run many times faster than interpreted JavaScript. This effectively provides a compiler in the browser. XML data can be merged using XSL style sheets to render HTML at faster speeds rather than at interpreted speeds. TIBCO General Interface makes extensive use of this technique to boost performance at runtime. Properly written TIBCO General Interface applications can run 10 times faster (or better) than if they were built using JavaScript alone.

Rapid Prototyping Tool

GI Builder and the included controls and widgets are so easy to use that they can be used to develop prototypes of new products and applications very rapidly. Because all components can consume raw XML files, the prototypes can be fully functional using static data. Additionally, the prototype can then be turned in to engineering to make it fully functional by integrating with the back-end services.

This development life cycle greatly reduces time to market for enterprise applications and allows for a separation of concern among groups. Business-savvy groups can use the IDE to build prototypes, and technical groups can then integrate the front end with the appropriate back-end data services or web services and deploy it to production.

2

Understanding General Interface Architecture

This chapter provides a high-level architecture of TIBCO General Interface and its framework components and describes how General Interface applications work in the browser.

One of the strengths of General Interface is its capability to work with XML and XSL. All widgets use XML/XSL to render the component onscreen. JavaScript is used for handling user actions. This strategy helps General Interface applications run faster than JavaScript code in the browser because the XSL processor used by the browser runs at high speeds, whereas the JavaScript processor runs outside the browser and must first be compiled every time and then executed. Additionally, GI Builder—the interactive development environment (IDE) that's included with TIBCO General Interface—makes it possible to visually build prototypes very quickly using more than 100 ready-to-use widgets from a component palette.

Applications that are built with General Interface should take advantage of General Interface's architecture for best performance. It is possible to build applications entirely in JavaScript using the framework APIs; however, the performance of JavaScript is about 10 times slower than that of XML/XSL processing. Therefore, it is important to understand how General Interface works and exploit it in building applications to get the highest levels of performance. General Interface's architecture includes many ways to use XSL processing to improve performance. TIBCO General Interface's JavaScript framework includes numerous classes and methods to load, cache, and parse XML documents as well as transform documents using XSL style sheets at runtime.

Model View Controller Architecture

Model-View-Controller (MVC) is a proven pattern for building graphical user interfaces since Smalltalk-80. GUI frameworks, such as Microsoft Foundation Classes (MFC), Java Swing, WinForms, and Struts for Java-based web applications, all use the MVC pattern. This pattern offers some key benefits to GUI developers: First, it modularizes the code and breaks a large problem down to many smaller ones and allows for faster team development. It also makes the code much more maintainable because each part of the code is dealing with its own set of variables and behaviors. One of the most important advantages of using MVC for GUI frameworks is that it makes the framework easily expandable and customizable. For example, it becomes possible to extend a View class to create a customized view. Multiple views can be attached to a single model if needed. Views can also use the observer pattern to update themselves when the model changes.

In an MVC pattern, three primary classes are involved: a Model class that owns the internal state of the data that drives the view, a View class that owns what is displayed on the screen and has direct access to make changes to it, and a Controller class that orchestrates user actions. When a user clicks a button, it is first felt by the corresponding View class. It then immediately passes it along with any parameters necessary to the Controller class. Logic to handle this click is in the Controller class, which performs the necessary steps and updates the Model class if necessary. The Model class then notifies the View class that something has changed, and the View class then picks up the new data and updates the display accordingly.

This architecture opens up the possibility for actions coming from anywhere—for example, a back-end process could invoke an action on the Controller to deliver a message that needs to be displayed to the user. Multiple different View classes can be associated with the same model to display the data in a different representation. For example, a Model class that represents tabular data could be displayed via two independent views— one that shows a grid onscreen and another that shows a chart from the same data. Figure 2.1 shows a high-level representation of the MVC pattern in use.

All controls and widgets in General Interface use XML as data and are driven by a combination of XSL style sheets and JavaScript code. General Interface defines a format called the *Common Data Format*, or CDF, which is a form of XML. General Interface also includes a large collection of XSL style sheets that transform the backing CDF into HTML elements such as grids, lists, and menus. JavaScript code that orchestrates the behavior of the widgets is structured in packages, classes, and interfaces. General Interface follows a style similar to the Prototype framework for JavaScript code to define interfaces and classes that support object-oriented concepts of inheritance, polymorphism, and encapsulation. This style makes JavaScript code look almost like Java code. However, keep in mind that JavaScript is not a true object-oriented language, and therefore not all the features of a modern language such as Java or C# are available to developers.

General Interface Application Life Cycle

A General Interface application begins by executing some JavaScript code that can be called the boot loader. In the General Interface package is a JavaScript file, `JSX30.js`, that contains the functions to bootstrap a General Interface application and begin running it. The Deployment utility generates the code to load this file using HTTP protocol with the appropriate parameters for the application. As the HTML page that contains the Gen-

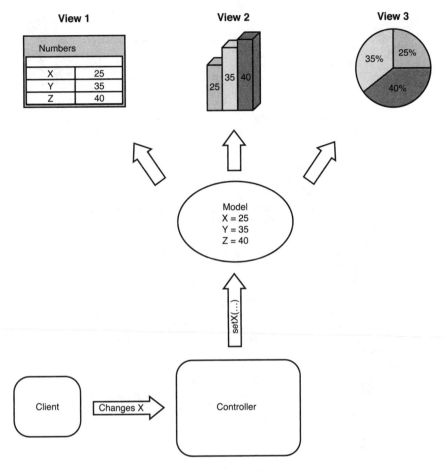

Figure 2.1   High-level representation of MVC.

eral Interface application is loaded by the browser, a call to JSX30.js is made, and it be-gins to load the application.

The first file that is loaded for any application is the config.xml file, which defines application files and various properties. Among other things, config.xml has a list of JavaScript files that begin to be loaded into browser memory. In the file config.xml is a reference to a file that defines the startup screen. The startup screen definition is also an XML file that contains the layout of the General Interface application as well as controls and widgets and/or subcomponents within it.

At this point, an instance is created of the global Application Controller, which is the main orchestrator for the application being loaded. It serves as the global context and contains all other widgets and controls for the application. Figure 2.2 shows the typical life cycle of a General Interface application.

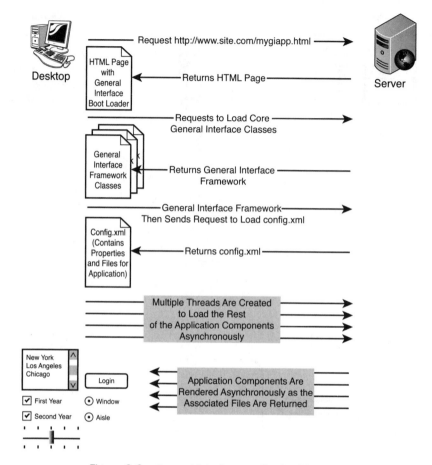

Figure 2.2   General Interface application life cycle.

General Interface supports a dynamic class loader, which loads only the JavaScript and XML files that are needed. This allows you to modularize your application to make sure it is responsive and does not have to download large files. Only the files needed for the opening screen are loaded, and instances of the startup screen and the controls in it are created and rendered; next, the execution control is passed on to the user, who then drives the application. Additional JavaScript and XML/XSL files are loaded and processed as needed.

Components such as dialogs and other controls contained within those dialogs do not need to be loaded initially. The General Interface framework provides methods to dynamically insert these components into the Application Object Model as needed. For example, when the user clicks the Save button, the application can call a method to display the Save dialog, which is defined in a separate XML file. This component XML file is loaded by General Interface into memory. After the file is loaded, General Interface instantiates JavaScript classes that are referenced in that file, and then it inserts the new component into the Application Object Model hierarchy and renders it onscreen. When the dialog is closed, it is removed from the Application Object Model. After they are downloaded, the components can be cached in the browser memory so that another fetch will not be required when this component is needed again.

General Interface also includes a utility to compress and obfuscate JavaScript files. In a nutshell, this utility takes in a number of JavaScript files and combines them into a single JavaScript file. It also changes the names of variables and methods to use as few characters as possible to reduce the size of the resulting JavaScript file. This is in direct contrast to the concept of dynamic class loading. Application developers have to analyze and understand the impacts of each strategy and adopt one that suits their requirements and environment. For very large applications, it is possible to use a hybrid approach, where classes are grouped into a few key groups and compressed using a merge utility into a few separate files that are loaded dynamically on demand.

Application Object Model

General Interface defines screens and controls at a higher level of abstraction than that of the HTML Document Object Model. This model, called the *Application Object Model (AOM)*, maps to the native browser's DOM. This enables General Interface applications to run in any browser where General Interface's AOM is implemented. Figure 2.3 shows a designer view of application canvas for a sample application in TIBCO General Interface, and Figure 2.4 shows the XML definition of the same appCanvas.

As you can see, every element's properties are defined in XML, and it is associated with a JavaScript class. As the General Interface controller loads the components, it creates an instance of the associated JavaScript class to handle events and behaviors for the component. This provides a great degree of encapsulation for classes and widgets. It is possible to make use of the familiar concepts of object-oriented programming to extend built-in widgets (or create new ones). As you build your canvas in GI Builder, it builds this file, and you can view a user-friendly representation of this file in the Component Hierarchy quadrant in the GI Builder.

Common Data Format

As stated earlier, all General Interface controls and widgets that consume data are driven by a backing XML model. The data must be in a format known as *Common Data Format*, or CDF. CDF is a very simple format that defines a few key elements and leaves the attribute space open. Attributes are mapped to data elements in controls. The main advantage of CDF is that it can drive any widget in TIBCO General Interface, which makes it possible to have the same backing CDF for a grid as well as a chart. The Model part of the MVC pattern in General Interface can be thought of as a CDF in TIBCO General Interface.

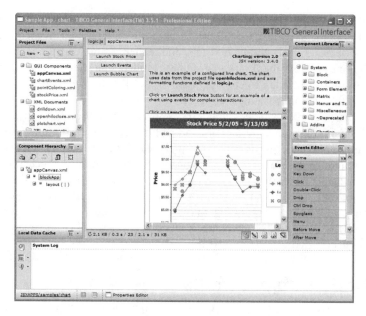

Figure 2.3   Application canvas in Design view.

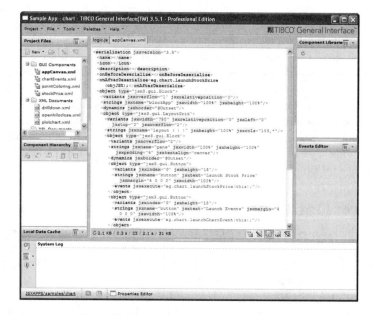

Figure 2.4   Application canvas in XML view.

JavaScript Object Notation (JSON) is a simple format for accessing and manipulating object properties. It is based on a subset of JavaScript Programming Language Standard, but is text based and is therefore language neutral. Because it is based on the JavaScript standard, it is inherently supported by TIBCO General Interface.

CDF Format also makes it very easy to manipulate the associated objects using a JSON paradigm. Each node in a CDF can be thought of as a JSON object where XML attributes map to JSON properties. It is possible, then, to use XSL/XPATH to manipulate this CDF when using an XSL style sheet, and at the same time, it's possible to update the fields using JSON syntax (for example, `obj.property = x`). Because TIBCO General Interface combines JavaScript and XML, this becomes a key convenience when dealing with the data structures in TIBCO General Interface applications.

JavaScript Framework

Prototype framework version 1.5 was released in January 2007 and introduced the concepts of object-oriented programming to JavaScript. Prototype framework started out as a small set of functions written in JavaScript to make it easy for developers to write modular code in JavaScript.

Object-oriented programming has been very successful in the rest of the development world, but the JavaScript language does not inherently support the concept of classes, interfaces, inheritance, and polymorphism. JavaScript does, however, have the capability to create objects that may have properties, and it does support the concept of a function pointer. So a clever group of people used those features as building blocks to create a framework in JavaScript that allows developers to use object-oriented concepts to write JavaScript code. For example, you could create a class called `Button` and have a method in it called `click()`, and extend the class to create other types of buttons, such as `ImageButton`, `RollOverImageButton`, and so on.

The Prototype framework consists of a single JavaScript file that defines various functions that can be used to define custom classes. The Prototype framework now includes support for AJAX by providing some classes to wrap an AJAX request and response object. Figure 2.5 shows the documentation page for General Interface's JavaScript framework, which is loosely based on the Prototype framework.

TIBCO General Interface's JavaScript framework adds a Java-like package structure and organizes the code in class files, interfaces, and packages. This goes a long way toward making JavaScript look and feel like Java. There is even a dynamic class loader in TIBCO General Interface that can download classes as needed. General Interface framework adds functions to signal to the General Interface class loader when another class is required. All JavaScript code is written in smaller classes. Although a single source code file can contain multiple class definitions, it is advisable to keep the files small and define only one class in a single source file. This also helps with dynamic class loading because each class can be loaded quickly when needed. Remember, the classes are in JavaScript files, which live on the server but are used on the client, so class loading is done using an HTTP request. After they are loaded in the client, the JavaScript files are cached by the browser. It would

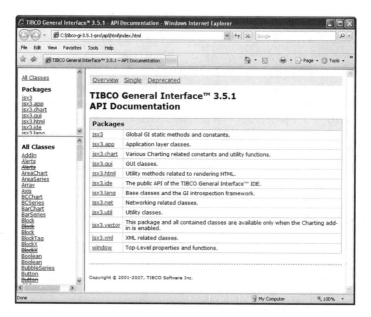

Figure 2.5   General Interface framework API documentation.

be nice if this could be compiled code and executed much faster than JavaScript on the client side. Also, a compiler would aid at development time. The IDE provided with General Interface offers some assistance in this regard, but it's not really a compiler.

For more details on how to take advantage of the object-oriented approach in the General Interface framework, refer to Chapter 7, "Object-Oriented JavaScript—Extending General Interface Widgets."

JavaScript API

TIBCO General Interface's JavaScript API is organized into packages similar to the Java Development Kit. The root package name for all JavaScript classes is `jsx3`. Base framework classes to manage defining classes and packages are in the `jsx3.lang` package. A word of caution here is that the concept of package is somewhat similar to that in Java, except that if a package is defined using the `jsx3.lang.package` it cannot be dynamically loaded by General Interface's class loader. TIBCO General Interface packages allow pulling together several classes into a single package and allow JavaScript programs to discover classes, methods, and properties of a package. Although that is a good feature, it is possible, and in fact even advisable, to not use a package at all. Packages can also be created by using appropriate namespaces in class names. The following subpackages are available:

- **Jsx3.app**—Contains the highest-level classes for a General Interface application; for example, the application controller and General Interface global cache among others.
- **jsx3.chart**—Contains classes related to General Interface charts.
- **jsx3.gui**—Contains GUI widget classes and event and notification-related classes.
- **jsx3.html**—Contains very few classes that are related to the HTML that's rendered by General Interface.
- **jsx3.ide**—Contains classes related to the GI Builder IDE.
- **jsx3.lang**—Contains the General Interface class framework, which can be used without the rest of General Interface to build reusable components in JavaScript.
- **jsx3.net**—Contains classes that allow an application to communicate with the back-end services.
- **jsx3.util**—Similar to the `java.util` package; contains simple utility classes such as `List`, `Iterator`, and so on.
- **jsx3.vector**—Contains classes related to vector graphics in General Interface. Available only if Charts are used.
- **jsx3.xml**—Contains General Interface's abstraction layer for XML documents and CDF.
- **window**—Allows access to browser-level JavaScript functions such as `window.alert()`.

Commonly Used Classes

TIBCO General Interface has a very rich set of features, and its framework includes numerous classes and methods. Product documentation includes a comprehensive API reference document similar to that available for Java. This section presents some of the more commonly used classes and APIs with specific use cases and sample code snippets.

Application Controller

General Interface has a high-level application controller that orchestrates various functions in a General Interface application. A single instance of this controller is created for every application. The name of this global controller class in General Interface is `jsx3.app.Server`. It is used frequently in custom code because it allows access to other parts of the same application. For example, from an event handling code in a Select component, if you need to call a method on the grid component of the same application, you could use the following:

```
this.getServer().findJSXByName('mygrid').getSelection();
```

In this statement, `this` refers to the instance of Select control that is making the call. If you are a Java or C++ developer, it's the same `this` pointer that is used to refer to the current instance of a class. Refer to Chapter 7 for details on writing custom classes in General Interface.

Cache

Cache is the global memory space that is available to an application with smart management similar to Java's garbage collection. In this class, General Interface has provided a very smart mechanism for storing data within the browser that can be accessed by any other function or at a later time. This class is also used to keep some key data for some of the controls. For example, the grid control keeps its backing data in an instance of the `jsx3.app.Cache` class. Applications can use this to store larger result sets locally in the client memory. However, care must be taken to not load too much into the client browser and avoid a memory overload of IE (or Firefox).

Custom Classes in JavaScript for General Interface

The exhaustive set of functions available in General Interface's framework makes it possible to write complex logic in a very few lines of JavaScript code that can also be embedded within the properties of controls similar to event handlers like `onClick` in HTML elements. JavaScript that accompanies any General Interface application can be written in the usual way in files with the `.js` extension. When you start a new project in General Interface, it opens a file `logic.js` in the workspace where small JavaScript scriptlets to handle event handling or validation logic can be placed. However, the best practice when writing JavaScript for General Interface is to develop JavaScript classes similar to Java classes. Each `.js` file should have only a single class defined in it. The way to define a class in General Interface is to use the `defineClass()` function from the `jsx3.lang` package. Listing 2.1 shows partial source code for a class written using TIBCO General Interface's framework:

Listing 2.1   Custom Class Defined in General Interface

```
/* File: CommandHandler.js
 * Description: Implements a command handler for online
 *             equity trading application
 *
 *             This class follows Command pattern to implement
 *             a generic handler for all menu items from
 *             the main trading window
 */
jsx3.lang.Class.defineClass (
"com.tibcobooks.gi.chapter2.CommandHandler", // name of class
com.tibcobooks.gi.chapter2.BaseHandler, // similar to "extends"
```

```
                              part of Java class definition
[], // Similar to "implements" part of Java class definition
function ( CommandHandler ) {
        CommandHandler.prototype.buyURL =
            'http://www.anilgrnani.com/gibook/chapter2/by';
        CommandHandler.prototype.sellURL =
            'http://www.anilgrnani.com/gibook/chapter2/sell';
        CommandHandler.prototype.init = function()
        {
            // this is the constructor in General Interface framework
        };
}
);
```

This framework can be used independently of General Interface by simply including some of the JavaScript files from the General Interface distribution. General Interface framework is open source, so there is no licensing nor cost implication of using it this way. It certainly makes JavaScript code much more modular and therefore easy to maintain.

The process of loading the class essentially downloads the JavaScript source file and executes it using the JavaScript method `evaluate()` to insert it dynamically into the current set of available JavaScript files. After the class has been loaded, other parts of the program can create instances of the class, or they may call any static methods or access static properties by directly referencing it with the fully qualified class name—for example:

```
com.tibcobooks.gi.chapter2.CommandHandler.sellURL =
  'http://www.anilgrnani.com/gibook/chapter2/newSellURL'
```

XSL Style Sheets

To deliver high performance, TIBCO General Interface relies heavily on the XML/XSL engine to render HTML instead of using DOM manipulation using JavaScript. It includes a large number of XSL style sheets in the distribution. Framework's XSL style sheets are stored in the JSX\xsl folder within the General Interface installation directory. A quick look in that directory shows the following xsl files:

```
cf_creator.xsl
cf_resolver.xsl
jsxlib.xsl
jsxmatrix.xsl
jsxmen.xsl
jsxselect.xsl
jsxtable.xsl
jsxtree.xsl
xml.xsl
```

Additionally, there are two subfolders: `ie` and `fx`. They contain XSL style sheets for the now deprecated classes List and Grid and are provided for backward compatibility with previous versions of General Interface.

Onscreen rendering of controls in General Interface is always done using these XSL style sheets. The XML data in CDF format is merged with one of these XSL style sheets to render the HTML for the browser. Editing these style sheets is not generally recommended because they are part of the General Interface product and may change with versions.

General Interface provides some hooks into these style sheets to allow customization. This technique helps the developer in another way—the developers do not have to write long and complex style sheets to do complete rendering; instead, they need to write only small fragments known as *value templates*, which are inserted by the General Interface runtime before running the merge with one of these prebuilt style sheets.

Value Templates

A common requirement when displaying large lists of data is to be able to apply styling depending on the contents of the cell. In Microsoft Excel this feature is presented as Conditional Formatting in the Tools menu in Office 97 through 2003 and in the Home tab in the Styles palette in Office 2007.

In General Interface applications, this sort of formatting or coloring of data is achieved using fragments of XSL style sheets known as *value templates*. Columns of a Matrix component have a property field called `value template` where XSL can be placed to affect the output during runtime. Value templates are discussed in detail in Chapter 8, "Advanced Features of Matrix."

XML Transformers

Back-end systems do not always produce CDF. They should not be expected to produce it, either. Therefore, General Interface runs the XML through an intermediate style sheet that can be supplied by developer. XML Transformer is a property of data-driven General Interface controls that can contain a reference to a style sheet, which will be used to transform XML data before rendering it onscreen using the General Interface style sheet for that control. This allows for very elegant application design where the back end can supply data in a standard XML format, and clients such as General Interface can transform that data to the format they can use. XML Transformer can also be used to manipulate the data before rendering it onscreen; for example, data can be sorted on several keys before passing on to the General Interface handlers. General Interface allows fields to be designated as sort keys. However, XML Transformers can be used to sort the data using a fixed XPath expression before applying the single column sort offered by General Interface.

Note that when you have full control over the back-end XML generation, and/or the sole purpose of generated XML is to feed it to TIBCO General Interface front end, it is best to produce CDF directly because it saves one step in General Interface processing. Transformers are a fast and efficient way to convert XML that is already being generated by some back-end application or when there are other client applications that require the full power of XML.

Chapter 4, "Working with XML and XSL," and Chapter 8 in this book discuss XML Transformers in more detail and provide a complete example of using XML Transformers in General Interface applications.

3

Quick Start
TIBCO General Interface

This chapter provides detailed instructions on building applications with TIBCO General Interface. TIBCO General Interface is a client-side framework and is completely independent of the back-end technology, so it is easy to use TIBCO General Interface with any type of back-end technology.

This chapter includes step-by-step instructions for building and packaging standalone TIBCO General Interface prototypes, as well as deploying them under Internet Information Services (IIS), Apache Web Server, and Apache Tomcat application server. Additionally, it includes a proposed directory structure along with scripts to deploy General Interface applications using the Apache ant tool from the command line.

Standalone prototypes can be distributed in a zip file so that anyone can extract the contents of the zip file and instantly begin using the prototype. Other types of deployments require a server such as Microsoft Internet Information Server, Apache Web Server, or Apache Tomcat. Although the examples in this chapter do not require any server-side technology, it is recommended that you install and set up Tomcat or Microsoft Internet Information Services to work with these.

Building and Packaging Standalone Prototypes

One of the many benefits of using TIBCO General Interface is that it is extremely easy to build standalone prototypes that can later be integrated with an appropriate back end. GI Builder is an excellent tool that can be used by product development teams to create fully functional prototypes. Deep technical knowledge of TIBCO General Interface is not required to build useful prototypes. Businesses do not have to invest a lot of resources in building throwaway prototypes to try out a new application or a new user interface. However, it is important to discover usability issues early in the prototype process because the farther a product is in its development cycle, the more expensive it is to make changes to the user interface. A prototype developed using TIBCO General Interface does not have to be thrown away. Most of it can be used directly in the final product. The tools included also make it easy to create and distribute prototype applications to focus groups or to business owners for evaluation and feedback.

To demonstrate how to build standalone prototypes with TIBCO General Interface, I will build a sample application and package it for distribution. This sample application displays a list of Dow 30 components in a table. The columns displayed are Symbol, Company Name, Industry, and Date Added. The goal of this chapter is to demonstrate how to build and distribute prototypes with General Interface and how to deploy General Interface applications IIS and Apache Tomcat. In this example, I will first use a simple XML file that contains the data. All the files for this example are available on the companion CD-ROM.

For this example, I will use a simple XML data format used by TIBCO General Interface controls. In TIBCO General Interface this format is called the Common Data Format (CDF). In later chapters you will see that a number of ways exist to convert any XML data into this format. TIBCO General Interface includes a tool that allows you to visually build mappings from data in XML documents to components onscreen. Alternatively, you can write XSL style sheets and place them in General Interface's processing queue.

In this chapter, I use a format that directly drives all components, including HTML forms, tables, menus, select controls, combo boxes, grids, and many other controls in TIBCO General Interface.

Installing TIBCO General Interface

GI Builder is an application that is written in the General Interface framework; therefore, it works in a browser. The operating system's security features prevent any web page from accessing the local hard disk, so special permissions must be configured to run GI Builder. To install General Interface, download the zip file from TIBCO's website and extract its contents to your hard drive. TIBCO publishes several versions on the download site. The first version that appears for download is the DEBUG version, which is discussed in more detail in Chapter 16, "Optimizing Performance."

Two other versions are available for download—a Standard version and a Maximum version. For samples in this book, you should use the Standard version. The difference between the Standard and Maximum versions is that the Standard version loads most (but not all) controls into the browser when a General Interface application is first launched; the Maximum version loads all General Interface controls and widgets at startup, which could increase the initial load time of an application. There is also a Minimum version, which loads only a bare minimum of classes, making the initial load quite fast while deferring loading of other classes as needed. Chapter 16 discusses how a custom build of General Interface can improve initial load performance by loading just the right number of classes upfront. Links to download TIBCO General Interface distribution package are as follows:

- **Standard**—http://power.tibco.com/content/GI/downloads/
  tibco-gi-3.5.1-pro.zip

- **Maximum**—http://power.tibco.com/content/GI/downloads/
  tibco-gi-3.5.1-pro-max.zip

After you download the Standard build, extract its contents to your hard drive. In the extracted folder are several files and subfolders, as shown in Figure 3.1.

Figure 3.1   Contents of the General
Interface distribution.

- Folder `api` contains the API documentation for JavaScript framework classes and functions.
- Folder `doc` contains General Interface documentation files in HTML format.
- Folder `JSX` contains all the framework files that are deployed with General Interface applications.
- Folder `legal` contains the official license.
- Folder `util` contains utilities, including `gi-merge.sh`, which can be used to create custom builds of General Interface for deployment.
- File `GI_Builder.hta` is the standalone file that launches the GI Builder tool.
- File `GI_Builder.html` and `GI_Builder.xhtml` are files that launch GI Builder inside a browser window.
- Files `jsx3.gui.window.html`, `jsx3.gui.window.xhtml`, `shell.html`, and `shell.xhtml` are templates used by GI Builder tool's Deployment Utility.

- File `logger.xml` has properties for General Interface's logging framework.

- File `readme.txt` is included, which provides some useful information about the version.

- File `tib_gi_release_notes.pdf` is the release notes for the current version.

Launching GI Builder

Several ways exist to launch GI Builder, which itself is a General Interface application. In the extracted folder, among other files and folders, are three files that can be used to launch the GI Builder application: `GI_Builder.hta`, `GI_Builder.html`, and `GI_Builder.xhtml`. Note that it may be necessary to change folder viewing options in Windows to view extensions. To do this, select Folder Options from the Tools menu in the folder window, click the View tab, and make sure that the check box labeled Hide Extensions for Known File Types in the Advanced Settings list is unchecked, as shown in Figure 3.2.

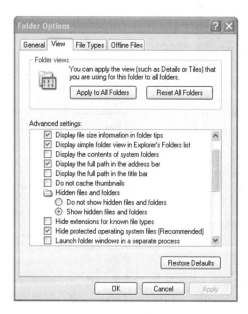

Figure 3.2   Changing Folder
options to view extensions.

`GI_Builder.html` file is included, but you cannot deploy it to a web server and access it remotely because it requires access to the local disk file system to open and/or save project files.

`GI_Builder.hta` is an IE application mode binary file that runs the GI Builder in a standalone mode. `GI_Builder.html` is an HTML file that can be opened in any browser. Double-clicking it launches it in the default browser for your desktop. It can also be dragged and dropped onto any browser icon on your desktop to open it with that browser. Alternatively, you can also launch your favorite browser and open this file by selecting Open from the File menu. Use XHTML launcher if you require XHTML output. You can generate XHTML in HTML mode, but you won't know if you did something wrong until you run it in XHTML. Running GI Builder in XHTML mode with IE7 actually requires that you change the extension of `GI_Builder.xhtml` back to html. IE7 uses the metadata tag at the beginning of HTML file content to decide the mode of rendering. So rename `GI_Builder.xhtml` to `GI_Builder_xhtml.html` and double-click to run in IE7.

I recommend using the standalone version by double-clicking `GI_Builder.hta` over other methods simply because you don't need to worry about browser settings if you use this method. To launch GI Builder in a browser, you will need to appropriately set up the browser security settings based on what browser and operating system you are using, as described in the following sections.

Internet Explorer 7 on Windows

From the Tools menu, select the Internet Options option, click the Advanced tab, and make sure that Allow Active Content to Run in Files on My Computer is checked, as shown in Figure 3.3.

Also under the Security tab, click Local Intranet, and then click the Custom Level button and make sure the following ActiveX controls and plug-in settings are enabled as shown in Figure 3.4:

- Binary and script behaviors
- Run ActiveX controls and plug-ins
- Script ActiveX controls marked safe for scripting

Mozilla Firefox on Windows

Mozilla Firefox will prompt you to override its default security settings and give you an option to allow or deny the privilege when you launch TIBCO General Interface for the first time. It gives you an option to remember the decision for GI Builder. Because General Interface needs this permission to run, you should check this box and click the Allow button. During the first startup, this dialog appears exactly three times—once for each type of security privilege that is required. Click the check box that says Remember This Decision, and click the Allow button to continue.

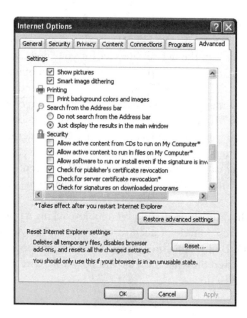

Figure 3.3   Security settings for running TIBCO
General Interface.

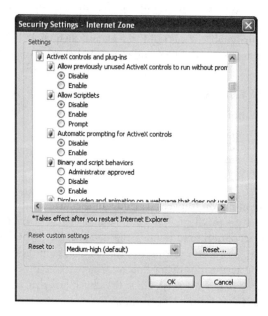

Figure 3.4   Custom-level
ActiveX settings.

Mozilla Firefox on Macintosh

Firefox on Macintosh will prompt for two additional privileges. Make sure to check the check box that says Remember This Decision, and click the Allow button. Firefox will continue and load GI Builder tool in the current window.

GI Workspace

When you launch GI Builder for the first time, you need to provided a path for it on your hard disk where you want to store your project files. Create a folder (c:\GIWorkspace) on your hard drive before launching GI Builder. You need to make sure that it is on the same drive as GI Builder because of the security requirements. When GI Builder prompts you for the workspace, supply the full path to this folder (c:\GIWorkspace) and click the Choose button. GI Builder may need to be restarted after the setting for the workspace is applied for the first time, and whenever it is changed. Figure 3.5 shows General Interface's Create or Locate a Workspace dialog.

Figure 3.5   General Interface's
Create or Locate a Workspace
dialog.

> **Note**
> It is quite convenient to make the General Interface workspace path the same as the folder where it is deployed locally. This enables you to edit the same files in TIBCO GI Builder and see the effect immediately by reloading the page in Tomcat.

After you provide the workspace path, GI Builder displays a blank workspace with a content area in the center and gray space for palettes on the left and right, as shown in Figure 3.6. General Interface's default workspace layout looks similar to the Java perspective in Eclipse. The main content area is for editing files and visually designing the GUI canvas using General Interface controls and widgets.

GI Builder will fill up the empty areas with various palettes when a project is opened. Several sample projects are included in the distribution. Open a sample to view all the palettes. Click the Project menu and select User Projects, Samples, Chart to open the sample project. You should see all the palettes in the General Interface sample project, as shown in Figure 3.7.

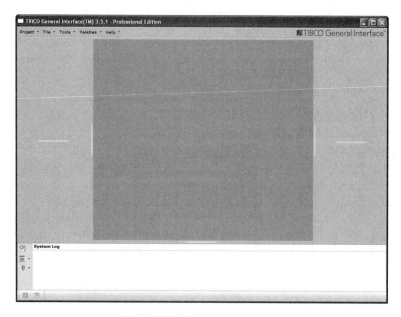

Figure 3.6   Blank GI workspace.

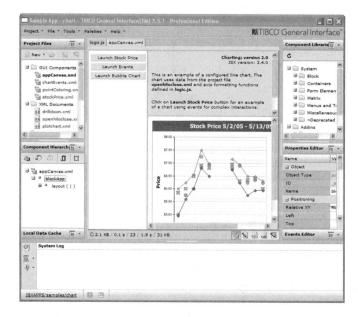

Figure 3.7   Chart sample application.

The top-left quadrant contains the Project Files palette, which shows the files in the project. Note that the Project Files palette shows only files created or added to the project and not the contents of the entire file system. Below it is the Component Hierarchy, which shows the Application Object Model of TIBCO General Interface's current project starting with `appCanvas.xml` at the top of the hierarchy. Note that this is different from the browser Document Object Model.

The top-right quadrant shows the Component Libraries palette, which includes all General Interface controls and widgets as well as Custom controls that can be added to the application screens. Below the Component Libraries palette is the Properties Editor, which shows the properties of the currently selected node in the Component Hierarchy (in the bottom-left quadrant).

GI Builder is very flexible about placement of these palettes. Users can customize and place them anywhere they like. Palettes can also be detached and opened in their own window, which can be minimized and maximized as needed.

Building the Application

To begin creating the sample application, launch the TIBCO GI Builder tool and from the Project menu select New Project. Type the name of the project: **dow30**. GI Builder creates the folder hierarchy for your new application. By default, you will see a blank root canvas for your new application. GI Builder is highly customizable, and you can adapt it to your style of working very easily as you get more comfortable working with it. For now, just use the default settings. After you create the project, the initial screen will look like Figure 3.8.

You can now begin to design the layout of your application. Follow these steps to create the dow30 application:

1. In the top-right quadrant titled `Component Libraries`, click the + sign next to System to expand the collection of widgets that are available in General Interface.

2. Expand the Matrix folder to show the set of controls related to the Matrix component.

3. Drag and drop the Grid component onto the canvas. You will see the default table that General Interface creates with some static data for countries.

4. Now click the + sign next to the matrix (General Interface names it matrix1 by default) in the Component Hierarchy (in the bottom-left quadrant) to view its child nodes. You will see two columns—mc2 and mc1.

5. Delete both column nodes. Select each node in the Component Hierarchy palette and click the Trash toolbar button at the top of that palette.

6. Click the matrix1 component in the Component Hierarchy to select it, and then in the Properties Editor on the right, scroll down until you see XML String property. Click the right mouse button over the name of the property (XML String) and select Reset/Clear from the context menu to clear the value.

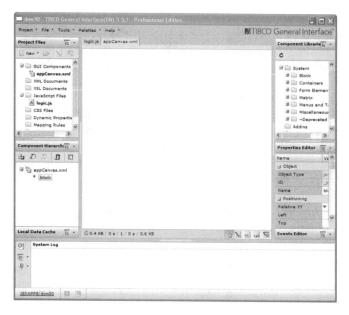

Figure 3.8   New project.

7. Open the file `chapter3/examples/dow30/JSXAPPS/dow30/xml/dow30.xml` in any text editor, such as Notepad, and copy its contents to the Clipboard by selecting the entire content and selecting Edit, Copy or by pressing Ctrl+C on the keyboard. Note that the contents are in CDF format ready for use by TIBCO General Interface, and the jsxid attribute of the data node is set to jsxroot to let General Interface know to render the records contained within this data node.

8. Now paste the contents as the value of XML String property in GI Builder. To do this, click in the text box for the value of XML String property and press Ctrl+V on the keyboard.

9. Expand the Columns group under the Matrix node in Component Library (top-right quadrant) by clicking the + sign.

10. Drag and drop a Text column onto the Grid in the canvas three times to add three new columns. General Interface will name them all textColumn by default.

11. Drag and drop a Date column onto the Grid in the canvas. General Interface will name it dateColumn and initialize it with default property values.

12. Click the right mouse button on the tab appCanvas and select Save and Reload.

   At this time the project window will look like Figure 3.9. Note that the blank Matrix appears in the content area and the matrix1 component appears in the Component Hierarchy palette.

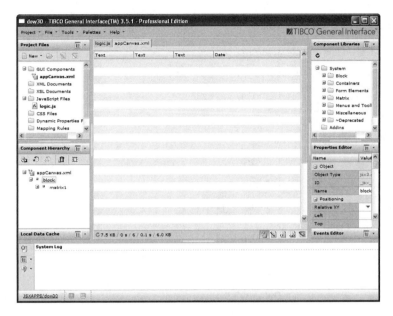

Figure 3.9   Project dow30 project window.

13. Change the Name property of the first textColumn in the Component Hierarchy to Ticker. This is a common property in many General Interface controls. It defines the name of the instance of the Control at runtime. In this example it refers to the instance of the Column object at runtime. This value can be used to locate this column object at runtime by using the JavaScript API provided by General Interface. I am not using this property for this example. But it's a good idea to give each object some meaningful name so that it's easy to access it in JavaScript if necessary.

14. Change the Att Name property of the first column in the Component Hierarchy to Ticker. This is critical for mapping values from CDF documents. General Interface will extract the value of the attribute whose name matches the value of this property to populate this column. In other words, the value associated with the attribute Ticker in the source XML document will be displayed in this column. Note that this is case sensitive.

15. Change the Caption property of the first column in the Component Hierarchy to Ticker. This is displayed in the column header.

16. Similarly, Change the Name, Att Name, and Caption properties of the remaining three column elements as follows:

Property	Value
Second Column Named textColumn	
Name	Company
Att Name	Company
Caption	Company
Third Column Named textColumn	
Name	Industry
Att Name	Industry
Caption	Industry
Fourth Column Named dateColumn	
Name	DateAdded
Att Name	DateAdded
Caption	Date Added

17. Select Save and Reload from the File menu once to make sure the project state is saved and the appropriate memory caches are updated. At this point your project will look like Figure 3.10.

Figure 3.10   Project dow30 with proper naming applied.

Deploying General Interface Applications

Now you are ready to deploy the sample application. The following sections describe how to deploy this application under various scenarios.

Deploying the Application as a Standalone Prototype

GI Builder includes a simple tool to create a full HTML page or a small fragment of HTML DIV or SPAN element that can be embedded in another HTML page. This utility can be used to create a prototype that needs to be distributed to potential reviewers and users. Follow these steps to create an HTML page that contains this application:

1. Open Windows Explorer and create a new folder for the application named `dow30prototype` in a location of your choice (C:\).

2. In GI Builder, select Deployment Utility from the Project menu. You should see the Deployment Utility dialog shown in Figure 3.11.

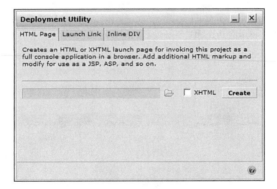

Figure 3.11   The Deployment
Utility dialog.

3. Click the Open Folder icon to browse and navigate to the newly created folder—`dow30prototype`.

4. Type in a name for the file `index.html` and click the Save button to dismiss the File Chooser dialog.

5. Click the Create button in the Deployment Utility to generate the HTML file containing the application.

6. Open this file `index.html` in a text editor such as Notepad. Note that it's a small HTML file with a script that contains a relative reference to the application in the GI Workspace:

```
<script type="text/javascript"
        src="../tibco-gi-3.5.1-pro/JSX/js/JSX30.js"
```

```
        jsxapppath="../GIWorkspace/JSXAPPS/dow30/" >
</script>
```

7. Note that `JSX/js/JSX30.js` is the boot loader for the General Interface framework and application. The attribute `jsxapppath` points to the application that will be loaded after the General Interface's top-level controller is loaded and begins executing. For a standalone deployment, we need to fix these references to be contained within the current folder. So change the `src` and `jsxapppath` values as follows:

```
<script type="text/javascript"
        src="JSX/js/JSX30.js"
        jsxapppath="JSXAPPS/dow30/" >
</script>
```

8. Assemble other components of the application into the newly created folder (`C:\dow30prototype`):

   a. Copy the JSX folder from the General Interface installation folder into this new folder.

   b. Copy logger.xml from the General Interface installation folder into this folder.

   c. Copy the JSXAPPS folder from GI Workspace into this folder. Because you do not need the sample applications that are shipped with General Interface in your package, delete the samples folder from within JSXAPPS. If you have any other applications besides dow30, delete them as well.

9. Double-click the file `index.html` to ensure that it brings up the General Interface application that was just built as it opens in the browser. The application should come up and display in the browser, as shown in Figure 3.12.

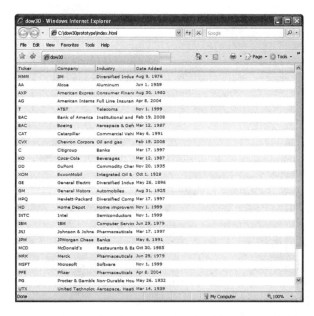

Figure 3.12   Application dow30 is displayed in the browser.

In Windows Explorer, navigate to the folder that contains this `dow30prototype` folder. Right-click the `dow30prototype` folder and select the Send To, Compressed file option to create a zip archive of this folder. Windows creates a file named `dow30prototype.zip` in the same folder where `dow30prototype` folder is contained. This is the packaged file ready to be distributed. Anybody can extract the contents of the folder and double-click `index.html` to bring up the General Interface prototype.

Deploying the Application Under IIS

Follow instructions available separately from Microsoft to install and configure IIS and create a website folder. IIS creates a `C:\InetPub\wwwroot` directory for the default website on the server. Open an Internet browser and type in the URL of the server in the address bar to ensure that the default website is working properly. If the name of the computer is localhost, the URL for the default website will be `http://localhost`. If the computer is connected to the Internet and a DNS entry has been configured to give it a name, such as www.tibcobooks.com, anybody on the Internet can type in www.tibcobooks.com to go to the website on that computer.

To deploy the prototype application, copy the entire folder `dow30prototype` inside the `wwwroot` folder for the default website. This is all that is needed to deploy any TIBCO General Interface application. Some additional features exist that pertain to application log windows and other deployment options, which are covered in Chapter 7, "Object-Oriented JavaScript: Extending General Interface Widgets."

After the application is deployed, verify it by going to the application URL—http://servername/dow30prototype; for example, if the name of the server is www.tibcobooks.com, the URL for the application will be www.tibcobooks.com/dow30prototype.

Deploying the Application Under Apache Web Server

The process of deploying General Interface applications under Apache Web Server is very similar to deploying under IIS, except that the directory structure of Apache Web Server is somewhat different. Web content is placed under the directory called the `DocumentRoot` directory in Apache. `DocumentRoot` is a configuration parameter that is set to point to the directory `<apache install directory>\htdocs` in a default install on Windows and in `/var/www/html` directory for a default installation on Linux.

Copy the entire folder `dow30prototype` to this `DocumentRoot` directory of the Apache website. For example, in Windows copy the entire folder to `<apache install directory>\htdocs` directory, and in Linux copy the entire folder to `/var/www/html` directory.

The URL to visit this page is very similar to the preceding deployment. If the name of the server is www.tibcobooks.com, the URL will be www.tibcobooks.com/dow30prototype.

Deploying the Application Under Tomcat

There are several ways to deploy this application to Tomcat. Manually deploying is very similar to deploying under Apache. Download and install Tomcat using the following steps:

1. Download JDK (version 1.6) from http://java.sun.com/javase/downloads/index.jsp and install it on your machine. Follow instructions at http://java.sun.com/javase/6/webnotes/install/index.html to install Java Development Kit on your machine. Make sure to download JDK and not just the Java Runtime Environment (JRE), because Tomcat requires JDK for some features.

2. Download Tomcat 5.5 from http://tomcat.apache.org/download-55.cgi by clicking the Zip link under Core in the Binary Distribution part of the page.

3. Extract the contents of this zip file into the C: drive.

4. Rename the `apache-tomcata-5.5.26` folder to **tomcat55** to keep it simple.

5. Edit the contents of the file `C:\tomcat55\bin\catalina.bat` and add the following three lines at the top of the file to set environment variables as per your setup:

```
set CATALINA_HOME=C:\tomcat55
set CATALINA_BASE=C:\tomcat55
set JAVA_HOME=C:\jdk1.6.0_03
```

6. Open an MS-DOS command prompt window and type the following commands to launch tomcat:

```
cd C:\tomcat55\bin
startup
```

If Tomcat started up successfully, you will see a window as shown in Figure 3.13.

Figure 3.13   The DOS window after starting Tomcat.

7. Open up a browser window and navigate to http://localhost:8080 to see the default Tomcat page as shown in Figure 3.14.

8. To create a new context in Tomcat, first copy the entire folder `dow30prototype` to the `C:\tomcat55\webapps` folder.

Figure 3.14   The default Tomcat page.

9. Now using a text editor such as Notepad, create a file named `dow30prototype.xml` in the folder `c:\tomcat55\conf\Catalina\localhost` with the following contents:

```
<?xml version="1.0" encoding="UTF-8"?>
<Context docBase="${catalina.home}/webapps/dow30prototype"/>
```

Tomcat automatically creates the new context and deploys the application.

10. After saving the preceding file, navigate to the URL—http://localhost:8080/ dow30prototype—using a browser to see the application running under Tomcat, as in Figure 3.15.

Deploying the Application as a WAR File Under Tomcat

TIBCO General Interface applications often need to communicate with back-end web applications or web services. J2EE applications are packaged in a Web Application Archive (war) file that makes it easy to deploy to any target application servers. In this section, I describe how to include a TIBCO General Interface application with all its components into a J2EE web project. Examples in following chapters build on this application and add J2EE application components that communicate with the General Interface front end.

To prepare a General Interface application to be deployed in a war file, begin by creating an empty folder, `dow30app`, and create two folders within it—`src` for any Java source code files and `WebContent` for HTML, JavaScript, CSS, and other content files including TIBCO General Interface files. Create a `build.properties` file with the environment variables as shown in Listing 3.1.

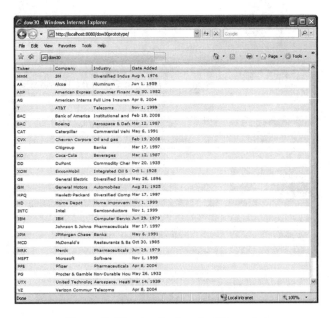

Figure 3.15   Application dow30 running
under Tomcat.

Note

All files are available on the companion CD-ROM.

Listing 3.1   Simple Properties File for a Basic `build.xml` File

```
# Ant properties for building and deploying to Tomcat 5.5
tomcat.home=C:\\Tomcat55
deploy.dir=${tomcat.home}\\webapps
tomcat.manager.url=http://localhost:8080/manager
tomcat.manager.username=admin
tomcat.manager.password=admin
```

ANT uses a `build.xml` file with targets for building and deploying web applications. Create a `build.xml` file that includes several useful targets. A sample `build.xml` file with commonly used targets is shown in Listing 3.2. Tomcat includes a jar file, `catalina-ant.jar`, which contains implementations of commonly used targets to manage web applications under Tomcat. Similarly, other J2EE application servers also include implementations of several tasks for ANT. Although the `build.xml` file that is included here is written for Tomcat targets, it is easy to adapt it to any other application server, such as BEA WebLogic, Sun Java System Application Server, JBoss, or GlassFish.

Listing 3.2   Basic `build.xml` for Sample Application

```xml
<?xml version="1.0"?>
<!-- ant build file for dow30app -->
<project name="dow30app" basedir="." default="usage">
  <property file="build.properties"/>
  <property name="src.dir" value="src"/>
  <property name="web.dir" value="WebContent"/>
  <property name="build.dir" value="${web.dir}/WEB-INF/classes"/>
  <property name="name" value="dow30app"/>
  <path id="master-classpath">
    <fileset dir="${web.dir}/WEB-INF/lib">
      <include name="*.jar"/>
    </fileset>
    <!-- include j2ee jar files -->
    <fileset dir="${tmcat.home}/common/lib">
      <include name="servlet*.jar"/>
    </fileset>
    <pathelement path="${build.dir}"/>
  </path>
  <!-- define tomcat tasks -->
  <taskdef name="deploy"
           classname="org.apache.catalina.ant.DeployTask">
    <classpath>
      <path
        location="${tomcat.home}/server/lib/catalina-ant.jar"/>
    </classpath>
  </taskdef>
  <taskdef name="undeploy"
           classname="org.apache.catalina.ant.UndeployTask">
    <classpath>
      <path
        location="${tomcat.home}/server/lib/catalina-ant.jar"/>
    </classpath>
  </taskdef>
  <taskdef name="reload"
           classname="org.apache.catalina.ant.ReloadTask">
    <classpath>
      <path
        location="${tomcat.home}/server/lib/catalina-ant.jar"/>
    </classpath>
  </taskdef>
  <taskdef name="list"
           classname="org.apache.catalina.ant.ListTask">
    <classpath>
      <path
        location="${tomcat.home}/server/lib/catalina-ant.jar"/>
    </classpath>
```

```
</taskdef>
<taskdef name="start"
         classname="org.apache.catalina.ant.StartTask">
  <classpath>
    <path
      location="${tomcat.home}/server/lib/catalina-ant.jar"/>
  </classpath>
</taskdef>
<taskdef name="stop"
         classname="org.apache.catalina.ant.StopTask">
  <classpath>
    <path
      location="${tomcat.home}/server/lib/catalina-ant.jar"/>
  </classpath>
</taskdef>
<target name="usage">
  <echo message=""/>
  <echo message="${name} build file"/>
  <echo message="------------------"/>
  <echo message=""/>
  <echo message="Available targets are:"/>
  <echo message=""/>
  <echo message="list      -- List Tomcat applications"/>
  <echo message="start     -- Start Tomcat application"/>
  <echo message="stop      -- Stop Tomcat application"/>
  <echo message="reload    -- Reload application in Tomcat"/>
  <echo message="build     -- Build the application
                (needed only if you have any Java Servlets)"/>
  <echo message="deploydir -- Deploy application as directory"/>
  <echo message="deploywar -- Deploy application as a WAR file"/>
  <echo message="undeploy  -- Undeploy application"/>
  <echo message=""/>
</target>

<!-- define common targets for Tomcat 5.5 -->
<target name="list" description="List Tomcat applications">
  <list url="${tomcat.manager.url}"
    username="${tomcat.manager.username}"
    password="${tomcat.manager.password}"/>
</target>

<target name="start" description="Start Tomcat application">
  <start url="${tomcat.manager.url}"
    username="${tomcat.manager.username}"
    password="${tomcat.manager.password}"
    path="/${name}"/>
```

```
  </target>

  <target name="stop" description="Stop Tomcat application">
    <stop url="${tomcat.manager.url}"
      username="${tomcat.manager.username}"
      password="${tomcat.manager.password}"
      path="/${name}"/>
  </target>

  <target name="reload" description="Reload application in Tomcat">
    <reload url="${tomcat.manager.url}"
      username="${tomcat.manager.username}"
      password="${tomcat.manager.password}"
      path="/${name}"/>
  </target>

  <!-- define project targets -->
  <target name="build" description="Compile java files">
    <mkdir dir="${build.dir}"/>
    <javac destdir="${build.dir}" debug="true"
      deprecation="false" optimize="false" failonerror="true">
      <src path="${src.dir}"/>
      <classpath refid="master-classpath"/>
    </javac>
  </target>

  <target name="deploydir" depends="build"
          description="Deploy application">
    <copy todir="${deploy.dir}/${name}"
          preservelastmodified="true">
      <fileset dir="${web.dir}">
        <include name="**/*.*"/>
      </fileset>
    </copy>
  </target>

  <target name="deploywar" depends="build"
    description="Deploy application as a WAR file">
    <war destfile="${name}.war"
        webxml="${web.dir}/WEB-INF/web.xml">
      <fileset dir="${web.dir}">
        <include name="**/*.*"/>
      </fileset>
    </war>
    <deploy url="${tomcat.manager.url}"
      username="${tomcat.manager.username}"
```

```
        password="${tomcat.manager.password}"
        path="/${name}" war="file:${name}.war"/>
  </target>

  <target name="undeploy"
          description="Undeploy application in Tomcat">
    <undeploy url="${tomcat.manager.url}"
      username="${tomcat.manager.username}"
      password="${tomcat.manager.password}"
      path="/${name}"/>
  </target>

</project>
```

After creating the directory structure and build files, copy the contents of the folder
dow30prototype from the previous section into the WebContent folder in the dow30app
directory. Leave the src folder empty for this example. It will be used when Java Servlets
are added to this application to provide dynamic data to the General Interface application.

Open an MS-DOS command prompt and start Tomcat by typing the command
startup.bat from the Tomcat install directory. A new DOS window will open.

Now open an MS-DOS command window and type the commands as shown in
Figure 3.16 to deploy the application to Tomcat.

Figure 3.16   Deploying Tomcat
Applications using ant.

After the application is successfully deployed, launch a web browser and type the URL into the address bar—http://localhost:8080/dow30app—to see the same application running under Tomcat.

Working with XML and XSL

In this chapter, I discuss how to use General Interface with XML and XSL. My approach is one of building from the ground up, so I will build a complete application with TIBCO General Interface using XML and XSL. All the code components required to build and run the examples are included on the companion CD-ROM.

One of the many powerful features of TIBCO General Interface is its capability to work with XML and XSL. Its XML Mapping Utility can be used to do the following:

- Parse a WSDL document and break it down into its parts (service call, input, and output).
- Map form elements to the input message to prepare an XML document for an HTTP or web service request.
- Map the incoming XML document from an HTTP or web service call to various GUI widgets (for example, a data grid) on the screen.

GI Builder includes a utility called XML Mapping Utility for creating a rule and generating JavaScript code to make the web service call. XML Mapping Utility saves all the necessary parameters, such as WSDL URL, web service URL, and input mappings and output mappings, into a serialized XML format. A mapping created using the XML Mapping Utility is called a *rule* and is placed into a folder named `rules`, which is created when the project is created by General Interface.

Architecturally, mappings work as shown in Figure 4.1.

GI Builder's XML Mapping Utility generates JavaScript code that loads the serialized rules file, prepares an input message using the mapping rules, and then makes the service call. The request message is prepared from the HTML elements or from the CDF data model. The request message may also be prepared by custom JavaScript code.

Then upon return, the output message from the HTTP or the web service call is parsed and placed into General Interface's internal data cache after applying the mapping rules to the output message. This cache is in the internal CDF format that can be used as a model for any General Interface control. The process of preparing an input message and parsing the output message involves the use of the XSLT processor and it is driven from

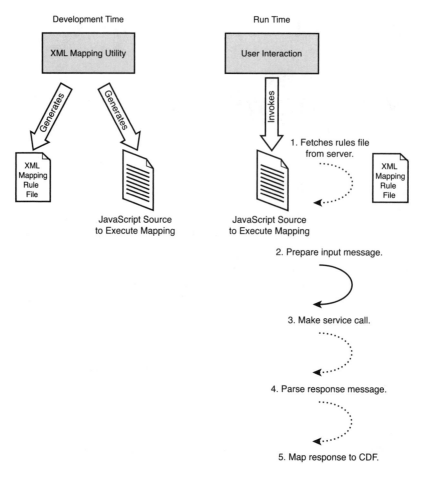

Figure 4.1   XML Mapping Utility explained.

the mapping rules file. Additionally, custom JavaScript code may be used to consume the output message and generate HTML content.

There is an option to compile this rule that results in generating an XSL style sheet for high-performance conversion of the message into the desired CDF format. Again, custom XSL mappings can be performed by developing JavaScript code and XSL style sheets as per requirements.

The JavaScript code that is generated by the XML Mapping Utility can be called from any JavaScript function, such as a Button component's Execute event script or from a custom JavaScript function. General Interface gives you an option to compile it into an XSL style sheet, which runs faster particularly for larger data sets. In this case, General Interface converts the rules file into corresponding XSL style sheets when the rule is compiled, and then at runtime, these XSL files are used to parse input and output messages.

XML Transformers

Most GUI components in General Interface can use an XML Transformer, which is an XSL style sheet that runs just before General Interface renders the component onscreen. The purpose of an XML Transformer is to convert source XML into CDF format.

To demonstrate XML Transformers, I am going to build the example from Chapter 3 using a simple XML Transformer. We will also learn about how to use XSL in General Interface and an XSL debugging utility that is part of GI Builder.

I will use a simple XML file for input data this time. The XML file can come from any database that supports XML output. In this case, I have used MySQL with phpMyAdmin to generate the output file using the *export table* option. A partial listing of this file with only two rows is shown in Listing 4.1, and the complete file is included on the companion CD-ROM.

Listing 4.1   XML Data File Showing Two Rows of `dow30` Data

```
<?xml version="1.0" encoding="utf-8" ?>
<dow30>
  <component>
    <Ticker>MMM</Ticker>
    <Company>3M</Company>
    <Industry>Diversified Industrials</Industry>
    <DateAdded>August 9, 1976</DateAdded>
  </component>
  <component>
    <Ticker>AA</Ticker>
    <Company>Alcoa</Company>
    <Industry>Aluminum</Industry>
    <DateAdded>June 1, 1959</DateAdded>
  </component>
</dow30>
```

Note that this XML file in Listing 4.1 does not use attributes. Instead it defines element names for data, which is more common in XML files. The entire document is enclosed within the tags `<dow30>` and `</dow30>` and each row is enclosed within the tags `<component>` and `</component>`. Elements `<Ticker>`, `<Company>`, `<Industry>`, and `<DateAdded>` are defined to hold the values for the symbol, company name, industry, and the date when the component was added to the DOW Jones Index.

TIBCO General Interface includes a JavaScript API to let you perform XSL transformations at runtime. Additionally, GI Builder includes a simple tool that can be used to test and debug the XSL style sheets. I will use the XSL style sheet in Listing 4.2 to convert the source XML file into CDF format, which is required by TIBCO General Interface controls.

Listing 4.2   XSL Style Sheet for Transforming XML into CDF

```xml
<?xml version="1.0" encoding="UTF-8" ?>
<xsl:stylesheet xmlns:xsl=
    "http://www.w3.org/1999/XSL/Transform" version="1.0">
  <xsl:output method="xml" indent="yes"/>
  <xsl:template match="dow30">
    <data jsxid="jsxroot">
    <xsl:apply-templates/>
    </data>
  </xsl:template>

<xsl:template match="component">
  <xsl:element name="record">
    <xsl:attribute name="jsxid">
      <xsl:value-of select="position()"/>
    </xsl:attribute>
    <xsl:for-each select="*">
      <xsl:attribute name="{name()}">
        <xsl:value-of select="."/>
      </xsl:attribute>
    </xsl:for-each>
  </xsl:element>
</xsl:template>

</xsl:stylesheet>
```

The XSL style sheet begins by creating a new document root element <data> with an attribute *jsxid* with a value of *jsxroot*. This is very important to note because General Interface controls ignore all other elements except the data node with this particular attribute value. This makes it possible to use any XML file in General Interface applications. This also makes it possible to cache larger XML documents that contain other application data and use the entire document as the model because General Interface will ignore everything else except this data node where the value of the *jsxid* attribute is *jsxroot*.

This style sheet looks for rows enclosed within the <component> tag and turns each child element into an attribute of the generated <record> element. Also note that this style sheet generates one <record> element for every row in the table. Recall from Chapter 3, "Quick Start TIBCO General Interface," that this is the CDF format as defined by TIBCO General Interface. Each <record> element in the CDF must have a unique value for the *jsxid* attribute. In an XML transformer, there is an automated way to generate a unique *jsxid* value for each <record> element. In this style sheet, I have used the position() function to generate unique *jsxid* values.

The following steps demonstrate how to test this style sheet and create the General Interface project that uses this XSL style sheet. Some of the initial steps are similar to what you did in Chapter 3. That's because this is another way to build the same application. The objective in Chapter 3 was to demonstrate how to create, deploy, and distribute simple General Interface applications, and the goal here is to demonstrate the use of XML transformers.

1. Launch GI Builder tool and select New Project from the Project menu and type the name of the project—**dow30xsl**. GI Builder will create the folder structure for the new application.

2. Drag and drop the Grid component from the Component Libraries onto the application canvas.

3. Delete column nodes mc1 and mc2 by selecting each node in the Component Hierarchy quadrant and clicking the Trash toolbar button at the top of that palette.

4. Click the matrix1 component in the Component Hierarchy to select it, and then in the Properties Editor scroll down until you see XML String property. Click the right mouse button over the name of the property (XML String) and select Reset/Clear from the context menu to clear the value.

5. Copy the file dow30components.xml (which is available on the companion CD) to the xml folder inside this project folder within your GI Workspace folder. Note that the contents are not in CDF format this time. This is the type of XML file that you will get from running a SQL query that can return data in XML format or from a database admin tool such as phpMyAdmin.

6. Copy the file dow30transformer.xsl (which is also available on the companion CD) to the xsl folder inside this project folder within your GI Workspace folder.

7. Drag and drop three Text column objects onto the Grid.

8. Drag and drop one Date column object onto the Grid.

9. Change the Name, Att Name, and Caption properties of the columns as follows:

Property	Value
First Column Named textColumn	
Name	Ticker
Att Name	Ticker
Caption	Ticker
Second Column Named textColumn	
Name	Company
Att Name	Company
Caption	Company
Third Column Named textColumn	
Name	Industry

Property	Value
Att Name	Industry
Caption	Industry
Fourth Column Named dateColumn	
Name	DateAdded
Att Name	DateAdded
Caption	Date Added

10. Select Save and Reload from the File menu once to make sure the project state is saved and the appropriate memory caches are updated. At this point your project will look like Figure 4.2.

Figure 4.2   Project `dow30xsl` after adding a Grid component and deleting columns.

So far you have created a simple grid with columns and no data. Follow these steps to display the data in the grid:

1. Select `matrix1` in the Component Hierarchy. The Properties palette shows the properties for this Matrix instance. Scroll down all the way to get to the XML/XSL section of properties.

2. Enter **xml/dow30components.xml** for the value of the XML URL property.

3. Enter **xsl/dow30transformer.xsl** for the value of the XML transformer property.

4. Select Save and Reload from the File menu to make sure the project state is saved and the appropriate memory caches are updated. At this point your project will look like Figure 4.3.

Note that all the data is populated properly in the Grid control exactly as we expected, even though the XML is not in CDF format. The Transformer style sheet was run first to convert the XML to CDF format, and then the View class of the Matrix component rendered it onscreen.

XML/XSL Merge Tool

GI Builder includes a simple tool to view the results of an XML/XSL merge. This can be used as a debugging tool for XSL style sheets. In General Interface, the output of XML data and Transformer XSL style sheet must always be a valid CDF model. You can view the output of the merge and make sure it confirms to CDF spec before plugging it into General Interface controls.

Alternatively, if the data onscreen does not quite reflect the data in the XML, you can use this tool to view the CDF that will be generated. Often, the first version of the XSL style sheet does not do the desired job. If you develop on a Linux or Mac platform, you can use the command `xsltproc` to test your XSL style sheet.

In GI Builder, you can test XSL style sheets using the XML/XSL Merge tool that's included. Selecting the menu option XML/XSL Merge Tool from the Tools menu in GI Builder will bring up the tool as shown in Figure 4.4.

XML/XSL Merge Tool is a Visual tool to see the results of an XML/XSL merge, and it offers many choices for the source XML as well as the XSL style sheet to use. The first tab Source (XML) has four option buttons indicating that the XML can come from either a URL, from GI Cache, as a result of a JavaScript call, or it can be directly typed into a text area provided there. Similarly, the XSL style sheet can be supplied using any of the preceding methods to the tool. Because processing in your application may involve multiple steps, the tool can use output from any of those steps.

Figure 4.3   Project `dow30xsl` after setting up the
XML file and XSL transformer.

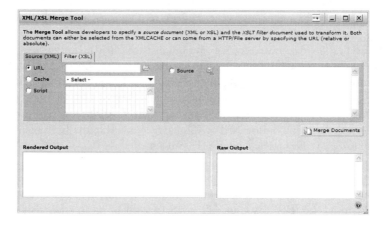

Figure 4.4   GI Builder's XML/XSL Merge tool.

Follow these steps to test the output of merging XML data and the XSL style sheet for this example:

1. Select the Source (XML) tab.

2. Select the URL option button.

3. Click the Folder icon to bring up the Open File dialog.

4. Navigate to the file `dow30components.xml` in the `xml` folder inside the `dow30xsl` application folder.

5. Select the Filter (XSL) tab.

6. Select the URL option button.

7. Click the Folder icon to bring up the Open File dialog.

8. Navigate to the file `dow30transformer.xsl` in the `xsl` folder inside the `dow30xsl` application folder.

9. Click the Merge Documents button to see the output of the merge in the Raw Output area, as shown in Figure 4.5.

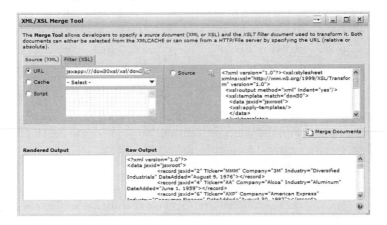

Figure 4.5   Output of XML/XSL Merge tool.

Note that the output of the merge is in CDF format.

XML Mapping Utility

If you do not know XSL, do not fret. GI Builder includes a tool to create mapping rules to populate General Interface controls from XML files. It can also generate JavaScript source code to invoke the mapping rule upon any user event. Follow these steps to build the same grid using the XML Mapping Utility:

1. Launch the GI Builder tool, and from the Project menu select New Project. Type the name of the project—**dow30map**. GI Builder creates the folder structure for the new application.

2. Drag and drop the Layout-Top/Over component from the Component Libraries onto the application canvas. This layout and others are available in the `Containers` folder. The functionality provided by layout components in General Interface is

similar to that provided by the Layout Manager in Java Swing. The different Layout elements can be used to divide the application canvas into separate areas. Application canvas must have a single root element. This root element may contain any number of container elements, which in turn can contain other components, including other containers. A Layout-Top/Over container divides the available canvas space into two spaces horizontally. You can then insert a Layout-Side/Side container in any of the areas to divide it into two areas vertically.

3. When you insert a Layout-Top/Over component into the canvas, you will see two panes that each correspond to an area of the canvas. Select this panel by clicking this node in the Component Hierarchy palette (in the bottom-left quadrant) and look at the Properties Editor palette (in the bottom-right quadrant). The property Rows Array shows how the area is split. The default value for this property is 100, * which means that the top 100 pixels of the area are allocated to the top pane and the remaining area is allocated to the bottom pane. Change it to 60, * for this example.

4. Drag a Button component from the Component Libraries palette onto the top pane in the canvas. You can find the Button component in the Form Elements folder inside the Component Libraries palette.

5. As you drag a component to the canvas, General Interface leaves it selected. Look at the Properties Editor palette and change the Relative XY property of the button to Absolute, and change the values for Left and Top properties to 20. This positions the button at a convenient location in the pane.

6. Drag a Grid component into the bottom pane.

7. Delete column nodes mc1 and mc2 by selecting each node in the Component Hierarchy palette and clicking the Trash toolbar button at the top of that palette.

8. Click the matrix1 component in the Component Hierarchy to select it, and then in the Properties Editor scroll down until you see the XML String property. Click the right mouse button over the name of the property (XML String) and select Reset/Clear from the context menu to clear the value. Also set the XML Cache property to dow30document. This is used to bind the CDF document that is the result of running the XML Mapping rule in the steps that follow.

9. Drag and drop three Text column objects onto the Grid. By default, General Interface fills in an XML string, which results in country names in this column. You can ignore this for now. The following steps take care of associating the right attribute name with the column.

10. Drag and drop one Date column object onto the Grid.

11. Change the Name, Att Name, and Caption properties of the columns as shown next:

Property	Value
First Column Named textColumn	
Name	Ticker
Att Name	Ticker
Caption	Ticker
Second Column Named textColumn	
Name	Company
Att Name	Company
Caption	Company
Third Column Named textColumn	
Name	Industry
Att Name	Industry
Caption	Industry
Fourth Column Named dateColumn	
Name	DateAdded
Att Name	DateAdded
Caption	DateAdded

12. Select Save and Reload from the File menu once to make sure the project state is saved and the appropriate memory caches are updated. At this point your project will look like Figure 4.6.

So far you have created a button and a simple grid with columns and no data. Now you will use the XML Mapping Utility to create a mapping rule and generate JavaScript code to run that rule to populate the data in the grid. Follow these steps:

1. Copy the `dow30components.xml` file from the companion CD into the `C:\InetPub` folder on your machine if you are using IIS. Or you can copy it to the `C:\tomcat55\webapps\ROOT` folder if you are using Tomcat for this example. Make sure you can retrieve the file in the browser by typing in its URL—http://local-host/dow30components.xml in IIS or in Tomcat using the URL http://local-host:8080/dow30components.xml.

2. From the Tools menu, select XML Mapping Utility. Figure 4.7 shows this utility.

3. There is one option button for WSDL and another for XML/XHTML/Schema. Select the XML/XHTML/Schema to map the XML file for this example.

4. Now the Utility shows two text fields: one for Outbound Document URL and one for Inbound Document URL. Outbound documents are request messages that

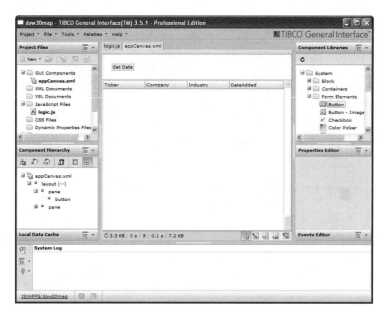

Figure 4.6   Project `dow30map` after creating the layout.

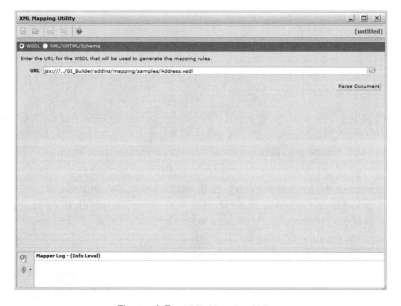

Figure 4.7   XML Mapping Utility.

can be sent to a web service, and inbound documents are what is returned from the web service as the response. In this example no outbound document exists, so click in the text field for outbound document and blank it out.

5. Type in the URL to the dow30components.xml file in the inbound document URL text field—http://localhost/dow30components.xml.

6. Click the Parse Document button. General Interface loads the XML file, parses it, and displays it in a hierarchical form as shown in Figure 4.8.

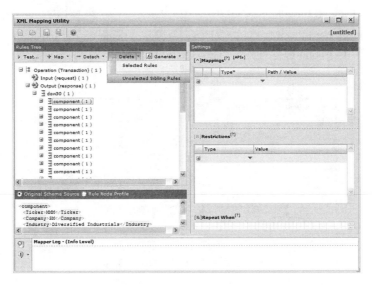

Figure 4.8   XML Mapping Utility after parsing the
XML document.

7. The XML file has a repeating structure, so General Interface shows all the nodes that it has parsed. With one component node selected, click the Delete menu in the Rules Tree and select Unselected Sibling Rule, as shown in Figure 4.8, to delete all but one node.

8. Click Operation (Transaction) in the Rules Tree on the left and type in the URL http://localhost/dow30components.xml in the Endpoint URL text field in the Settings area on the right; then select GET in the Method pop-up menu.

9. Click dow30 node in the Rules Tree and select CDF Document in the Type menu in the Settings area. Type in the name **dow30document** in the Path/Value text field. This is the name of the cache element. This is the model for the Matrix component. The Matrix component that will display this data must be bound to this same name. In other words, the XML Cache property of the matrix1 component must also be set to dow30document. If you recall, that's what we just did in step 8 in the first set of steps in this section.

10. Click the `component` node in the Rules Tree and select CDF Record in the Type menu in the Settings area. Leave the Path/Value text field empty because all nodes in the CDF are automatically named `record`.

11. Click the `Ticker` node in the Rules Tree and select CDF Attribute in the Type menu in the Settings area; then type in the name of this attribute—**Ticker**.

12. Similar to Ticker, map `Company`, `Industry`, and `DateAdded` nodes to CDF Attributes with their corresponding names.

    The mapping rule has been created. Now you are ready to test this rule:

13. Click the Test button in the Rules Tree section to bring up the Test Interface for the XML Mapping Utility as shown in Figure 4.9.

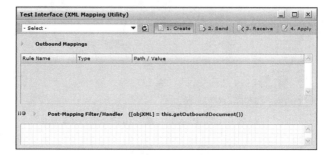

Figure 4.9   Test Interface (XML Mapping Utility).

14. Select Operation (Transaction) from the pull-down menu and click the green triangle below it to start the test. General Interface will go through each of the phases of the test and display the output. After the test is complete, you can click each of the tabs to view each step's processing and output.

15. Close the Test Interface and click the disk icon in the XML Mapping Utility to save this rule. Save this rule in the `rules` folder inside the application folder and give it the name **dow30map2.xml**.

16. Select Operation from the Generate menu in the Rules Tree to generate JavaScript code to run this rule. General Interface displays a dialog stating that the generated JavaScript code has been copied to the Clipboard.

17. Close the XML Mapping Utility and click the `logic.js` tab in the work area. Then click below the first comment line and press Ctrl+V to paste the JavaScript code from the Clipboard.

Note that General Interface generates a complete package definition for this code. Also note that General Interface generates default function handlers for success, error, and invalid call conditions. Depending on the response from the service call in the Operation, General Interface's function fires an appropriate event. Listing 4.3 shows that the main service function subscribes to these events and registers handler functions. (more on this in Chapter 8, "Advanced Features of Matrix").

Bold lines in Listing 4.3 show that the main service function subscribes to these events and registers handler functions. The default handler for success condition simply displays an alert.

In this example, when the service returns successfully, we want to repaint the matrix that displays the response. So we need to edit the onSuccess handler appropriately. After making required changes, the JavaScript code will look like the code in Listing 4.3.

Listing 4.3   Code for Running the `dow30mapping` Rule

```
/* place JavaScript code here */
jsx3.lang.Package.definePackage(
  "com.tibcobooks.gi.chapter4.service",
  function(service) {
     service.call = function() {
       var objService = dow30map.loadResource("dow30map2_xml");
       objService.setOperation("");

       //subscribe
       objService.subscribe(jsx3.net.Service.ON_SUCCESS,
           service.onSuccess);
       objService.subscribe(jsx3.net.Service.ON_ERROR,
           service.onError);
       objService.subscribe(jsx3.net.Service.ON_INVALID,
           service.onInvalid);
       objService.doCall();
     };

     service.onSuccess = function(objEvent) {
       var srvr = objEvent.target.getServer();
       var mat = srvr.getJSXByName("matrix1");
       mat.repaint();
     };

     service.onError = function(objEvent) {
       var myStatus = objEvent.target.getRequest().getStatus();
       objEvent.target.getServer().alert("Error",
        "The service call failed. The HTTP Status code is: "
        + myStatus);
     };
```

```
service.onInvalid = function(objEvent) {
  objEvent.target.getServer().alert("Invalid",
    "The following message node just failed validation:\n\n"
    + objEvent.message);
};


}
);
```

1. Now we need to hook up a call to this method when the button Get Data is clicked. To do this, click the button in the Component Hierarchy palette and click the Events Editor in the bottom-right quadrant to bring up the Events Editor palette.

2. In the Execute field, type in the code to make the call to the service function:

   `com.tibcobooks.gi.chapter4.service.call();`

3. Click Save and Reload from the File menu to save your work and reload all the scripts.

4. Click the Get Data button in the canvas, and General Interface runs the rule and populates the data in the Grid, as shown in Figure 4.10.

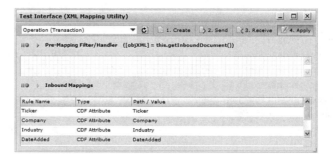

Figure 4.10   Project dow30map after
clicking the Get Data button.

Component Gallery

TIBCO General Interface has a rich set of components with which to build web applications. In this chapter, we look at the different components that are available out of the box for use in building rich Internet applications. Much of this text is available as online help in the product. It is here for reference along with some usage comments based on experience with the product.

TIBCO General Interface components are a superset of simple HTML controls and have a number of smart features over and above the simple controls available in HTML. Each of these components has a large set of properties and event handlers, which can be used to customize their look and feel and behavior. All components are implemented using a Model-View-Controller (MVC) pattern, which makes it very easy to update their view dynamically by changing the model.

General Interface components also support a number of useful events, such as the `onBeforeShow` event for the menu control, which makes it possible to alter the menu dynamically based on context just before the menu is displayed. We will look at the details of each component and how to use them in the sections that follow.

A sample application is included on the companion CD-ROM, which shows some of the commonly used controls. Simply open the `index.html` file in the folder `chapter5\ examples\componentgallery` to view the samples for this chapter.

Component Categories

At the highest level, General Interface divides components into three broad categories: System, Addins, and User.

The System category is reserved for out-of-the box components provided by General Interface. A large number of widgets are available with TIBCO General Interface. Every component has an XML representation and a JavaScript class associated with it. As you drag and drop components on the canvas, GI Builder constructs an XML file (`appCanvas.xml` by default) that contains the GI Application Object Model. All components have some common properties as well as events. Details of every built-in component are included in the "System Components" section that follows.

The Addins category is used by plug-in modules such as Charting. GI Builder has a pluggable architecture where new components can be developed and plugged in to General Interface. Each plug-in gets its own subcategory for the set of components it adds to the basic collection provided by General Interface. To view the charting components, from the File menu select Project Settings and click the Add-ins icon in the left navigation bar; check the check box for the Charting plug-in and click Save. General Interface prompts you to restart GI Builder for the changes to take effect. After restarting the browser, you will see additional components in the Addins category in the Component Libraries palette.

The last category, User, is for controls created by users. Business enterprises might need to build business-specific controls, such as a control to look up a company's stock symbol and share it among many applications. All user-developed controls are displayed in the User category of components. You can also create some common controls such as buttons with a specific style, place them in the User category, and use them in multiple General Interface applications to get a consistent look and feel.

System Components

In GI Builder, the System category is visually subdivided into several subcategories:

- Block
- Containers
- Form Elements
- Matrix
- Matrix Column
- Menus and Toolbars
- Miscellaneous
- ~Deprecated

TIBCO General Interface controls are closely modeled after the Java Swing framework. However, JavaScript classes for components have a very flat hierarchy. At the top level is `jsx3.gui.Block`, which derives from `jsx3.gui.Painted`.

Controls in the ~Deprecated subcategory are included for backward compatibility with earlier versions of TIBCO General Interface. These controls should not be used in new applications.

All components of TIBCO General Interface as available in TIBCO General Interface Builder are described in this section. Default properties in the sections that follow are the key properties set by GI Builder when you drag and drop that control onto the application canvas. General Interface follows an inheritance hierarchy of classes; therefore, many properties are inherited by several components.

Block

The Block subcategory contains only block, label, and image components.

Figure 5.1 shows all the components in the Block subcategory.

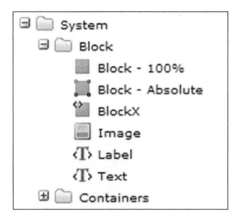

Figure 5.1   Components in
the Block subcategory.

Block—100%

Name	Block—100%
JavaScript class name	`jsx3.gui.Block`
Description	Simple block, relatively positioned with overflow=scroll.
Default properties	• Overflow = scroll • Name = block • Width = 100% • Height = 100% • Positioning = Relative
Usage Notes	Renders an HTML `div` element. Use it to hold other components. Inherits style elements from parent. Supports a large number of properties relating to positioning, size, and many more. Always apply custom styles to the highest-level element and have them trickle down for fast performance. Block can be used to hold custom HTML. Simply set the text property value as the custom HTML to be displayed in the Block.

Block—Absolute

Name	Block—Absolute
JavaScript class name	`jsx3.gui.Block`

Description	Simple block, absolutely positioned with overflow=scroll.
Default properties	▪ Background Color = Solid Medium ▪ Overflow = scroll ▪ Name = block ▪ Width = 100% ▪ Height = 100% ▪ Left = 0 ▪ Right = 0 ▪ Positioning = Absolute

BlockX

Name	BlockX
JavaScript class name	`jsx3.gui.BlockX`
Description	A simple BlockX control with a prefilled XML string. Content is generated by an XML/XSL merge.
Default properties	▪ Background Color = Solid Light ▪ Padding = 8 Pixel ▪ Positioning = Absolute ▪ Left = 10 ▪ Top = 10 ▪ Width = 100 ▪ Height = 100 ▪ Load XML Asynchronously = true ▪ Load XSL Asynchronously = true ▪ Name = blockX ▪ Content = `<helloworld/>`
Usage Notes	This element automatically shows XML formatted. Ideal for displaying XML data to users.

Image

Name	Image
JavaScript class name	`jsx3.gui.Image`
Description	Block object with `src` attribute set to reference an image. Overflow is set to expand.
Default properties	▪ Name = image ▪ Image Source = `jsx:///images/icons/logo_234_18.gif`
Usage Notes	Renders an HTML `img` tag with path relative to General Interface application path.

Label

Name	Label
JavaScript class name	`jsx3.gui.Block`

Description	Block object with Text/HTML property.
Default properties	▪ Positioning = Relative ▪ Overflow = expand ▪ Name = label ▪ Content = [label]

Text

Name	Text
JavaScript class name	`jsx3.gui.Block`
Description	Block with long Text/HTML property. Relatively positioned, so text will wrap around other relatively positioned objects.
Default properties	▪ Name = text ▪ Width = 100% ▪ Content = [Lorem ipsum ...]

Containers

The Containers subcategory includes a number of components that can contain other components and controls. Layout containers enable you to create different types of layouts for your application, and Tabs and Tab Panes enable you to create tabbed pages easily.

Figure 5.2 shows all the components in the Containers subcategory.

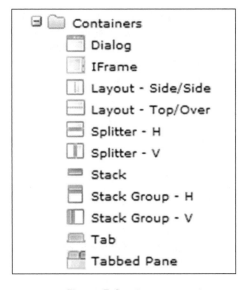

Figure 5.2   Components in the Containers subcategory.

Dialog

Name	Dialog
JavaScript class name	`jsx3.gui.Dialog`
Description	Dialog box. (Set Modal property for a modal dialog.)
Default proper-ties	▪ Background Color = Solid Medium Gray ▪ Width = 431 ▪ Height = 318 ▪ Z-Index = 5100 ▪ Window State = Maximized ▪ Name = dialog
Contains	▪ An instance of `jsx3.gui.WindowBar` and a Block for laying out other components. ▪ The WindowBar in turn contains three instances of `jsx3.gui.ToolbarButton`—Maximize, Minimize, and Close.
Default event handlers	Toolbar buttons have the following event handlers by default: ▪ Maximize: `this.getAncestorOfType (jsx3.gui.Dialog).doMaximize (this);` ▪ Minimize: `this.getAncestorOfType (jsx3.gui.Dialog).doMinimize (this);` ▪ Close: `this.getAncestorOfType (jsx3.gui.Dialog).doClose (this);`
Usage Notes	Renders a floating div with a very high Z index to ensure it floats on top of other contents on screen. Div is styled to look like a dialog box. When a Modal dialog is rendered, it blocks user interactions on the rest of the window, and a translucent pane covers the contents behind the dialog.

iFrame

Name	iFrame
JavaScript class name	`jsx3.gui.iFrame`
Description	Displays an HTML resource in a region of the application.
Default proper-ties	▪ Name = iframe ▪ Source = about: blank
Usage Notes	Renders a standard HTML iFrame element. The URL property points to the URL that will fill the contents of the iFrame. All requirements to be in an iFrame must be met by the URL.

Layout—Side/Side

Name	Layout—Side/Side
JavaScript class name	`jsx3.gui.LayoutGrid`
Description	Two side-by-side panes in an adaptive layout grid.
Default properties	▪ Positioning = Absolute ▪ Left = 0 ▪ Top = 0 ▪ Overflow = hidden ▪ Name = layout (l) ▪ Columns Array = 100,* ▪ Width = 100% ▪ Height = 100%
Contains	Two instances of `jsx3.gui.Block,` one on each vertical side, each with the following properties: ▪ Border = Outset ▪ Overflow = scroll ▪ Name = pane ▪ Width = 100% ▪ Height = 100%
Usage Notes	Values for the Columns array can also be specified as percentages; for example, 30%, 70%. This component is ideal for dividing the available area into two columns. All properties can be changed dynamically. A pane that slides open can be created by using a value of 0,* for hiding the left pane initially and then changing the value dynamically to 100,* (or 50%, 50%). Although the default component has two panes, any number of columns can be created by manipulating the columns array. For example, setting a value of 100,100,* for a columns array divides the available area into three columns; the first two are of size 100, and the rest of the area is given to the third column. The wildcard character * can appear anywhere. A value of 100, *, 100 can be used to create two columns of equal size on either side with the rest of the area available for content in the middle.

Layout—Top/Over

Name	Layout—Top/Over
JavaScript class name	`jsx3.gui.LayoutGrid`

Description	Two top-over-bottom panes in an adaptive layout grid.
Default properties	• Positioning = Absolute • Left = 0 • Top = 0 • Overflow = hidden • Name = layout (–) • Rows Array = 100,* • Width = 100% • Height = 100%
Contains	Two instances of `jsx3.gui.Block,` one on each horizontal side, each with the following properties: • Border = Outset • Overflow = scroll • Name = pane • Width = 100% • Height = 100%
Usage Notes	Values for Rows array can also be specified as percentages; for example, 30%, 70%. This component is ideal for dividing the available area into two horizontal parts. All properties can be changed dynamically. A pane that slides open horizontally can be created by using a value of *, 0 for hiding the bottom pane initially and then changing the value dynamically to 100,* (or 50%, 50%). Although the default component has two panes, any number of columns can be created by manipulating the columns array. For example, setting a value of 100,100,* for rows array divides the available area into three horizontal parts; the first two are of size 100, and the rest of the area is given to the third part. The wildcard character * can appear anywhere. A value of 100, *, 100 can be used to create two parts of equal size on either side, with the rest of the area available for content in the middle.

Splitter—V

Name	Splitter—V
JavaScript class name	`jsx3.gui.Splitter`
Description	Splitter (side-by-side panes)
Default properties	• Orientation = vertical • Left = 0 • Top = 0 • Name = splitter (l) • Sub container 1 Percentage = 50%

Contains	Two instances of `jsx3.gui.Block,` one on each horizontal side, each with the following properties:
	▪ Border = Inset
	▪ Overflow = scroll
	▪ Name = pane
	▪ Width = 100%
	▪ Height = 100%
Usage Notes	Splitter components are identical to the Layout components. Splitter—V divides the area into two columns with a divider that can be dragged by the user at runtime. A Splitter cannot have more than two parts.

Splitter—H

Name	Splitter—H
JavaScript class name	`jsx3.gui.Splitter`
Description	Splitter (top/bottom panes)
Default properties	▪ Orientation = Horizontal
	▪ Left = 0
	▪ Top = 0
	▪ Name = splitter (I)
	▪ Sub container 1 Percentage = 50%
Contains	Two instances of `jsx3.gui.Block,` one on each horizontal side, each with the following properties:
	▪ Border = Inset
	▪ Overflow = scroll
	▪ Name = pane
	▪ Width = 100%
	▪ Height = 100%
Usage Notes	Splitter components are identical to the Layout components. Splitter—V divides the area into two columns with a divider that can be dragged by the user at runtime. A Splitter cannot have more than two parts.

Stack Group—V

Name	Stack Group—V
JavaScript class name	`jsx3.gui.StackGroup`
Description	Stack group with two vertical (side-by-side) stack items. Some AJAX toolkits refer to this control as Accordion.
Default properties	▪ Orientation = Vertical
	▪ Positioning = Absolute
	▪ Name = stackgroup

Contains	Two instances of `jsx3.gui.Stack`, which are displayed vertically. Stacks are named `stack` and contain the text Stack 1 and Stack 2, respectively. Each Stack in turn contains an instance of a Block with the following properties: ■ Overflow = scroll ■ Load Type = Paint on Show ■ Name = pane ■ Background Color = #FFFFFF
Usage Notes	Stack Groups can be used to display different types of information in the same space while keeping a clear separation of content.

Stack Group—H

Name	Stack Group—H
JavaScript class name	`jsx3.gui.StackGroup`
Description	Stack group with two horizontal (top/over) stack items. Some AJAX toolkits refer to this control as Accordion.
Default properties	■ Orientation = Horizontal ■ Positioning = Absolute ■ Name = stackgroup
Contains	Two instances of `jsx3.gui.Stack`, which are displayed horizontally. Stacks are named `stack` and contain the text Stack 1 and Stack 2, respectively. Each Stack in turn contains an instance of a Block with the following properties: ■ Overflow = scroll ■ Load Type = Paint on Show ■ Name = pane ■ Background Color = #FFFFFF
Usage Notes	Horizontal stack groups are similar to Vertical stack groups. GI Builder uses stack groups for palettes in the two bottom quadrants.

Tab

Name	Tab
JavaScript class name	`jsx3.gui.Tab`
Description	Tab for use with TabbedPane container.
Default properties	■ Height = 18 ■ Name = tab ■ Content = [caption] ■ Background Color = #D8D8E5

Contains	An instance of Block with the following properties:
	▪ Background Color = Solid Medium gray
	▪ Overflow = Hidden
	▪ Positioning = Absolute
	▪ Load Type = Paint on Show
	▪ Name = pane
	▪ Width = 100%
	▪ Height = 100%
Usage Notes	Use Tabs to create multiple pages with quick navigation by clicking the tab. Any number of Tabs can be added to a TabbedPane container.

Tabbed Pane

Name	Tabbed Pane
JavaScript class name	`jsx3.gui.TabbedPane`
Description	Tabbed pane with three Tab children.
Default properties	▪ Selected Tab Index = 0
	▪ Name = tabbedpane
Contains	Three child elements of type Tab, each with the following properties:
	▪ Z-Index = 3
	▪ Height = 20
	▪ Name = tab
	▪ Content = [caption]
	▪ Background Color = #E8E8F5
	Each Tab in turn contains a Block with the following properties:
	▪ Background Color = Solid Medium Gray
	▪ Overflow = Hidden
	▪ Positioning = Absolute
	▪ Left = 0
	▪ Top = 0
	▪ Name = pane
	▪ Width = 100%
	▪ Height = 100%
Usage Notes	In BEA WebLogic Portal, this type of collection is called a Book. A Tabbed Pane may contain any number of Tabs, which may in turn contain other components to define the user interactions.

Form Elements

The Form Elements subcategory contains all the elements that can be placed in forms in General Interface. Note that General Interface includes a number of custom controls, such as Date Picker, Time Picker, Color Picker, Slider, and so on, in addition to the simple Form controls that are available in HTML. Even though HTML form elements can easily be used in General Interface applications, you should use the form elements that are provided in this library instead of using HTML form elements, because General Interface's controls add a lot of features and functionality over and above those provided by HTML form elements.

Figure 5.3 shows all the components in the Form Elements subcategory.

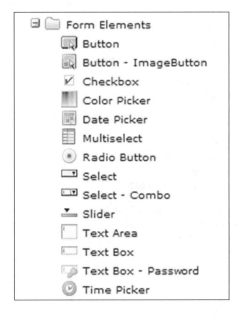

Figure 5.3   Components in
the Form Elements subcategory.

Button

Name	Button
JavaScript class name	`jsx3.gui.Button`
Description	A `jsx3.gui.Button` object.
Default properties	▪ Height = 18 ▪ Name = button ▪ Content = [button text] ▪ Margins = 0 4 0 0
Default event handlers	▪ Execute = `alert ('hello');`

Checkbox

Name	Checkbox
JavaScript class name	`jsx3.gui.CheckBox`
Description	A `jsx3.gui.CheckBox` object.
Default properties	▪ Height = 18 ▪ Name = checkbox ▪ Contents = [checkbox label] ▪ Margins = 0 4 0 0
Default event handlers	▪ Execute = `jsx3.out ('mycheck','the jsxexecute method was fired for checkbox,'+this.getId ());`

Color Picker

Name	Color Picker
JavaScript class name	`jsx3.gui.ColorPicker`
Description	An HSB color picker GUI control, instance of `jsx3.gui.ColorPicker`.
Default properties	▪ Border = Outset ▪ RGB Color = #FF0000 ▪ Name = colorPicker

Select—Combo

Name	Select—Combo
JavaScript class name	`jsx3.gui.Select`
Description	Combo/Select box. Allows the user to enter text manually or move through the list of options with type ahead.
Default properties	<ul><li>Width = 150</li><li>Height = 18</li><li>Type = Combo</li><li>Asynchronous loading of XML= true</li><li>Name = combo</li><li>Value = a</li><li>XML URL = `jsx:///xml/sample.xml`</li><li>Margin = 0 4 0 0</li></ul>
Default event handlers	<ul><li>On Mouse Down = `this.style.backgroundColor=''`</li><li>On Key Up = `jsx3.out ('a server call could be made here to perform a lookup on the value, ' + this.childNodes [0].value + '.');`</li></ul>

Date Picker

Name	Date Picker
JavaScript class name	`jsx3.gui.DatePicker`
Description	Date Picker object.
Default properties	<ul><li>Width = 100</li><li>Positioning = Relative</li><li>Height = 18</li><li>Name = datePicker</li><li>Margins = 0 4 0 0</li></ul>

Button—Image Button

Name	Button—Image Button
JavaScript class name	`jsx3.gui.ImageButton`
Description	A `jsx3.gui.ImageButton` object.

Default properties	▪ Width = 16 ▪ Height = 16 ▪ Name = imagebutton ▪ Image = jsx:///images/imagebutton/off.gif ▪ Mouse over Image = jsx:///images/imagebutton/over.gif ▪ Mouse down Image = jsx:///images/imagebutton/down.gif ▪ On image = jsx:///images/imagebutton/on.gif ▪ Disabled image = jsx:///images/imagebutton/disabled.gif
Default event handlers	▪ Execute = alert ('Execute');

Multiselect

Name	Multiselect
JavaScript class name	jsx3.gui.Block
Description	Multiselect object.
Default properties	▪ Border = Inset ▪ Width = 150 ▪ Height = 200 ▪ Overflow = scroll ▪ Name = multi1 ▪ Margins = 0 4 0 0 ▪ Background Color = #FFFFFF
Contains	An instance of jsx3.gui.Matrix with the following properties: ▪ Selection Model = Multi Select ▪ Load XML asynchronously = true ▪ Header height = 0 ▪ Name = matrix ▪ Focus Style = '' ▪ XML = default XML for a sample list Embedded matrix object contains a single Column object with the following properties: ▪ Name = column ▪ Cell Padding = 2 ▪ Bound CDF attribute name = jsxtext

Text Box—Password

Name	Text Box—Password
JavaScript class name	`jsx3.gui.TextBox`
Description	Password text box
Default properties	• Height = 18 • Name = password • Margins = 0 4 0 0

Radio Button

Name	Radio Button
JavaScript class name	`jsx3.gui.RadioButton`
Description	Radio button object, with default property for Radio Group.
Default properties	• Height = 18 • Selected = 0 • Positioning = Relative • Name = radio • Content = [radio button text] • Group Name = group1 • Margins = 0 4 0 0

Select

Name	Select
JavaScript class name	`jsx3.gui.Select`
Description	Select box object
Default properties	• Width = 150 • Height = 18 • Load XML asynchronously = true • Name = select • XML URL = `jsx:///xml/sample.xml` • Margins = 0 4 0 0

Slider

Name	Slider
JavaScript class name	`jsx3.gui.Slider`

Description	Horizontal slider form control.
Default properties	• Value = 0 • Positioning = Relative • Orientation = horizontal • Name = slider • Length = 200

Text Area

Name	Text Area
JavaScript class name	`jsx3.gui.TextBox`
Description	Text box object with Type property set to Text Area and Wrap = True.
Default properties	• Width = 200 • Height = 72 • Type = Text Area • Name = textarea • Margins = 0 4 0 0

Text Box

Name	Text Box
JavaScript class name	`jsx3.gui.TextBox`
Description	Text box object.
Default properties	• Height = 18 • Name = textbox • Margins = 0 4 0 0

Time Picker

Name	Time Picker
JavaScript class name	`jsx3.gui.TimePicker`
Description	Time picker object.
Default properties	• Positioning = Relative • Height = 18 • Hours = 0 • Minutes = 0 • Seconds = 0 • Milliseconds = 0 • Name = timePicker • Margins = 0 4 0 0

Matrix

Matrix is one of the most powerful components in TIBCO General Interface, and it is probably the most commonly used in applications of all types. A matrix is used to display tabular data onscreen. General Interface's MVC approach makes it possible to have multiple views associated with the same data model. It is possible to attach a matrix and a chart to the same backing data model in General Interface. Additionally, a matrix can display hierarchical data as well in a Tree view. Because General Interface is built with XML in mind, the Tree view is included that can display hierarchical XML data. All data for General Interface controls must be in CDF format. This subcategory includes all Matrix-related components, as well as a subcategory Matrix Column that contains Column types that can be added to a matrix.

Figure 5.4 shows all the components in the Matrix subcategory.

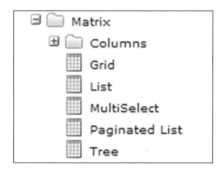

Figure 5.4   Components in
the Matrix subcategory.

Grid

Name	Grid
JavaScript class name	`jsx3.gui.Matrix`
Description	Matrix instance configured to allow for spreadsheet-like functionality, such as cell-based edits.
Default properties	• Name = matrix1 • Body border = 1 px solid #DFDFEF • Header border = 1 px solid #DFDFEF • Background Color = #EFEFFF • Paging Model = 2 – Pass • Selection Model = Not selectable • Load XML asynchronously = true • Content = default XML with sample data

Contains	Two sample columns mc1 and mc2 with the following properties: • Border = Outset • Background = Bevel TopDown • Background Color = Solid Disabled • Width = 30 • Resizable = false • Padding = 2 • Cell Padding = 2

Default event handlers	• On before edit = jsx3.log ('EVENT: (jsxbeforeedit). Record:'
	  + strRECORDID);
	• On after edit = jsx3.log ('EVENT: (jsxafteredit).
	  Record:' + strRECORDID + '. New Value:' + strNEWVALUE);

List

Name	List
JavaScript class name	jsx3.gui.Matrix
Description	Matrix instance configured to allow for List-type functionality. Additionally describes custom XSLT templates (for example, "value template"), borders (body, data cell, and header cell), auto-adjusting column widths paging (2-pass model) selection (multi-row) alternating row colors (jsx_rowbg1 and jsx_rowbg2) custom focus style event binding (execute), and XSLT uri-resolver template (resolving image URLs at runtime).
Default properties	• Name = matrix1 • Body border = 1 px solid #DFDFEF • Header border = 1 px solid #DFDFEF • Background Color = #EFEFFF • Paging Model = 2 – Pass • Selection Model = Multi-row • Load XML asynchronously = true • Focus style = font-weight: bold • Contents = default XML with sample data
Contains	Two sample columns mc1 and mc2 with the following properties: • Border = Outset • Background = Bevel TopDown • Background Color = Solid Disabled • Width = 30 • Resizable = false • Padding = 2 • Cell Padding = 2

Default event handlers	• Execute = jsx3.log ('EVENT: (jsxexecute). Record:' + strRECORDID);

MultiSelect

Name	MultiSelect
JavaScript class name	jsx3.gui.Matrix
Description	Matrix instance configured to allow for multiselect-type functionality.
Default properties	• Name = matrix1 • Body border = 1 px solid #DFDFEF • Header border = 1 px solid #DFDFEF • Background Color = #EFEFFF • Paging Model = 2 – Pass • Selection Model = Multi-row • Load XML asynchronously = true • Focus style = font-weight: bold • Contents = default XML with sample data
Contains	Two sample columns mc1 and mc2 with the following properties: • Border = Outset • Background = Bevel TopDown • Background Color = Solid Disabled • Width = 30 • Resizable = false • Padding = 2 • Cell Padding = 2
Default event handlers	Select = jsx3.log ('EVENT: (jsxselect). Record:' + strRECORDID);

Paginated List

Name	Paginated List
JavaScript class name	jsx3.gui.Matrix
Description	Matrix instance configured to allow for Paginated List–type functionality. Additionally describes customizing the scroll info label, custom row heights, and paging (paged model, including panel, row, and paint-queue configuration).

Default properties	■ Name = matrix1 ■ Body border = 1 px solid #DFDFFF ■ Header border = 1 px solid #DFDFFF ■ Background Color = #EFEFFF ■ Paging Model = Paged ■ Selection Model = Single Row ■ Paint queue size = 3 ■ Rows per panel = 50 ■ Panel pool size = 5 ■ Load XML asynchronously = true ■ Scroll info label = - viewing countries {0} to {1} of {2} - ■ Focus style = font-weight: bold ■ Contents = default XML with sample data
Contains	Two sample columns mc1 and mc2 with the following properties: ■ Border = Outset ■ Background = Bevel TopDown ■ Background Color = Solid Disabled ■ Width = 30 ■ Resizable = false ■ Padding = 2 ■ Cell Padding = 2
Default event handlers	Select = jsx3.log ('EVENT: (jsxselect). Record:' + strRECORDID);

Tree

Name	Tree
JavaScript class name	jsx3.gui.Matrix
Description	Matrix instance configured to allow for tree-type functionality. Additionally describes event binding (toggle), custom background, drag and drop, and on-demand (stepped) paging.
Default properties	■ Name = matrix1 ■ Background Color = Solid Light ■ Header Height = 0 ■ Load XML asynchronously = true ■ Rendering Model = hierarchical ■ Paging Model = Stepped (hierarchical) ■ Can drag from = Enabled ■ Can drop to = Enabled ■ Selection Model = Multi-row ■ Contents = default XML with sample data
Default event handlers	Toggle = jsx3.log ('EVENT: (jsxtoggle).' + strRECORDID + '.Open:' + bOPEN);

Matrix Column

The Matrix Column object can be used as a column in any type of matrix. General Interface defines a number of standard types of columns. Matrix columns support the concept of an edit mask. Any class that implements the Form interface can be used as an edit mask. When the user clicks in a cell with an edit mask, the mask is shown to the user for interaction and when the user clicks out, the value is inserted back into the cell. A single floating div is associated with each column mask that moves where the user clicks. Therefore, if a matrix has 200 rows, there will not be 200 floating div elements corresponding to each row. Figure 5.5 shows all the components in the Matrix—Column subcategory.

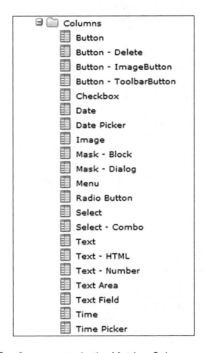

Figure 5.5   Components in the Matrix—Columns subcategory.

Mask Block

Name	Mask Block
JavaScript class name	`jsx3.gui.Matrix.Column`
Description	Example of using a Block as an edit mask for a matrix column. A Block with a single child of type `jsx3.gui.Form` is supported out-of-the-box. For more complex behavior, implement the methods `getMaskValue()`, `setMaskValue()`, and `getMaskFirstResponder()`. See the API documentation for `jsx3.gui.Matrix.BlockMask`.

Default properties	• Border = Outset
	• Background = Bevel TopDown
	• Background Color = Solid Disabled
	• Name = blockMaskColumn
	• Width = 150
	• Header label = Value
	• Padding = 2
	• Cell padding = 2
	• Bound CDF attribute name = jsxvalue

Contains	A Block with the following properties:
	• Background Color = Solid Medium
	• Border = Dashed
	• Width = 200
	• Height = 25
	• Z-Index = 1
	• Name = block
	• Padding = 5
	The Block in turn contains a Slider object with the following properties:
	• Smallest Value = 0
	• Positioning = Relative
	• Orientation = Horizontal
	• Name = slider
	• Length = 100%

Button

Name	Button
JavaScript class name	`jsx3.gui.Matrix.Column`
Description	Renders a clickable button in each row of a column using the `jsx3.gui.Button` class. In the EXECUTE event, the CDF record ID is available with `this.emGetSession().recordId`. Honors the `@jsxdisabled` and `@jsxnomask` CDF attributes.
Default properties	• Border = Outset
	• Background = Bevel TopDown
	• Background Color = Solid Disabled
	• Name = buttonColumn
	• Width = 100
	• Header label = Button
	• Padding = 3
	• Cell padding = 1
	• Value Template = @empty

Contains	An instance of `jsx3.gui.Button` with the following properties: ▪ Name = buttonMask ▪ Button text = Execute
Default event handlers	▪ Execute = `jsx3.log('Clicked on button mask in row' +` `this.emGetSession().recordId + '.');`
Usage Notes	Use this to render an action button in each row. As stated in the description, if a CDF record contains an attribute `jsxnomask` this button is not rendered in that row. Similarly, if a CDF record contains an attribute `jsxdisabled`, an inactive button is rendered that cannot be clicked.

Checkbox

Name	Checkbox
JavaScript class name	`jsx3.gui.Matrix.Column`
Description	Renders a check box in each row of a column. Sets the CDF attribute speci- fied in the path property to 0 or 1 based on the checked state. Honors the `@jsxdisabled` and `@jsxnomask` CDF attributes.
Default proper- ties	▪ Border = Outset ▪ Background = Bevel TopDown ▪ Background Color = Solid Disabled ▪ Name = checkboxColumn ▪ Width = 100 ▪ Header label = Checkbox ▪ Bound CDF attribute name = checked ▪ Cell text alignment = center ▪ Padding = 3 ▪ Cell Padding = 1 ▪ Value Template = @empty
Contains	An instance of `jsx3.gui.CheckBox` with the following properties: ▪ Name = checkboxMask
Usage Notes	Use this to render a Checkbox control in each row. As stated in the descrip- tion, if a CDF record contains an attribute `jsxnomask`, this button is not rendered in that row. Similarly, if a CDF record contains an attribute `jsxdisabled`, an inactive Checkbox is rendered that cannot be clicked.

Select—Combo

Name	Select—Combo
JavaScript class name	`jsx3.gui.Matrix.Column`
Description	Combo that selects one of a set of enumerated values. `jsxid` is the key; `jsxtext` is the text.
Default properties	• Border = Outset • Background = Bevel TopDown • Background Color = Solid Disabled • Name = comboColumn • Width = 100 • Header label = Combo • Padding = 2 • Cell Padding = 2 0 0 6 • Value Template = @empty • Format Handler = @lookup • Bound CDF attribute name = jsxvalue
Contains	An instance of `jsx3.gui.Select` object with the following properties: • Type = Combo • Name = selectMatrix • Contents = default XML with sample data

Date

Name	Date
JavaScript class name	`jsx3.gui.Matrix.Column`
Description	Renders a date according to a configurable date format. The data model can store the dates as epoch seconds or a string format recognized by the JavaScript `Date.parse()` method. Supported format handlers include @date, @date,short, @date,medium, @date,long, and @date,full.

Default properties	■ Border = Outset ■ Background = Bevel TopDown ■ Background Color = Solid Disabled ■ Name = dateColumn ■ Width = 100 ■ Header label = Date ■ Padding = 2 ■ Cell Padding = 2 ■ Bound CDF attribute name = date ■ Value Template = @empty ■ Format Handler = @date
Usage Notes	Dates are formatted automatically in this type of column. However, sorting by date is done using XSL and is not likely to be what you need.

Date Picker

Name	Date Picker
JavaScript class name	`jsx3.gui.Matrix.Column`
Description	Extends the Date column with a DatePicker edit mask.
Default properties	■ Border = Outset ■ Background = Bevel TopDown ■ Background Color = Solid Disabled ■ Name = datePickerColumn ■ Width = 100 ■ Header label = Date ■ Padding = 2 ■ Cell Padding = 2 ■ Bound CDF attribute name = date ■ Value Template = @empty ■ Format Handler = @date
Contains	An instance of `jsx3.gui.DatePicker` with the following properties: ■ Format = Medium ■ Name = datePicker

Button—Delete

Name	Button—Delete
JavaScript class name	`jsx3.gui.Matrix.Column`
Description	Renders an image in each row that when clicked causes the CDF record to be deleted from the matrix.

Default properties	▪ Border = Outset ▪ Background = Bevel TopDown ▪ Background Color = Solid Disabled ▪ Name = imageButtonColumn ▪ Width = 100 ▪ Header label = Delete ▪ Padding = 3 ▪ Cell Padding = 1 ▪ Value Template = @empty
Contains	An instance of `jsx3.gui.ImageButton` with the following properties: ▪ Name = `imageButtonMask` ▪ Image = `jsx:///images/list/delete.gif`
Default event handlers	The ImageButton has the following event handlers: ▪ Execute = `this.getParent().getParent().deleteRecord(this.emGetSession().recordId, true);`

Mask—Dialog

Name	Mask Dialog
JavaScript class name	`jsx3.gui.Matrix.Column`
Description	Example of using a dialog as an edit mask for a matrix column.
Default properties	▪ Border = Outset ▪ Background = Bevel TopDown ▪ Background Color = Solid Disabled ▪ Name = dialogMaskColumn ▪ Width = 150 ▪ Header label = Value ▪ Padding = 2 ▪ Cell Padding = 2 ▪ Bound CDF attribute name = jsxvalue
Contains	An instance of the standard `jsx3.gui.Dialog`.
Default event handlers	Contained dialog has Image buttons with the following event handlers: ▪ Close button handler = `this.getParent().getParent().commitEditMask(objEVENT);`

Image

Name	Image
JavaScript class name	`jsx3.gui.Matrix.Column`
Description	A column that renders an HTML image. Path is relative to the project.

Default properties	■ Border = Outset
	■ Background = Bevel TopDown
	■ Background Color = Solid Disabled
	■ Name = imageColumn
	■ Width = 20
	■ Header label = Image
	■ Value Template = @image
	■ Padding = 3
	■ Cell Padding = 1
	■ Bound CDF attribute name = jsximg

Button—ImageButton

Name	Button—ImageButton
JavaScript class name	`jsx3.gui.Matrix.Column`
Description	Renders a clickable button in each row of a column using the `jsx3.gui.ImageButton` class. In the EXECUTE event, the CDF record ID is available with `this.emGetSession().recordId`. Honors the @jsxdisabled and @jsxnomask CDF attributes.
Default properties	■ Border = Outset
	■ Background = Bevel TopDown
	■ Background Color = Solid Disabled
	■ Name = imageButtonColumn
	■ Width = 100
	■ Header label = ImageButton
	■ Padding = 3
	■ Cell Padding = 1
	■ Value Template = @empty
Contains	An instance of `jsx3.gui.ImageButton` with the following properties:
	■ Width = 16
	■ Height = 16
	■ Name = imageButtonmask
	■ Image = `jsx:///images/imagebutton/off.gif`
	■ Mouse over image = `jsx:///images/imagebutton/over.gif`
	■ Mouse down image = `jsx:///images/imagebutton/down.gif`
	■ On image = `jsx:///images/imagebutton/on.gif`
	■ Disabled image = `jsx:///images/imagebutton/disabled.gif`
Default event handlers	The contained ImageButton has the following event handlers:
	■ Execute = `jsx3.log('Clicked on the button mask in row' + this.emGetSession().recordId + '.');`

.Column

n menu in each row of a column using the
ass. In the EXECUTE event, the CDF record ID is available
ssion().recordId. Honors the @jsxdisabled and
ributes.

TopDown
Solid Disabled
n

name = Menu

mpty

gui.Menu with the following properties:

s
ult XML with sample data

t has the following event handlers:
('Executed menu item' + strRECORDID + 'in
etSession().recordId + '.');

olumn

in each row of a column. Only one row may be sets the CDF attribute specified in the path property to 0
ked state. Honors the @jsxdisabled and @jsxnomask
CDF attributes.

Default properties	<ul><li>Border = Outset</li><li>Background = Bevel TopDown</li><li>Background Color = Solid Disabled</li><li>Name = radioColumn</li><li>Width = 100</li><li>Header label = Radio</li><li>Bound CDF attribute name = radioed</li><li>Cell text alignment = center</li><li>Padding = 3</li><li>Cell Padding = 1</li><li>Value Template = @empty</li></ul>
Contains	An instance of `jsx3.gui.RadioButton` with the following properties:<ul><li>Name = radioMask</li></ul>

Select

Name	Select
JavaScript class name	`jsx3.gui.Matrix.Column`
Description	Selects one of a set of enumerated values. `jsxid` is the key; `jsxtext` is the text.
Default properties	<ul><li>Border = Outset</li><li>Background = Bevel TopDown</li><li>Background Color = Solid Disabled</li><li>Name = selectColumn</li><li>Width = 100</li><li>Header label = Select</li><li>Padding = 2</li><li>Cell Padding = 3 0 0 4</li><li>Value Template = @empty</li><li>Format Handler = @lookup</li><li>Bound CDF attribute value = jsxvalue</li></ul>
Contains	An instance of `jsx3.gui.Select` with the following properties:<ul><li>Name = selectMask</li><li>Contents = default XML with sample data</li></ul>

Text

Name	Text
JavaScript class name	`jsx3.gui.Matrix.Column`
Description	A plain text column.
Default properties	■ Border = Outset ■ Background = Bevel TopDown ■ Background Color = Solid Disabled ■ Name = textColumn ■ Width = 100 ■ Header label = Text ■ Padding = 2 ■ Cell Padding = 3 ■ Bound CDF attribute name = jsxtext

Text Area

Name	Text Area
JavaScript class name	`jsx3.gui.Matrix.Column`
Description	An editable plain text column. The edit mask can be larger than the data cell.
Default properties	■ Border = Outset ■ Background = Bevel TopDown ■ Background Color = Solid Disabled ■ Name = textareaColumn ■ Width = 100 ■ Header label = Text ■ Padding = 2 ■ Cell Padding = 3 ■ Bound CDF attribute name = jsxtext
Contains	An instance of `jsx3.gui.TextBox` with the following properties: ■ Height = 80 ■ Type = Text Area ■ Name = textareaMask

Text Field

Name	Text Field
JavaScript class name	`jsx3.gui.Matrix.Column`

Description	An editable plain text column.
Default properties	• Border = Outset • Background = Bevel TopDown • Background Color = Solid Disabled • Name = textColumn • Width = 100 • Header label = Text • Padding = 2 • Cell Padding = 3 • Bound CDF attribute name = jsxtext
Contains	An instance of `jsx3.gui.TextBox` with the following properties: • Name = textMask

Text—HTML

Name	Text—HTML
JavaScript class name	`jsx3.gui.Matrix.Column`
Description	Renders as HTML. Uses format handler @unescape (for Firefox) and value template @unescape (for IE), which makes it possible to include HTML characters such as < in the CDF attribute value.
Default properties	• Border = Outset • Background = Bevel TopDown • Background Color = Solid Disabled • Name = htmlColumn • Width = 100 • Header label = HTML • Value Template = @unescape • Padding = 2 • Cell Padding = 2 • Bound CDF attribute name = jsxtext • Format Handler = @unescape
Usage Notes	The difference between this and Text column is that you can render any HTML, including another div element within this cell, whereas in Text column you can render only plain text. Because of this, it is possible to dynamically control the styling of this element, but it is not possible to control the styling of Text cell.

Text—Number

Name	Text—Number
JavaScript class name	`jsx3.gui.Matrix.Column`
Description	Formats a number. One of `@number`, `@number,integer`, `@number,percent`, and `@number,currency`.
Default properties	<ul><li>Border = Outset</li><li>Background = Bevel TopDown</li><li>Background Color = Solid Disabled</li><li>Name = numberColumn</li><li>Width = 100</li><li>Header label = Number</li><li>Value Template = @empty</li><li>Padding = 2</li><li>Cell Padding = 2</li><li>Bound CDF attribute name = jsxtext</li><li>Format Handler = @number, integer</li></ul>
Usage Notes	Unless you need sorting and formatting of numbers, use Text column. Formatting of each cell is done using JavaScript methods (all format handlers are JavaScript methods), which makes rendering much slower than that for Text column. best results can be achieved by formatting the number in the server and having an unformatted number available in the CDF to sort against. A Matrix column can display one CDF attribute and can be sorted using a different CDF attribute.

Time

Name	Time
JavaScript class name	`jsx3.gui.Matrix.Column`
Description	Renders a time according to a configurable date format. The data model can store the dates as epoch seconds or a string format recognized by the `JavaScript Date.parse()` method. Supported format handlers include @time, @time,short, @time,medium, @time,long, and @time,full.

| Default proper-
ties | ▪ Border = Outset
▪ Background = Bevel TopDown
▪ Background Color = Solid Disabled
▪ Name = timeColumn
▪ Width = 100
▪ Header label = Time
▪ Padding = 2
▪ Cell Padding = 2
▪ Bound CDF attribute name = time
▪ Format Handler = @time
▪ Value Template = @empty |

Time Picker

Name	Time Picker
JavaScript class name	`jsx3.gui.Matrix.Column`
Description	Extends the Time column with a TimePicker edit mask.
Default proper- ties	▪ Border = Outset ▪ Background = Bevel TopDown ▪ Background Color = Solid Disabled ▪ Name = timeColumn ▪ Width = 100 ▪ Header label = Time ▪ Padding = 2 ▪ Cell Padding = 2 ▪ Bound CDF attribute name = time ▪ Format Handler = @time, short ▪ Value Templates = @empty
Contains	An instance of `jsx3.gui.TimePicker` with the following properties: ▪ Name = timePicker ▪ Background Color = #FFFFFF

Button—ToolbarButton

Name	Button—ToolbarButton
JavaScript class name	`jsx3.gui.Matrix.Column`
Description	Renders a clickable button in each row of a column using the `jsx3.gui.ToolbarButton` class. In the EXECUTE event, the CDF record ID is available with `this.emGetSession().recordId`. Honors the @jsxdisabled and @jsxnomask CDF attributes.

Default properties	▪ Border = Outset ▪ Background = Bevel TopDown ▪ Background Color = Solid Disabled ▪ Name = tbButtonColumn ▪ Width = 100 ▪ Header label = ToolbarButton ▪ Padding = 3 ▪ Cell Padding = 0 ▪ Value Templates = @empty
Contains	An instance of `jsx3.gui.ToolbarButton` with the following properties: ▪ Name = tbButtonMask ▪ Image = `jsx:///image/tbb/open.gif` ▪ Margins = 0 0 0 0
Default event handlers	Contained toolbar button has following event handlers: ▪ Execute = `jsx3.log('Clicked on button mask in row' +` `this.emGetSession().recordId + '.');`

Menus and Toolbars

The Menus and Toolbars subcategory contains components that can be used to create those user-interface elements. General Interface applications look and behave like, and in many ways rival, their desktop counterparts. General Interface includes a complete set of GUI elements to build desktop-like applications that run in the browser.

Figure 5.6 shows all the components in the Menus and Toolbars subcategory.

Figure 5.6   Components in the Menus and
Toolbars subcategory.

Menu

Name	Menu
JavaScript class name	`jsx3.gui.Menu`
Description	Menu object.
Default properties	▪ Load XML asynchronously = true ▪ Name = menu ▪ Tooltip = menu ▪ Menu label = menu ▪ Content XML = default menu items

Toolbar

Name	Toolbar
JavaScript class name	`jsx3.gui.WindowBar`
Description	Toolbar object, use for collecting sets of buttons into navigable groups.
Default properties	▪ Bar Type = Toolbar ▪ Name = toolbar

Menu Bar

Name	Menu Bar
JavaScript class name	`jsx3.gui.WindowBar`
Description	Menu Bar object, used to group multiple menus.
Default properties	▪ Bar Type = Menu Bar ▪ Name = menuBar

Taskbar

Name	Taskbar
JavaScript class name	`jsx3.gui.WindowBar`
Description	Taskbar object. Will hold an icon representation of open and minimized dialogs. Use LayoutGrid to position at the bottom of your app, or as desired.

Default properties	• Bar Type = Taskbar • Name = taskBar

Toolbar Button

Name	Toolbar Button
JavaScript class name	`jsx3.gui.ToolbarButton`
Description	Toolbar Button contains both text and icon.
Default properties	• Name = toolbar button • Image = `jsx:///images/tbb/open.gif` • Text label = [text]
Default event handlers	• Execute = `window.alert ('button clicked');`

Miscellaneous

The Miscellaneous subcategory includes sound controls and a simplified version of a Matrix control for lightweight requirements.

Figure 5.7 shows all the components in the Miscellaneous subcategory.

Figure 5.7   Components in
the Miscellaneous subcategory.

Sound

Name	Sound
JavaScript class name	`jsx3.gui.Sound`
Description	A sound component that can be played programmatically.
Default properties	• Volume = 50% • Name = sound • URL = `jsx:///sounds/beeps.wav`

Sound Button

Name	Sound Button
JavaScript class name	`jsx3.gui.Button`
Description	A button that plays a sound when pressed.
Default properties	• Height = 18
Contains	A single child element of type Sound with the following properties: • Volume = 50% • Name = sound • URL = `jsx:///sounds/beeps.wav`
Default event handlers	• Execute = `this.getChild(0).play();`

Table

Name	Table
JavaScript class name	`jsx3.gui.Table`
Description	Prebuilt table control.

Default proper-ties	■ Background = Bevel TopDown ■ Header height = 29 ■ Selection Model = Single Row ■ Font size = 10 ■ Load XML asynchronously = true ■ Name = abc ■ Column profile = default column definitions for six columns ■ Header style = background=color: #DFDFFF ■ Font weight = normal ■ Background Color = #FAFAFF ■ Font name = Verdana ■ Color = #232743 ■ Padding = 12 ■ Border = Solid 1px gray ■ Text alignment = right ■ Content = default XML containing sample data ■ Row style = background-color: #FAFAFF ■ Alternate row style = background-color: #EFEFFF
Default event handlers	■ Select = jsx3.log('The target record that was just clicked is' + this.getSelectedIds()); ■ Change = jsx3.log('The selected records are' + this.getSelectedIds()); ■ Execute = jsx3.log('The table was executed on record:' + strRECORDID + '. The selected rows are' + this.getSelectedIds());
Usage notes	This is a lightweight version of the Table and lacks many of the features available in the Matrix component. One important difference is that its column structure is driven by a separate column profile rather than being defined at design time like Matrix. This makes it possible to customize the column set that is displayed in this Table component.

Tree

Name	Tree
JavaScript class name	jsx3.gui.Tree
Description	Prebuilt tree control with custom icons.
Default proper-ties	■ Load XML asynchronously = true ■ Name = tree ■ Width = 100% ■ Height = 100% ■ Value = 1 ■ Content = default XML containing sample data

Component Properties

TIBCO General Interface Components support a very large number of properties. Many properties are inherited by all components. Additionally, each component supports its own set of properties. Listed next are some common properties, along with their default value and the corresponding CDF attribute name for each.

Object

Object Type	The JSX foundation class that this object is an instance of.		`jsxinstance-of`
ID	The unique, system-assigned ID for this object.		`_jsxid`
Name	Sets the name assigned by the developer to identify this object.		`jsxname`

Positioning

Relative XY	Sets whether to place this object relatively or absolutely with respect to its container.	Relative (`<code>jsx3.gui.` `Block.RELATIVE` `</code>`)	`jsxrelative-position`
Left	Sets the position of this object from the left edge of container. If this object is absolutely positioned, this value is applied as an implied pixel or a percentage. For example, `<code>10</code>` or `<code>15%</code>`.	If absolutely positioned, the default is 0. If relatively positioned, the default is empty.	`jsxleft`

Top	Sets the position of this object from the top edge of container. If this object is absolutely positioned, this value is applied as an implied pixel or a percentage. For example, `<code>10</code>` or `<code>15%</code>`.	If absolutely positioned, the default is 0. If relatively positioned, the default is empty.	jsxtop
Width	Sets the width of the control as implied pixels or a percentage. For example, `<code>100</code>` or `<code>25%</code>`.		jsxwidth
Height	Sets the height of the control in pixels or percentage. For example, `<code>100</code>` or `<code>25%</code>`.		jsxheight
Z-Index	If this object is absolutely positioned, sets the CSS z-index. The z-index sets the stack order of an element.	`<code>1</code>`	jsxzindex

List/Grid

Grow By	Sets whether a new row is appended to the view when a new record is added to the CDF document for the list. In the case of a grid, a new row is also appended when the last row in the grid gets cursor focus.	`<code>true (jsx3.Boolean.TRUE)</code>`	jsxgrowby
Word Wrap	The word wrapping for this object. If set to `<code>True</code>`, text wraps.	`<code>true (jsx3.Boolean.TRUE)</code>`	jsxwrap
Sort Path	Sets the attribute path to sort on, such as `<code>@jsxtext</code>`.		jsxsortpath
Sort Column Index	Overrides sortpath. Specifies the zero-based index for the child column to sort on.		jsxsort-column

Sort Data Type	Sets the default data type for columns in this list/grid.	Text (`<code>jsx3.gui.Column.TYPETEXT</code>`)	`jsxsorttype`
Sort Direction	Sets whether the grid is sorted ascending (a–z) or descending (z–a).	Ascending (`<code>jsx3.gui.List.SORTASCENDING</code>`)	`jsxsort-direction`
CSS			`css`
CSS Override	Convenience method for extending this object. CSS properties affecting layout, including `<code>border-width, padding, margin, width, and height</code>` are strongly discouraged, as they may interfere with the framework's internal box models. Because some controls are composited from multiple HTML elements, some styles might not cascade to nested elements. `  <b>Instance Properties</b>` are the preferred method for applying styles.		`jsxstyle-override`

CSS Rule Name	Sets the named CSS rule(s) to use. Rules that specify `<code>border-width, padding, margin, width,` and `height</code>` are strongly discouraged. Multiple rules may be specified, delimited with a space. For example, `<code>label emphasis</code>`. Because some controls are composited from multiple HTML elements, some rule styles might not cascade to nested elements. `  <b>Dynamic Properties</b>` are the preferred method for applying global styles.		`jsxclassname`
Display	Sets the CSS display property. When set to None, content is hidden and the container collapses.	Block (`<code>jsx3.gui. Block.DISPLAYBLOCK </code>`)	`jsxdisplay`
Visibility	Sets the CSS visibility property. When set to Hidden, content is hidden.	Visible (`<code>jsx3.gui. Block.VISIBILITY- VISIBLE</code>`)	`jsx- visibility`

Font

Font Name	Sets the name of the font family.	`<code>jsx3.gui.Block .DEFAULTFONTNAME </code>`	`jsxfontname`
Font Size	Sets the point size of the font.	`<code>jsx3.gui.Block .DEFAULTFONTSIZE </code>`	`jsxfontsize`
Font Weight	Sets the weight of the font, such as bold or normal.	Normal (`<code>jsx3.gui. Block.FONTNORMAL </code>`)	`jsxfont- weight`

| Color | Sets the color of the font. Accepts CSS values, such as pre-defined color names, RGB, or hexadecimal values. For example, `<code>red</code>`, `<code>rgb(255,0,0)</code>`, or `<code>#ff0000</code>`. | `<code>jsx3.gui.Block .DEFAULTCOLOR</code>` | jsxcolor |

Box

BG Color	Sets the background color. Accepts CSS values, such as pre-defined color names, RGB, or hexadecimal values. For example, `<code>red</code>`, `<code>rgb(255,0,0)</code>`, or `<code>#ff0000</code>`.	The default background color specified in the static field, `<code>` `DEFAULTBACKGROUND-` `COLOR</code>`, of the component class. For example, the default background color for a list is #f3f2f4 and is specified in `<code>jsx3.gui.List.` `DEFAULTBACKGROUND-` `COLOR</code>`. See the API documentation for the component. For some components, this prop-erty is empty.	jsxbgcolor
Background	Sets the CSS background defini-tion, such as `<code>background-` `image:url(abc.gif);back-` `ground-repeat:repeat-` `x;</code>`.		jsxbg
Padding	Sets the whitespace gap between the outer edge/border of this ob-ject to its inner content. Specified as one- or four-pixel values (top, right, bottom, and left). For exam-ple, `<code>5</code>` or `<code>8 4 8 4</code>`.		jsxpadding

Margin	Sets the gap between this object's border and its bounding box. Specified as one- or four-pixel values (top, right, bottom, and left). For example, <code>2</code> or <code>4 2 4 2</code>. CSS syntax is also supported but reduces performance.		jsxmargin
Border	Sets the CSS border definition. Specified as one- or four-value sets (top, right, bottom, and left). Specified as style width color. For example, <code>solid 1px red;dashed 2px red;double 3px black; solid 1px red;</code>.		jsxborder
Text Align	Sets the alignment of any contained object or text.	Left (<code>jsx3.gui.Block.ALIGNLEFT</code>)	jsxtext-align
Overflow	Sets the CSS overflow for this object, which defines how its onscreen view behaves when the contents are larger than the specified width and/or height.	Expand (<code>jsx3.gui.Block.OVERFLOWEXPAND</code>)	jsxoverflow

XML/XSL

XML Cache Id	Sets the cache ID for the XML document this object is mapped to.	Unique ID assigned by the system	jsxxmlid
XML String	Sets an XML document as a string.		jsxxml
XML URL	Sets the URL for the resource. This resource is synchronously loaded when this object is painted onscreen.		jsxxmlurl

XML Transformers	A comma-separated list of XSLT transformers. The source XML will be transformed in series by each of the transformers listed here before being placed in the XML cache. Each transformer is either a URI to an XSLT file or the XML cache ID of an XSLT document.		`jsxxmltrans`
Share Resources	If set to Share, this object does not delete its associated document from the cache when removed from the DOM.	Cleanup (`<code>jsx3.xml.Cacheable.CLEANUP-RESOURCES</code>`)	`jsxshare`
XML Async	If set to Asynchronous and the XML data source of this control is loaded from a URL, the data is loaded asynchronously and a loading message is displayed in this control until the data loads.	Synchronous (`<code>jsx3.Boolean.FALSE</code>`)	`jsxxmlasync`
XML Bind	If set to Bound, this control automatically repaints every time its XML cache document changes.	Not Bound (`<code>jsx3.Boolean.FALSE</code>`)	`jsxxmlbind`
XSL Cache Id	Sets the cache ID for the XSL document this object is mapped to.	Unique ID assigned by the system	`jsxxslid`
XSL String	Sets the XSL document as a string.		`jsxxsl`
XSL URL	Sets the URL for the resource. This resource is synchronously loaded when this object is painted onscreen.		`jsxxslurl`

Accessibility

Tab Index	Sets the tab index. It represents the group this component belongs to when tabbing between controls.		`jsxindex`
Tooltip	Sets the text displayed when hovered over this object (text only).		`jsxtip`

Text/HTML	Sets the text/HTML content of this object.		`jsxtext`
Tag Name	Sets the HTML tag to use when rendering this object onscreen.	`<code>span</code>`	`jsxtagname`
Cursor	Sets the CSS cursor definition, such as `<code>default</code>`, `<code>wait</code>`, or `<code>col-resize</code>`.		`jsxcursor`
Bound Menu	Sets the `jsxname` property for the context menu instance to display on a right-click.		`jsxmenu`
Enabled	Sets whether the view for this item is enabled and mouse/keyboard events will be listened to.	Enabled (`<code>jsx3.gui. Form.STATEENABLED </code>`)	`jsxenabled`
Value	Sets the value/content for the form control.		`jsxvalue`
Can Drag From	If `<code>true (1)</code>` (Enabled), this object supports drag events and allows any contained item to be dragged and dropped on another container supporting drop.	Disabled (`<code>jsx3.Boolean. FALSE</code>`)	`jsxdrag`
Can Drop On	If `<code>true (1)</code>` (Enabled), this object can be the target of drop events.	Disabled (`<code>jsx3.Boolean. FALSE</code>`)	`jsxdrop`

Column Interactions

Sortable	If Sortable, the list/grid can be sorted when a column header is clicked.	Sortable (`<code>jsx3.Boolean. TRUE</code>`)	`jsxsort`
Reorderable	If Reorderable, the columns in the list/grid can be reordered by the user at runtime.	Reorderable (`<code>jsx3.Boolean. TRUE</code>`)	`jsxreorder`

Resizable	Sets whether the columns in the list/grid can be resized by the user at runtime.	Resizable (`<code>jsx3.Boolean.TRUE</code>`)	jsxresize
Can Move	If `<code>true (1)</code>` (Moveable), this object can be moved around the screen. This is not the same as drag and drop.	Fixed (`<code>jsx3.Boolean.FALSE</code>`)	jsxmove
Can Spy	If `<code>true (1)</code>`, this object can be spyglassed. A spyglass displays HTML returned from the `jsxspy` event when a spyglassed object is hovered over.	`<code>false (jsx3.Boolean.FALSE)</code>`	jsxspy
Path	Sets the selection path for this column of data. Typically this is simply the name of the attribute, such as `<code>jsxtext</code>`, `<code>social</code>`, or `<code>phone</code>`.	`<code>@jsxid</code>`	jsxpath
XSL Template	Sets the XSLT fragment for any custom template to render the cells for this column.		jsxxsl
Separator	Precedes this item with a vertical separator to designate a new button group.	Normal (`<code>jsx3.Boolean.FALSE</code>`)	jsxdivider
Image	Sets the URI of the image for this object		jsximage
Word Wrap	Sets the word wrapping for this object.	Wrap (`<code>jsx3.gui.TextBox.WRAPYES</code>`)	jsxwrap

Resize

Resizable	Determines whether the dialog can be resized by the user at run-time.	Resizable (`<code>jsx3.Boolean.TRUE</code>`)	jsxresize

Min Width	Sets the minimum width of the dialog when resized. Units are implied pixels and only positive integers are allowed.		jsxminx
Min Height	Sets the minimum height of the dialog when resized. Units are implied pixels and only positive integers are allowed.		jsxminy
Max Width	Sets the maximum width of the dialog when resized. Units are implied pixels and only positive integers are allowed.		jsxmaxx
Max Height	Sets the maximum height of the dialog when resized. Units are implied pixels and only positive integers are allowed.		jsxmaxy

Metadata

Load Type	Sets the load type of this DOM branch.	Normal (`<code>jsx3.app.Model.LT_NORMAL</code>`)	jsxloadtype
Annotation	The annotation comment visible in the Component Hierarchy palette.		jsxannota-tion
Help ID	A unique ID for use with context-sensitive help.		jsxhelpid

Active BG Color	Sets the background color to use when the cursor is moved over this object. Accepts CSS values, such as predefined color names, RGB, or hexadecimal values. For example, `<code>red</code>`, `<code>rgb(255,0,0)</code>`, or `<code>#ff0000</code>`.	The default color specified in the static field, `<code>DEFAULTACTIVE COLOR</code>` or `<code>ACTIVECOLOR </code>`, of the component class. For example, `<code>jsx3.gui.Tab. DEFAULTACTIVECOLOR </code>`. See the API documentation for the component.	`jsxactive-color`
Idle BG Color	Sets the background color to use when the cursor is not over this object. Accepts CSS values, such as predefined color names, RGB, or hexadecimal values. For example, `<code>red</code>`, `<code>rgb(255,0,0)</code>`, or `<code>#ff0000</code>`.	The default inactive color specified in the static field, `<code>DEFAULTI- NACTIVECOLOR</code>` or `<code>INACTIVECOLOR </code>`, of the component class. For example, `<code>jsx3.gui.Tab. DEFAULTINACTIVE- COLOR</code>`. See the API documentation for the component.	`jsxinactive-color`
Disabled BG Color	Sets the background color to use when in a disabled state. Accepts CSS values, such as predefined color names, RGB, or hexadecimal values. For example, `<code>red</code>`, `<code>rgb(255,0,0)</code>`, or `<code>#ff0000</code>`.	The default disabled background color specified in the static field, `<code>DEFAULTDIS- ABLEDBACKGROUND- COLOR</code>`, of the component class. For example, `<code>jsx3.gui.Form. DEFAULTDISABLEDBACK- GROUNDCOLOR</code>`. See the API documentation for the component.	`jsxdisabled-bgcolor`

Disabled Color	Sets the font color to use when this object is in a disabled state. Accepts CSS values, such as pre-defined color names, RGB, or hexadecimal values. For example, `<code>red</code>`, `<code>rgb(255,0,0)</code>`, or `<code>#ff0000</code>`.	The default disabled color specified in the static field, `<code>DEFAULT-DISABLEDCOLOR</code>`, of the component class. For example, `<code>jsx3.gui.Form.DEFAULTDISABLED-COLOR</code>`. See the API documentation for the component.	`jsxdisabled-color`
Key Binding	Sets the key binding (keyboard shortcut) for this form control, which is specified as a '+' delimited string. For example, `<code>ctrl+s</code>`. See API documentation for `<code>jsx3.gui.Form.doKey-Binding()</code>`.		`jsxkeycode`
Required	Determines whether the form input field is required.	Optional (`<code>jsx3.gui.Form.OPTIONAL</code>`)	`jsxrequired`

6

Sharing Assets Across Multiple Applications

This chapter describes a best practices approach for building reusable TIBCO General Interface components. Detailed instructions are included on how to build and use such components.

Often it is necessary to create common components that can be used in multiple applications within an enterprise. You can create simple widgets using the visual designer and save them as components that can be used in any application. In Chapter 5, "Component Gallery," you saw that General Interface components have many properties that are editable in the GI Builder. Just as you create complete User Interfaces with GI Builder, you can also create components using the GI Builder.

Components can also have JavaScript code associated with them. Small scriptlets can be embedded within the event handler properties in General Interface components. However, for more complex components, it is cleaner and more manageable to have a separate JavaScript file. You will build custom components using JavaScript classes in Chapter 7, "Object-Oriented JavaScript—Extending General Interface Widgets." In this chapter, you build custom components using the visual designer and then use them to build multiple applications.

Advantages of Sharing Components

There are several advantages to building smaller independent components instead of building a large, monolithic application. Smaller components are easier to design, debug, and test. It is possible to develop components in parallel and reduce the overall project timeline. It is also much easier to maintain smaller components because the code is easier to follow and change. Deploying a smaller component is also easier than deploying a whole application.

Additionally, a well-designed component can also be reused in other applications that require similar user interface elements.

In the software industry, there are companies (such as Infragistics and Telerik) whose sole business is to build and market software components. A well-designed component that can be plugged in to any application dramatically reduces the time needed to build new applications. Components should be a part of an overall enterprise strategy because it is possible to accelerate the pace of innovation within an enterprise by reusing existing components.

Shared Components in General Interface

Widgets included with General Interface are very generic controls that can be used in any line of business. More specific business-related components can be built by enterprise developers. For example, a Stock Quote widget can be very useful in a financial services company because it is used by many financial applications. Similarly, a Book Detail widget can be very useful in a book publishing business.

General Interface's MVC architecture makes it possible to build independent components. Each component has a model, a view, and a controller. CDF is a common data model for all components. Various attributes can be defined for use in specific components. Views in General Interface are often defined using XML and XSL. General Interface's components are serialized into XML format. GI Builder creates a serialized representation of the canvas design as you drag other components into it. In addition, the controller for a component is built using JavaScript.

The XML file for each component allows you to provide a class name that will serve as the controller for the component. General Interface framework includes classes that can be extended to create custom controllers for custom components. At runtime, when General Interface loads a component's XML, it dynamically loads the controller class associated with it and creates a new instance of it for each new instance of the component. This allows the application to be loaded without having to load all the components and the JavaScript. Components and their controllers are loaded automatically as needed by the runtime.

For example, assume that you have a custom dialog with its own XML definition and a custom controller class in JavaScript. This dialog needs to be displayed only when the user clicks a button. The button is part of the initial screen that is loaded when the application is loaded. But the dialog and the associated JavaScript class are not loaded until the user clicks the button. This makes the initial loading of the application screen faster because only the opening screen needs to be loaded. Furthermore, General Interface framework provides ways to load the components in the background using asynchronous calls. We discuss these techniques in more detail in Chapter 16, "Optimizing Performance."

Building Shared Components with GI Builder

You can build components in GI Builder much the same way as you build full applications, except that components must be saved in their own XML files. When you open a new project with GI Builder, it creates a new file called `appCanvas.xml` by default to hold the User Interface components for the application. To create a new component, you need to select File, New, GUI Component option, or press the Ctrl+N key on the keyboard. GI Builder gives you a new canvas to draw your new component into. You can assemble the controls for your new component in this new canvas, change properties as desired, and save this file as an XML file.

To share this new component with other applications, recall from Chapter 5 that user-defined controls go into the User category in the Component Libraries palette. User controls that need to be shared must be placed in the Prototypes directory inside the GI Workspace directory. Anything that is placed in this directory is available for use in all General Interface applications.

There are four modes of persistence for a component within a drawing canvas—Transient, Embedded, Reference, and Reference-Asynchronous.

- Transient persistence implies that this particular component will first be removed from the DOM tree when the canvas being designed is saved to disk. A transient component may be displayed in the current GI Builder window, but when the canvas is first loaded—whether in General Interface or in the browser at runtime—it will not appear. It will be loaded on demand when required. Use this for components that need to be displayed upon certain events and that are then disposed, such as dialogs or alerts.

- Embedded mode of persistence ensures that the control or component will be saved to disk and will always appear whenever this canvas is displayed by General Interface. GI Builder essentially copies the XML for the component into the XML for the canvas, and thereafter it never looks at the original component XML.

- Reference mode of persistence is used for inserting external components into the canvas. Any components that are included using this mode are included by reference only, which means that whenever the canvas is displayed, the latest version of the referenced component will be loaded from the original component file. The component can be independently updated, and the updates will be automatically loaded when the canvas is repainted.

- Reference-asynchronous mode is a variation on the basic reference mode. It tells General Interface to load this component asynchronously from a separate file. This ensures better performance; however, component dependencies must be carefully considered when using this mode. For example, if the Grid component requires a Select component to draw itself, the Select component must be loaded before the Grid component. If Grid and Select components are set up with reference-asynchronous mode, there is no guarantee which one will load first. Therefore, the Grid initialization may not always be consistent.

It is obvious that the best persistence modes for shared components are reference or reference-asynchronous because they ensure that the latest copy of the component will be loaded whenever the canvas is loaded.

To insert a component using reference mode, you cannot simply drag and drop it onto the canvas. You must click the right mouse button on the container and select Import, Reference, or the Import, Reference-Asynchronous option from the menu.

Unfortunately GI Builder does not allow you to change an Embedded control to be a Reference control. It does allow you to convert a control's persistence mode from Reference to Embedded or Transient.

It is possible to edit the XML file for the canvas in a plain text editor; however, you must be very careful when manipulating files outside of GI Builder because some inadvertent error may make it impossible to open the file in GI Builder again. You must know the format of the file quite well before attempting to make such a change. The format of General Interface's XML screen definition files is very simple and easy to follow.

GI Builder also does not support giving your new component a unique name or icon. However, it is easy to do that by editing the component's XML definition using a plain text editor. Both the name and a reference to the icon image file are stored in the XML file.

Sample Applications

To demonstrate shared components, we will first build some common components and then develop the user interface screens for two separate General Interface applications using those shared components.

The first application is an online banking application that has a tabbed pane with two tabs. One tab displays an overview and the other tab displays details of an account. The second application is an online investing application with two tabs. One tab displays balances and the other displays positions. We will use a red color scheme for our applications.

Both sample applications have several common components, including an announcements panel, a customer service panel, and a banner ad panel. We will use shared tabbed pane and tab components to provide a common look and feel across both the applications.

Follow the steps outlined in the next section to create the shared components and then the two applications.

Building the Announcements Panel

The Announcements panel is a shared component that will be used in both applications. The following steps demonstrate how to build this component for our applications:

1. Launch GI Builder and start a new project by selecting New Project from the Project menu in the main menu bar.

2. Give this project a name—**Banking**—even though the components will not be part of this project.

3. Select File, New, GUI Component from the menu bar to begin building a new component. GI Builder will create a new [untitled] canvas as the starting point of this new component.

4. Drag and drop a Layout—Top/Over component into this new canvas.

5. Change the Rows Array property of this layout component to `20,*`.

6. Change the Text/HTML property of the first pane to Announcements.

7. Change the Font Weight property of the first pane to Bold.

8. Change the BG Color property of the first pane to #DDDDDD.

9. Drag and drop four label controls onto the second pane.

10. Change the Name property of the four labels to announce, announce2, announce3, and announce4, respectively.

11. Change the Text/HTML property of the four labels to Use Our New Spanish Version, Mobile Banking Is Here, Invest with 0 Dollar Trades, and No Interest for Six Months, respectively.

12. Change the Relative XY property of all four labels to Absolute.

13. Change the Left property of all four labels to 20.

14. Change the Top property of the four labels to 4, 22, 40, and 58, respectively.

15. Change the Color property of all four labels to #5555FF.

16. Change the Border property of all four labels to @Outset Bottom. To do this, click the right mouse button on the name of the property (Border) and select @Outset Bottom from the menu. This gives each label an underline.

17. Change the Cursor property of all four labels to @Hand. To do this, click the right mouse button on the name of the property (Cursor) and select @Hand from the menu. This sets the cursor to the hand cursor when the mouse is hovered over this item.

18. Open the Events Editor palette and change the Click event handler for all four labels to `alert('hello');` to display a simple alert when a link is clicked. To do this, you will need to select each label while the Events Editor palette is open and type in the code for the handler—`alert('hello')`—into the text field for the Click event property.

19. Select Save As from the File menu and save this file as **announcements.xml** in the **prototypes** directory under the **root** workspace directory.

Your project will look like Figure 6.1.

Close the **announcements.xml** by selecting File, Close from the menu. Follow the instructions in the next section to build the Customer Service panel.

Figure 6.1   Announcements panel component.

Building the Customer Service Panel

The Customer Service panel is also a shared component that will be used in both applications. The following steps demonstrate how to build this component for our applications:

1. Select File, New, GUI Component from the menu bar to begin building a new component. GI Builder will create a new [untitled] canvas as the starting point of this new component.

2. Drag and drop a Layout—Top/Over component into this new canvas.

3. Change the Rows Array property of this layout component to **20,***.

4. Change the Text/HTML property of the first pane to Customer Service.

5. Change the Font Weight property of the first pane to Bold.

6. Change the BG Color property of the first pane to #DDDDDD.

7. Drag and drop four label controls onto the second pane.

8. Change the Name property of the four labels to service1, service2, service3, and service4, respectively.

9. Change the Text/HTML property of the four labels to Manage Alerts, Stop Check Payment, Transfer Money, and Open a New Account, respectively.

10. Change the Relative XY property of all four labels to Absolute.

11. Change the Left property of all four labels to 20.

12. Change the Top property of the four labels to 4, 22, 40, and 58, respectively.

13. Change the Color property of all four labels to #5555FF.

14. Change the Border property of all four labels to @Outset Bottom. To do this, click the right mouse button on the name of the property (Border) and select @Outset Bottom from the menu. This gives each label an underline.

15. Change the Cursor property of all four labels to @Hand. To do this click the right mouse button on the name of the property (Cursor) and select @Hand from the menu. This sets the cursor to the hand cursor when the mouse is hovered over this item.

16. Open the Events Editor palette and change the Click event handler for all four labels to `alert('hello');` to display a simple alert when a link is clicked. To do this, you will need to select each label while the Events Editor palette is open and type in the code for the handler—`alert('hello')`—into the text field for the Click event property.

17. Select Save As from the File menu and save this file as **custservice.xml** in the prototypes directory under the root workspace directory.

Your project will look like Figure 6.2.

Close the file `custservice.xml` by selecting File, Close from the menu.

Figure 6.2   Customer Service panel component.

Building the Ad Banner

Ad Banner is another shared component that will be used in both applications. The following steps demonstrate how to build this component for your applications.

1. Select File, New, GUI Component from the menu bar to begin building a new
   component. GI Builder will create a new [untitled] canvas as the starting point of
   this new component.

2. Drag and drop a Block—Absolute component into this new canvas.

3. Change the Width property of this block component to 200.

4. Change the Overflow property to Hidden.

5. Change the Cursor property of the block to @Hand. To do this, click the right
   mouse button on the name of the property (Cursor) and select @Hand from the
   menu. This sets the cursor to the hand cursor when the mouse is hovered over
   this item.

6. Open the Events Editor palette and change the Click event handler for this block
   to `alert('hello');` to display a simple alert when a link is clicked. To do this, you
   will need to select the block while the Events Editor palette is open and type in the

code for the handler—**alert('hello')**—into the text field for the Click event property.

7. Drag and drop three label controls onto the block.

8. Change the Name property of the three labels to label1, label2, and label3, respectively.

9. Change the Font Size property of label1 to 82.

10. Change the Font Name property of label1 to Times.

11. Change the Text/HTML property of label1 to 0.

12. Change the Left, Top, and Width properties of label2 to 45, 25, and 145, respectively.

13. Change the Text/HTML property of label2 to Zero Dollar Trades.

14. Change the Font Size property of label2 to 16.

15. Change the Left, Top, and Width and Height properties of label3 to 45, 50, and 145, respectively.

16. Change the Text/HTML property of label3 to Apply Today.

17. Change the Font Size property of label3 to 16.

18. Change the Font Weight property of label3 to Bold.

19. Select Save As from the File menu and save this file as **bannerad.xml** in the prototypes directory under the root workspace directory.

Your project will look like Figure 6.3.

Close the **custservice.xml** file by selecting File, Close from the menu.

Building the Custom Tabbed Pane

The Tabbed Pane is another shared component that will be used in both applications. The following steps demonstrate how to build this component for your applications:

1. Select File, New, GUI Component from the menu bar to begin building a new component. GI Builder will create a new [untitled] canvas as the starting point of this new component.

2. Drag and drop a Tabbed Pane component into this new canvas.

3. Change the BG Color property of the Tabbed Pane component to @Solid Shadow.

4. Delete two of the tab nodes by clicking each one and then clicking the Trash icon in the menu bar. We will prepare one tab component and then clone it.

5. Change the Active BG Color property of tab1 to #CA5050.

6. Change the Idle BG Color property of tab1 to #9898A5.

7. Change the Font Color property of tab1 to #FFFFFF.

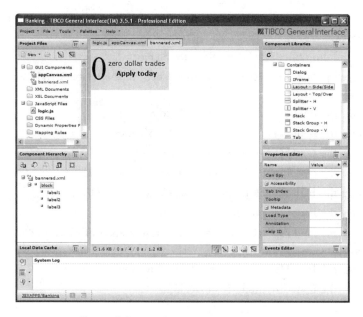

Figure 6.3   Ad Banner panel component.

8. Drag and Drop a Layout—Top/Over component into the pane and change the Rows Array property to 8,* to divide the available area into two panes.

9. Change the BG Color property of the top pane to #CA5050.

10. Drag and drop a Layout—Side/Side component into the second pane below to divide the content area into two columns.

11. Change the Name property of the second tab to tab1.

12. Select tab1 and make a copy of it by clicking the right mouse button on it and selecting the Clone option from the menu.

13. Change the Name property of the second tab to tab2.

14. Select Save As from the File menu and save this file as `redtabbedpane.xml` in the prototypes directory under the root workspace directory.

Your project will look like Figure 6.4.

Close the `redtabbedpane.xml` file by selecting File, Close from the menu.

At this point, you have created the common components. If you see the names of these files in the Project Files palette under GUI Components, click the right mouse on each and select Dereference from the menu to remove them from there.

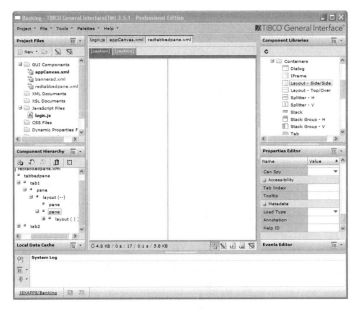

Figure 6.4   Red TabbedPane component.

Editing Component XML Files

When you save a file in the `prototypes` directory, it is saved with the original component name and icon. For these custom components, it's best to give them a different
name and icon to distinguish them from the built-in General Interface components. GI
Builder does not support renaming these. You must open the file in a plain text and
change the name. To do this for the announcements panel component, open up the file
`announcements.xml` in the `prototypes` directory in any text editor such as Notepad and
edit the line as shown (the name to be changed is shown in bold text):

```
<serialization jsxversion="3.5" xmlns="urn:tibco.com/v3.0">
    <name><![CDATA[Announcements Panel]]></name>
```

Similarly assign meaningful names (for example, Banner Ad, Customer Service panel,
and Red TabbedPane) to the other custom components previously built.

You can also create custom icons for your components. Because the sample custom
components are based on existing General Interface components, their icons are already
available in the General Interface distribution. Create a directory named `images` in your
GI Workspace folder, and then create a subdirectory named `prototypes` inside the images
directory. Now copy the images `block-abs.gif`, `layout-over.gif`, and
`tabbedpane.gif` from the `GI_Builder\images\prototypes` directory into this newly
created directory. You can also change these images to something more appropriate for
the custom components. For example, you could change the color of the tab to red for
the Red TabbedPane component.

It is also important to close and restart GI Builder after building custom components and setting up their icons and names. You will see the components in the Users subcategory in the Component Libraries after you close GI Builder and start it again, as shown in Figure 6.5.

Figure 6.5   Custom components in the User category.

Follow the steps in the next section to build the Banking application.

Building the Banking Application

This is the first application to use the shared components. It will have two red tabs.

1. Build the Banking application's screen in `appCanvas.xml`. Click the appCanvas tab to start designing the main screen.
2. Give this project a name—**Banking**.
3. Drag and drop a Red Tabbed Pane component from the User category into this new canvas.
4. Change the Text/HTML property of the two tabs to Overview and Details, respectively.
5. Drag a Layout—Top/Over component into the left pane and set its Rows Array property to `100,200,*` to divide it into three parts.
6. Clone one of the panes by clicking the right mouse button on a pane within the Layout component and selecting Clone. You will see three panes in the Layout control after this.
7. Drag the Banner Ad component into the top pane, the Announcements Panel component into the middle pane, and the Customer Services component panel into the

bottom pane within the left layout component. The right pane is for the actual content of the Overview information about the bank account.

8. Click the Details tab and drag the Customer Service panel component into the left side panel. The right side panel is for details of account.

9. Select Save and Reload from the File menu to save the application.

10. Use the deployment utility to create an HTML page to launch this application—`banking.html`.

Your project will look like Figure 6.6.

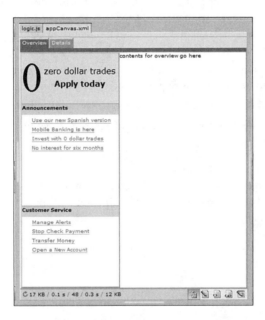

Figure 6.6   Banking application.

Building the Investing Application

This is the second application that will make use of the shared component that we built earlier.

1. Launch GI Builder and start a new project by selecting New Project from the Project menu in the main menu bar.

2. Give this project a name—**Investing**.

3. Drag and drop a Red Tabbed Pane component from the User category into this new canvas.

4. Change the Text/HTML property of the two tabs to Balances and Positions, respectively.

5. Drag a Layout—Top/Over component into the left pane and set its Rows Array property to 120,120,* to divide it into three parts.

6. Clone one of the panes by clicking the right mouse button on a pane within the Layout component and selecting Clone. You will see three panes in the Layout control after this.

7. Drag the Banner Ad component into the bottom pane, the Announcements panel component into the middle pane, and the Customer Services component panel into the top pane within the left layout component. The right pane is for the actual content of the Balances information about the trading account.

8. Click the Positions tab and remove the Layout—Side/Side component from the pane because the entire area is required to display the Positions.

9. Select Save and Reload from the File menu to save the application.

10. Use the deployment utility to create an HTML page to launch this application—investing.html.

Your project will look like Figure 6.7.

All files for the project are included on the companion CD. A complete HTML file named index.html that can be used to launch either application is also included. Figures 6.8 and 6.9 show the applications running in the browser.

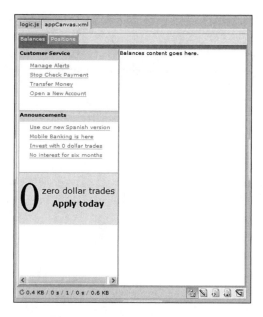

Figure 6.7   Investing application.

Figure 6.8   Banking application running
in the browser.

Figure 6.9   Investing application running in the browser.

7

Object-Oriented JavaScript— Extending General Interface Widgets

This chapter discusses TIBCO General Interface's JavaScript framework. All applications built using General Interface can take advantage of the functions available with TIBCO General Interface to build object-oriented modules in JavaScript. In fact, this framework can also be used for non-General Interface applications by including some key JavaScript source files supplied with General Interface.

A common problem that exists with JavaScript code is that it's not very easy to write modular code. Or should I say that it is very easy to write nonmodular code in JavaScript? The object-oriented programming model promotes componentization and reuse of components. Because JavaScript does not inherently support classes, code tends to be very procedural, and reuse involves copying and pasting lines and lines of code into another file and then hacking it for the new requirements. Maintaining such programs is also a nightmare because two or more copies of very similar code exist. When a bug is found in one program file, the same bug probably exists in all the copies that were made.

Object-oriented programming has long been established as a proven technique for effective componentized software development. It greatly enhances productivity by promoting reuse of components, and it allows plug and play among software components.

An object-oriented program defines classes, each having a well-defined set of properties and methods. Then at runtime, instances of classes are created on demand. Each instance is referred to as an object. Each object can have its own set of properties and methods. All properties and methods of a class are inherited by all subclasses, which can in turn define additional properties and methods.

Even though JavaScript is not an object-oriented language, TIBCO General Interface includes a framework to develop complex JavaScript programs using object-oriented principles. JavaScript code that is included with TIBCO General Interface is written using the same framework. This chapter describes the model used by TIBCO General Interface for its JavaScript components.

Prototype Inheritance

JavaScript was designed as a scripting language to allow some programmability of HTML page elements within the browser. JavaScript supports the concept of prototypes. It also supports the concept of function pointers. Using these capabilities it is possible to create programming constructs similar to those in other object-oriented programming languages such as C++, Java, or C#.

TIBCO General Interface provides functions in JavaScript that can be used to create new classes, interfaces, and packages. General Interface's framework also supports loading of JavaScript classes dynamically. Underneath the hood, these are JavaScript functions that take advantage of the prototype inheritance feature of JavaScript.

JavaScript allows prototype inheritance. Every JavaScript function essentially defines a class. For example, consider the function `Animal`:

```
function Animal(name, age) {
this.name = name;
this.age = age;
}
```

The function `Animal` defines a new class called `Animal`. Classes defined in C++ or Java use a constructor to create a new instance of the class. Every new function in JavaScript can be thought of as a constructor of a new class. In JavaScript, the instance of a class is defined to be the `prototype` property of the class. Methods that are intended to be inherited may be defined as fields of the prototype:

```
Animal.prototype.getName = function() { return this.name; };
Animal.prototype.getAge = function() { return this.age; };
Animal.prototype.speak = function() { window.alert('base class') };
```

A new instance of the class will create a copy of the `prototype` object, including any fields and methods placed in it. Thus, a new function `Dog` may inherit all fields and methods defined for `Animal` as follows:

```
function Dog(name, age) {
this.name = name;
this.age = age;
}
```

Then all methods may be inherited by setting the prototype field of the new class function:

```
Dog.prototype = new Animal();
```

Any additional methods can now be added to the `Dog` class:

```
Dog.prototype.wagtail = function() { window.alert('wag tail'); };
```

Also, methods can now be overridden by redefining them:

```
Dog.prototype.speak = function() { window.alert('bark'); };
```

Another subclass of `Animal` is defined next to further illustrate the concept of inheritance in JavaScript:

```javascript
function Cat(name, age) {
  this.name = name;
  this.age = age;
}


Cat.prototype = new Animal();
Cat.prototype.purr = function() { window.alert('purr'); };
Cat.prototype.speak = function() { window.alert('meow'); };
```

After the classes have been defined as shown previously, they may be used as follows in other JavaScript code:

```javascript
function Zoo() {
    var c1 = new Cat('kitty',3);
    var c2 = new Cat('miffy',4);
    var d1 = new Dog('Tommy',5);
    var d2 = new Dog('Mufasa',6);
    window.alert('c1 is called ' + c1.getName() +
                'c1 is ' + c1.getAge() + ' years old' +
                'c1 says ' + c1.speak() );
    window.alert('c2 is called ' + c2.getName() +
                'c2 is ' + c2.getAge() + ' years old' +
                'c2 says ' + c2.speak() );
    window.alert('d1 is called ' + d1.getName() +
                'd1 is ' + d1.getAge() + ' years old' +
                'd1 says ' + d1.speak() );
    window.alert('d2 is called ' + d2.getName() +
                'd2 is ' + d2.getAge() + ' years old' +
                'd2 says ' + d2.speak() );
}
```

JavaScript also supports an inheritance-aware `instanceof` operator similar to Java and C# that can be used to test whether a class inherits from another class. Given the preceding definitions of classes and the sample source code, the following Boolean expressions will evaluate to `true`:

```javascript
c1 instanceof Cat        // will be true
c2 instanceof Animal     // will be true
d1 instanceof Animal     // will be true
d2 instanceof Dog        // will be true
```

Whereas the following Boolean expressions will evaluate to `false`:

```javascript
c1 instanceof Dog        // will be false
d1 instanceof Cat        // will be false
```

Similar to Java and C#, all classes in JavaScript implicitly extend the `Object` class, so the following statements are also `true`:

```
c1 instanceof Object        // will be true
c2 instanceof Object        // will be true
d1 instanceof Object        // will be true
d2 instanceof Object        // will be true
```

Defining Classes in General Interface

Although the prototype inheritance previously described is very powerful, it is not very easy to comprehend. It also does not provide any constrained framework or guidelines for defining classes like C++, Java, or C#. Based on the preceding principles, a simple framework called the prototype framework was created to allow building classes in JavaScript. But even that framework lacked the sophistication of a fully object-oriented language such as Java or C#.

TIBCO General Interface includes a framework that exploits the previous principles to make it easier to create classes, interfaces, and packages. It also includes ways to do reflection to discover methods available in a class, and the accompanying documentation promotes development in JavaScript along similar lines, as done with Java and C#. General Interface's framework and best practices make programming in JavaScript like programming with Java. The framework even includes some basic packages and classes that are included in Java—for example, utility classes such as list, vector, and others.

In TIBCO General Interface, the method `jsx3.lang.Class.defineClass()` is used to define a new class in JavaScript. It takes four arguments: first is the full name of the class being defined; second is the base class, if any; third is a list of all interfaces that it implements; and the last argument is the function body that defines the class. The following listing defines a new class:

```
com.tibcobooks.gi.Example:


jsx3.lang.Class.defineClass(
  "com.tibcobooks.gi.Example", // the full name of the class to create
  com.tibcobooks.gi.Base, // this class extends com.tibcobooks.gi.Base
  [com.tibcobooks.gi.Comparable,
   com.tibcobooks.gi.Testable], // implemented interfaces
  function(Example) { // argument of this function must be "Example"
    // every class must define an init method since it
    // is called automatically by the constructor of the class
    Example.prototype.init = function(arg1) {
      this.arg1 = arg1;
    };
    // define an instance method like this:
    Example.prototype.instanceMethod = function() {
      ...
```

```
    };
    // define an abstract method like this:
    Example.prototype.abstractMethod = jsx3.Method.newAbstract();
    // define a static method like this:
    Example.staticMethod = function() {
      ...
    };
    // define a static field like this:
    Example.STATIC_FIELD = "...";
    // define an instance field like this:
    Example.prototype.instanceField = "...";
  }
);
```

Note that this file should be placed in a directory structure represented by com/tibcobooks/gi under the root folder js, where all JavaScript files are stored. So this file should be in a folder named gi, which will be in a folder named tibcobooks in a folder named com inside the folder named js in the application directory as created by GI Builder.

Defining Interfaces in General Interface

General Interface supports the concept of interfaces in the same way as Java and other object-oriented languages. An *interface* is a contract that ensures that a certain number of methods will be available in a class that implements that interface. Clients can interact with any class that implements that interface without having to worry about the implementation details.

General Interface is not exactly equivalent to Java interface. Unlike in Java, General Interface interfaces may contain concrete instance methods. When a class implements an interface, the instance methods of the interface are mixed into the class. A mixed-in method will override a method of the same name inherited from the superclass but will not override a method defined in the implementing class or mixed in from an interface coming earlier in the arrImplements parameter to Class.defineClass().

In TIBCO General Interface, the method jsx3.lang.Class.defineInterface() is used to define a new interface in JavaScript. It takes three arguments: first is the full name of the interface being defined; second is the base interface, if any; and the third is the function that defines the interface. This function takes two arguments: the constructor of the interface and its prototype. The following listing defines a new interface com.tibcobooks.gi.IExample:

```
jsx3.Class.defineInterface('com.tibcobooks.gi.IExample',
     null, function(IExample, IExample_prototype) {
  IExample_prototype.getInstance = jsx3.Method.newAbstract();
  IExample_prototype.getPrice = jsx3.Method.newAbstract();
});
```

Note that all methods in an interface must be defined using `jsx3.Method.newAbstract()` so that General Interface framework can ensure that implementing classes provide an implementation for the method.

Defining Packages in General Interface

Similar to interfaces and classes, the method `jsx3.lang.definePackage()` allows developers to define a full package. Although this function is available, I would highly discourage the use of a package for custom applications.

The only additional feature a package provides is the capability to use reflection to find all available classes in a package. The disadvantage of using a package is that a package cannot be loaded dynamically by General Interface's runtime layer. Therefore, if all custom classes are wrapped in a package definition, the application cannot take advantage of a powerful performance optimization technique of using dynamic class loading. Dynamic class loading is discussed further in Chapter 16, "Optimizing Performance."

General Interface Event Model

Internet browsers allow custom applications to respond to various user interface events from the mouse and keyboard. It is possible to respond to these events using JavaScript functions; however, these are very low-level events for a complex application. General Interface provides a mechanism that can be used to generate and respond to application-level events.

General Interface framework includes an interface `jsx3.util.EventDispatcher`, which provides four essential methods of General Interface's event model: `publish()`, `subscribe()`, `unsubscribe()`, and `unsubscribeAll()`. Many classes in the General Interface framework implement this interface to allow clients to subscribe to events that they publish.

For example, the class `jsx3.net.Request` is used to make requests to the server-side components. It implements the `EventDispatcher` interface and allows clients to subscribe to success and failure events. When a request to the server is completed successfully, it publishes the success event to all listeners in sequence to give each subscriber a chance to perform any appropriate action when the request is successful. When a request fails, it publishes the failure event similarly.

This mechanism allows a very high degree of independence and modularity among classes. This makes it easy to build loosely coupled classes that can easily be plugged in to any application. This is especially useful for GUI controls that might need to publish application-level events. For example, a button component publishes an event when the button is clicked, and also when the right button is clicked over it.

In TIBCO General Interface terminology, these high-level events are known as Model events. GI Builder includes a palette that allows developers to insert their methods to be called in response to events published by a component. Various Model events are published by many classes in General Interface. A reference document available with the product includes all events published by all classes. Figure 7.1 shows this event reference document.

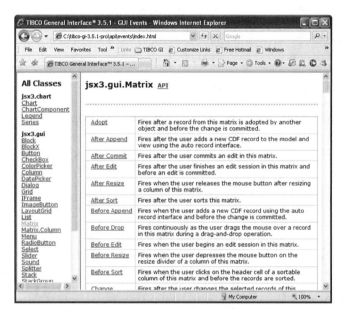

Figure 7.1   GUI Events Reference documentation.

The Model event defined by the GUI controls are actually the implementation of the `jsx3.gui.Interactive` interface and `jsx3.util.EventDispatcher` interface. The `Interactive` interface provides the serialization storage for the model event handler, whereas the `EventDispacher` interface provides the publish/subscribe mechanism.

What you see in the GI Builder IDE is the GUI-based interface to configure and edit the handler to various model events that a GUI control publishes.

Additionally, every application built using General Interface has a single controller object that is an instance of the class `jsx3.app.Server`, and GI Builder assigns it the same name as that of the application. This instance helps keep the events published within a single application from being passed on to handlers in other applications, even if they choose the same name for the event. Note that it is best to use a separate namespace for events of an application to avoid clashes with other General Interface applications on the same page.

All application code can use the publish and subscribe methods available in the `Server` object to publish and subscribe to application events. Sample code included later in this chapter shows how custom components and classes can be built that can easily be plugged in to any application.

Best Practices

Most General Interface applications require little or no JavaScript code. The extensive controls and widgets provided with General Interface support JavaScript scriptlets in their event handlers to call an application function in response to user interaction. Although these functions can be written in simple JavaScript files, it is best to organize all code in a Java-like class structure. GI Builder even opens up a file `logic.js` by default for any JavaScript code for the application, but that's meant only for very simple applications that do not require a lot of JavaScript code.

Generally speaking, if one method has more than 20 to 30 lines, and a single class has more than 100 to 200 lines of code, it is best to break it down to smaller components (classes in General Interface framework). Many advantages exist to writing code in this way. Code written this way can be easily reused in other applications. It is also much easier to test and maintain code that's written as small independent components.

Directory Structure

JavaScript code for General Interface applications should follow a directory structure similar to that used by Java programs. When GI Builder creates a new project, it creates a directory named `js` for all JavaScript files. All JavaScript files should be placed in this directory using a structure like Java programs. For example, if the application has three logically separate modules named Dialogs, Filters, and Tabs, divide the project into the three directories, as shown in Figure 7.2.

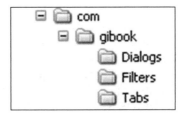

Figure 7.2   Recommended directory structure for a General
Interface project with three modules.

JavaScript Files

Although it is possible to define multiple classes and interfaces in a single JavaScript file, it is best to follow Java best practices when defining classes and limit one class per JavaScript file. TIBCO General Interface includes a tool that can collapse a number of files into a single file later if necessary. Individual files make it possible to load a single class on demand as needed, and larger files make it possible to load everything upfront. So depending on the user experience requirements, you will be able to load classes on demand or load them all upfront if each class is defined in its own file.

Dynamic Class Loading

The TIBCO General Interface bootstrap application loader loads only files that are tagged for automatic loading when an application is first loaded in the browser. All other classes and interfaces are loaded on demand. User interface components that are defined by XML files can also be loaded on demand. Any classes referenced in serialized XML screen definitions are loaded when the object is deserialized.

This feature makes it possible to reduce the initial loading time for a complex application that might require many files and lines of JavaScript code. Without this feature, all JavaScript will need to be loaded in one single large JavaScript file, which could take a long time to download over a slow network connection.

Application-Level Events

Model events provide a way to develop components that can be used in any application. Instead of calling a method in another part of the application, publish an application-level event and then have the other part of the application subscribe to it. This ensures that the two classes are loosely coupled and can be used independently of each other.

The component that publishes the event can be used in another application without any changes to the code. The new application only needs to provide a handler for the event published by the component. Additionally, the handler can be made to respond to the model event regardless of how it is published.

For example, a hotkey may be associated with a menu event, and the same handler will be invoked as long as the same event is published by both the menu as well as the hotkey. General Interface framework includes a class named `jsx3.gui.Hotkey` that can be used to invoke methods in response to a special combination of keys being pressed.

Sample Code

This section demonstrates how to build a reusable component MultiSelectMenu using object-oriented JavaScript code and a publish-subscribe event model using TIBCO General Interface framework. The sample includes a simple example that makes use of the MultiSelectMenu component.

MultiSelectMenu

TIBCO General Interface's `jsx3.gui.menu` includes a feature that allows a check mark to be placed next to an item when it is selected. However, no class or property exists that would give it functionality of a multiselect menu. For example, a menu for font styles could include four menu items: Normal, Italic, Bold, and Underline, and the functionality desired is such that when Normal is selected, all other items should be unchecked, and when any item other than Normal is selected, it adds on to the selection so that all three items—Italic, Bold, and Underline—may be selected at the same time.

To implement this functionality, we will create a new GUI component with an associated JavaScript class implemented using General Interface framework. This component will be placed in the prototypes directory so any application can use it. The entire project with the MSMenu component is included in the examples directory for this chapter.

This section will take you through four major steps for building this component:

1. Building a GUI component
2. Writing the JavaScript class
3. Setting up Project Classpath
4. Updating the associated class

Building the GUI Component

First, create a GUI component: Launch GI Builder and create a new project, and then select File, New, GUI Component to begin creating this component. Drag and drop a Menu object from the Menus and Toolbars subcategory under the System category in the Component Libraries palette.

Change the XML for this menu to include four options and set the event handler for the Execute event to call a method of its instance—
`this.executeRecord(strRECORDID)`. Our custom class will override this method to implement the special behavior for this multiselect menu. The Menu class that's part of TIBCO General Interface allows you to place a call to a JavaScript method in the jsxexecute attribute of its associated CDF. Our MSMenu will not have this feature; instead, it will override this `executeRecord` method to implement the special functionality needed for a multiselect menu. After making all the changes, save the component into prototypes directory and name it **MSMenu.xml**. Now open it up in a text editor and make some additional changes to give it a unique name and description in the Component Libraries palette. The file will look like the following code. (Make sure you do not update the class name until after the last step in this section; otherwise, the project will not load correctly.)

```
<serialization jsxversion="3.5" xmlns="urn:tibco.com/v3.0">
  <name><![CDATA[MSMenu]]></name>
  <icon><![CDATA[images/prototypes/menu.gif]]></icon>
  <description><![CDATA[Multiselect Menu object.]]></description>
  <onBeforeDeserialize></onBeforeDeserialize>
  <onAfterDeserialize></onAfterDeserialize>
  <object type="com.tibcobooks.gi.MSMenu'">
    <variants jsxxmlasync="1"></variants>
    <strings jsxname="msmenu" jsxtip="msmenu" jsxtext="msmenu"
      jsxxml="&lt;data jsxid=&quot;jsxroot&quot;&gt;&#xA;
```

```
&lt;record jsxid=&quot;1&quot;
jsxtext=&quot;Normal&quot;/&gt;&#xA;
&lt;record jsxid=&quot;2&quot;
jsxtext=&quot;Italics&quot;/&gt;&#xA;
&lt;record jsxid=&quot;3&quot;
jsxtext=&quot;Bold&quot;/&gt;&#xA;
&lt;record jsxid=&quot;4&quot;
jsxtext=&quot;Underline&quot;/&gt;&#xA;
&lt;/data&gt;">
    </strings>
    <events jsxexecute="this.executeRecord(strRECORDID);">
    </events>
  </object>
</serialization>
```

There are a few interesting things to note in the preceding block of code. First, all the changes you need to make in a text editor are highlighted. Additionally, note the XML attributes `<onBeforeDeserialize>` and `<onAfterDeserialize>`. These elements allow developers to provide a method that can be called when this component is first loaded in memory and when a new instance is created in memory, respectively. For example, a custom class can provide methods to do some initialization as soon as it is loaded, or to subscribe to some events as soon as a new instance is created.

Writing the JavaScript Class

Now write a JavaScript class that uses `jsx3.gui.Menu` as the base class and overrides the `executeRecord` method. You can use the File, New, JavaScript File menu item to begin creating this class. Store this file in the prototypes directory using a package-like structure under the directory named `js`.

Note that the code for this class must be written using General Interface's framework. The final code will be as follows:

```
/*
 * File: msmenu.js
 *
 * Implements a multi select menu where
 * multiple items may be selected.
 * Item with an id of '1' is assumed to imply
 * "uncheck all" When any item other than
 * the '1' item is selected, it is checked
 * and the '1' item is unchecked. Whenever
 * the first item is selected all other items
 * are unchecked except the first item.
 *
 * Publishes model event MENU_CHANGED whenever
 * anything changes in the menu.
 *
```

```
   * @author Anil Gurnani
   *
 */


// make sure jsx3.gui.Menu is loaded beforehand
jsx3.require("jsx3.gui.Menu");


jsx3.lang.Class.defineClass (
"com.tibcobooks.gi.MSMenu", // name of this class
jsx3.gui.Menu, // base class
null, // no special interface is implemented
function(MSMenu) {

  MSMenu.eventName = "com.tibcobooks.gi.MSMenu.CHANGED";
  MSMenu.unselectAllJSXID = '1';

  // constructor
  MSMenu.prototype.init = function() {
  }

  // instance methods
  MSMenu.prototype.executeRecord = function(strRecordId) {
      if( strRecordId == com.tibcobooks.gi.MSMenu.unselectAllJSXID ) {
          // deselect all first
          var xmlDoc = this.getXML();
          var rootNode =
          xmlDoc.selectSingleNode("//data[@jsxid='jsxroot']")
          var iter = rootNode.getChildIterator();
          while( iter.hasNext() ) {
            this.deselectItem(iter.next().getAttribute("jsxid"));
          }
      } else {
          this.deselectItem(com.tibcobooks.gi.MSMenu.unselectAllJSXID);
      }
      this.selectItem(strRecordId);
       this.publish({id:com.tibcobooks.gi.MSMenu.eventName,
         subject:com.tibcobooks.gi.MSMenu.eventName,target:this});
  }
}
);
```

Note how the class instance method `executeRecord` uses the General Interface framework API to iterate through all items and turn them off if Normal is selected. Also note how the class defines some useful static variables that can be used by clients.

Setting Up the Project Classpath

After writing the class, it is important to tell GI Builder (and the General Interface run-time) where the new class is before it will work. To do this, we need to set up `classpath` for the project. You can do this by going to the Project Settings dialog from the Project menu. Figure 7.3 shows this dialog and what values need to be entered. The first entry that includes prototypes is for the `MSMenu` class, and the second entry shown in the picture will be used for the `StyleChanger` class that will be built in the next section.

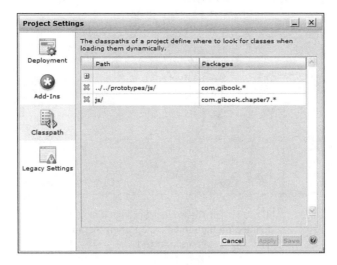

Figure 7.3   Setting `classpath` for
General Interface project.

Updating the Associated Class

After the `classpath` has been updated, GI Builder will need to be restarted. Close GI Builder and update the class name before opening it again. The class name for a compo-nent cannot be changed in GI Builder, so open up the XML file again in a text editor and change the associated class.

Building a Sample Using MultiSelectMenu

Now we will build a sample that makes use of this multiselect menu. The companion CD includes a sample project including a class `StyleChanger` to demonstrate how to use this MultiSelectMenu component. Create a Top/Over layout in the main panel, drag and drop this MSMenu component into the top pane, and place a label with words "Hello World." Set the text size to 82 to get large text.

There are two JavaScript files in this project. The project makes use of several interest-ing features of TIBCO General Interface framework:

- It uses a custom component MSMenu defined previously.

- It defines Classpath to include MSMenu and StyleChanger classes into the Classpath.
- It uses the Project Settings dialog (see Figure 7.4) to set the `onLoadScript` method to `main()`.

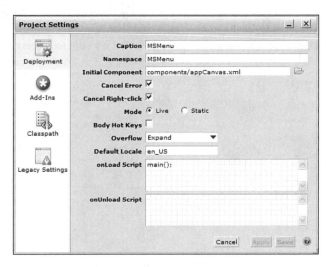

Figure 7.4   The Project Settings dialog to
define a method to be called when the app
is first started.

- It uses a Java-like directory structure for JavaScript files. Note how the class `com.tibcobooks.gi.chapter7.StyleChanger` is defined in a matching directory structure.
- It uses General Interface's Publish and Subscribe mechanism to subscribe to events published by the custom component MSMenu. Note how the `init` function in the following code subscribes to events published by MSMenu. Also note that the `init` method is invoked whenever a new instance of this class is created by General Interface. Thus, it functions similarly to the constructors in Java and C#.

```
/*
 * File: StyleChanger.js
 *
 * @author Anil Gurnani
 *
 */

jsx3.require("com.tibcobooks.gi.MSMenu");

jsx3.lang.Class.defineClass (
```

```
"com.tibcobooks.gi.chapter7.StyleChanger", // name of this class
null, // no base class
null, // no special interface is implemented
function(StyleChanger) {

    // constructor
    StyleChanger.prototype.init = function() {
       var mm = MSMenu.getJSXByName("stylemenu");
       mm.subscribe(com.tibcobooks.gi.MSMenu.eventName, this, this.changeStyle );
       jsx3.log('done init')
    }


    // instance methods

    StyleChanger.prototype.changeStyle = function(eventObject) {
        var menuObject = eventObject.target;
        var label = MSMenu.getJSXByName("label");
        var xmlDoc = menuObject.getXML();
        var rootNode = xmlDoc.selectSingleNode("//data[@jsxid='jsxroot']")
        var iter = rootNode.getChildIterator();
        var labeltext = 'Hello World';
        while( iter.hasNext() ) {
            var jsxid = iter.next().getAttribute("jsxid");
            if( menuObject.isItemSelected(jsxid) ) {
                if( jsxid != com.tibcobooks.gi.MSMenu.unselectAllJSXID )
                { // style is set
                    if( jsxid == '2' ) { // Italics
                        labeltext = '<i>'+labeltext;
                    }
                    if( jsxid == '3' ) { // Bold
                        labeltext = '<b>'+labeltext;
                    }
                    if( jsxid == '4' ) { // Underline
                        labeltext = '<u>'+labeltext;
                    }
                }
                // nothing to do for Normal style
            }
        }
        label.setText(labeltext, true);
        jsx3.log('done changeStyle')
    }
}
);
```

Advanced Features of Matrix

The Matrix component in General Interface is one of the most powerful components. I have heard some people refer to it as Table on Steroids. It is actually even more than that. This chapter provides an in-depth look at this very versatile component.

The TIBCO General Interface Matrix component can render data in a tree view as well as in a grid view, and it has numerous properties and features packed into it.

`Matrix.Column` class represents a column of a matrix. General Interface packs in a number of predefined column types that can be inserted into a matrix, including Date, Time, Button, DatePicker, and many more.

The Matrix component enables developers to render large tables in smaller chunks for better performance. It can also get data asynchronously from the server. Figure 8.1 shows high-level sequence in rendering a Matrix component.

This chapter explores various stages of the Matrix rendering sequence and other advanced features of the Matrix component of TIBCO General Interface's framework.

Rendering Tabular Data

In its simplest and default form, a matrix renders tabular data as an HTML table onscreen. As we saw earlier, the CDF data for rendering a table looks like the XML file shown in Listing 8.1.

Listing 8.1   Simple Tabular Data in CDF Format

```
<data jsxid="jsxroot">
    <record jsxid="1" Ticker="IBM"
            Company="International Business Machines"/>
    <record jsxid="2" Ticker="MSFT"
            Company="Microsoft"/>
</data>
```

A Matrix component can be created to display the data in Listing 8.1 as an HTML table in the browser. The larger XSL style sheet that is a part of the General Interface

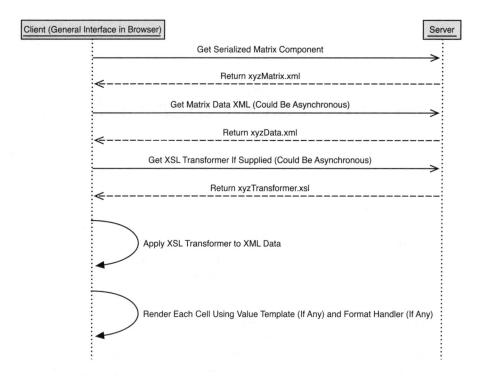

Figure 8.1   Typical sequence in rendering a Matrix component on-screen.

framework is able to dynamically convert the XML into HTML. The attributes can be associated with each column using the Att Name property of each column.

Several other properties are in the CDF Mapping section of the properties of a matrix column.

There is a property for Att Type, which tells General Interface what type of data is going to be in this column. If the column is going to have numeric data, the Att Type should be set to Numeric to signal that the data should be treated as a number when sorting.

There is another property for Sort Att Name. This is the name of an attribute that will be used to sort the table if the user asks to sort on this column by clicking its header. Note that if there is nothing in this property, General Interface will use the data for this attribute to sort the table. This property allows you to specify a separate attribute whose value will determine the sort order. This is especially useful if you are displaying numbers with formatting elements, such as commas and currency signs or dates and times. An easy way to allow sorting by any of those columns is to have an additional attribute in the CDF that keeps the sort order using the raw numbers and instructs General Interface to use it by setting the Sort Att Name property of the column. General Interface defines format handlers (discussed in a later section in this chapter), which can be used to display numerical values in Date, Currency, or other formats similar to Microsoft Excel.

Another commonly used property of the Matrix component is its Paging Model. A matrix is rendered based on the Paging Model. Possible values for Paging Model are No Paging, 2-Pass, Chunked, Paged, and Stepped (hierarchical).

When the Paging Model is set to No Paging, General Interface renders the contents of the entire matrix in a single HTML table whenever it is repainted. This can be slow for large tables. Rendering performance is the major cause of slowness in web-based applications. General Interface includes many ways to detect and fix performance bottlenecks caused by this. You will see some techniques in Chapter 16, "Optimizing Performance."

When the Paging Model is set to 2-Pass, General Interface renders an outer `<div>` tag in the first pass with no data in it. After that, it renders the actual data in the `<table>` tag in the second pass. This improves perceived performance.

If the Paging Model is set to Chunked, General Interface renders an outer `<div>` tag first, and then it renders smaller parts of the data in groups of tables in chunks so that the browser does not get overwhelmed. The developer can adjust the number of rows per chunk to find the optimal setting for the data to be displayed. This improves the perceptible performance even more. This works similar to the `layout: auto` style element supported by Internet Explorer. By default, Internet Explorer waits for the last row in a table before rendering it onscreen because it determines row dimensions (height and width) based on the widest and tallest row in the entire table. But if the layout element of the style is set to auto, Internet Explorer assumes that the first row defines the dimensions and continues to render each row using that fixed format.

Finally the Stepped (hierarchical) mode is used to render hierarchical data as tree nodes.

Rendering a Tree Structure

The Matrix component of TIBCO General Interface can also be used to render hierarchical content such as a directory listing. The Tree component in the Component Libraries palette is an instance of the Matrix component with predefined property values for rendering a hierarchical XML as a tree.

To render as a tree, the XML data must have second-level record elements within the top-level record elements. These record elements must be inside the enclosing data element, similar to the structure for tabular data. Listing 8.2 shows a sample XML with nested record elements:

Listing 8.2   Simple Hierarchical Data in CDF Format

```
<data jsxid="jsxroot">
  <record jsxid="1" jsxtext="rootnode" jsxopen="1"
          jsximg="GI_Builder/images/icon_7.gif">
    <record jsxid="2" jsxtext="node a" jsxopen="1"
            jsximg="GI_Builder/images/icon_7.gif">
```

```
        <record jsxid="3" jsxtext="node b"
                jsximg="GI_Builder/images/icon_7.gif">
          <record jsxid="4" jsxtext="node c"
                  jsximg="GI_Builder/images/icon_7.gif">
            <record jsxid="5" jsxtext="node d"
                    jsximg="GI_Builder/images/icon_16.gif"/>
          </record>
        </record>
        <record jsxid="6" jsxtext="node e"
                jsximg="GI_Builder/images/icon_7.gif">
          <record jsxid="7" jsxtext="node f with a lot of text"
                  jsximg="GI_Builder/images/icon_7.gif">
            <record jsxid="8" jsxtext="node g"
                    jsximg="GI_Builder/images/icon_16.gif"/>
          </record>
        </record>
      </record>
    </record>
</data>
```

Data shown in Listing 8.2 will be rendered as a tree with nodes. Note that the `jsximg` attribute contains the name of a file with an icon for that node. Each node in a tree can have its own icon file. Figure 8.2 shows how this tree will be rendered by General Interface.

Note that the Paging Model must be set to Stepped (hierarchical) for rendering a tree, which automatically rules out Paged and Chunked models for a tree. It is not possible to render a tree structure in chunks or pages because it's a hierarchical structure. The best way to make a tree perform faster is to have a limited number of nodes in it.

Stepped paging helps the tree render faster by rendering only the contents of a branch in the tree when the given branch is toggled open by the user. If stepped paging is not used on a tree, even branches that are closed will be painted—the content will be hidden from view—thus, performance will be affected.

Using XML Transformers

Although General Interface's CDF format is built upon XML, it is somewhat specific to General Interface. Many standards-based systems including database servers generate more generic XML. In a typical service-oriented enterprise, a large number of web services generate XML for consumption by any client. There are two ways to pass this XML to TIBCO General Interface.

Generic XML can be transformed on the server side using some translators and then passed in CDF format to TIBCO General Interface. Alternatively, generic XML data can be directly passed to TIBCO General Interface's Matrix component, which is configured to use an XSL style sheet (known in General Interface as the XML Transformer).

Figure 8.2   A simple tree component rendered in a browser.

The first method would involve passing the TIBCO General Interface calls through some server-side component that could then transform the results on the way back. On the other hand, the second method could be used without any such server-side component.

Another advantage of using a transformer is that more of the processing will be pushed to the client side.

In addition, TIBCO General Interface allows programs to maintain data locally on the client side. Typically, such data is useful in generic XML format and is therefore maintained in its original XML form on the client side. If the underlying XML changes as a result of some user action, it is necessary to run the data through XML transformer again to convert it to CDF format required by TIBCO General Interface's Matrix component.

The example in Chapter 4 included an XSL style sheet to transform simple XML into CDF format. Listing 8.3 shows that style sheet.

Listing 8.3   Simple XSL Style Sheet to Convert XML to CDF Format

```
<?xml version="1.0"?>
<xsl:stylesheet xmlns:xsl="http://www.w3.org/1999/XSL/Transform" version="1.0">
  <xsl:output method="xml" indent="yes"/>
  <xsl:template match="dow30">
    <data jsxid="jsxroot">
    <xsl:apply-templates/>
    </data>
```

```
  </xsl:template>

<xsl:template match="component">
  <xsl:element name="record">
    <xsl:attribute name="jsxid">
      <xsl:value-of select="position()"/>
    </xsl:attribute>
    <xsl:for-each select="*">
      <xsl:attribute name="{name()}">
        <xsl:value-of select="."/>
      </xsl:attribute>
    </xsl:for-each>
  </xsl:element>
</xsl:template>

</xsl:stylesheet>
```

Note that the style sheet in Listing 8.3 generates XML output in the CDF format. The style sheet first looks for the root node `<dow30>` of the XML data and outputs the CDF root element `<data>` with a `jsxid` of `jsxroot`. It then looks for all `component` elements and turns them into `record` elements as required by TIBCO General Interface.

Also note that it generates a `jsxid` for each record using its position.

TIBCO General Interface supports an easier way of generating unique `jsxids` for each row of the data. If an attribute named `jsxassignids` exists in the `<data>` element of a CDF, TIBCO General Interface automatically generates unique `jsxid` values for each row in the matrix.

Another useful artifact of XML Transformer is that you can set up an automatic sort based on some attributes using an XSL style sheet. For example, if you were displaying a dynamic list of stock positions and wanted to make sure that the initial display is sorted by stock symbol, you could put the following `xsl` statement in the XML Transformer (assuming that the CDF attribute for stock symbol is `symbol`):

```
<xsl:sort select="symbol">
```

Note that you can have a complex sort path here involving multiple CDF attributes to accomplish multicolumn sorts—for example, first sort by symbol, then sort by date, and so on.

Using Value Templates

All matrix columns have a property called Value Template, which can contain a template XSL style sheet. This style sheet gets merged with the larger style sheet that is used to render the table on screen.

Value Templates are used to change the styles of individual cells based on the contents. For example, if you wanted to show negative numbers in red and positive numbers in green, you could write a small Value Template that checks the value of current cell and applies a different color depending on its value.

Listing 8.4 shows a fragment of the larger XSL style sheet that is used to render a matrix in TIBCO General Interface.

Listing 8.4   Partial Listing of File `jsxmatrix.xsl` Included with TIBCO General Interface

```
<!-- the TR element -->
<tr JSXDragId="{$jsx_cdfkey}"
  JSXDragType="{$jsx_drag_type}"
  id="{$jsx_id}_jsx_{$jsx_cdfkey}"
  jsxid="{$jsx_cdfkey}"
  jsxrownumber="{$jsx_row_number}"
  jsxtype="record" style="{$jsx_rowbg}{$jsx_style}">
  <xsl:if test="@jsxtip and $jsx_no_tip != '1'">
    <xsl:attribute name="title">
      <xsl:value-of select="@jsxtip"/>
    </xsl:attribute>
  </xsl:if>
  <xsl:choose>
    <xsl:when test="$jsx_use_categories='0' or
          @jsxcategory='0' or
          (not(@jsxcategory='1') and not(record))">
    </xsl:when>
  </xsl:choose>
</tr>
</xsl:template>

<!--
CELL VALUE TEMPLATE(S): These templates are dynamically
  generated by the Matrix class or can be created by the
  developer and bound to a given column. These templates
  return the text content that will go inside the associated
  CELL template. The developer can create this template in
  order to have more fine-grain control over the format
  and content of the cell.
-->

</xsl:stylesheet>
```

Partial listing of the file `jsxmatrix.xsl` shows how a `<tr>` element is rendered onscreen. The comment included shows where Value Templates are inserted into this larger XSL style sheet as the table is rendered onscreen.

One important point to note is that the Value Template is executed just before the data is actually rendered onscreen. At this point the XML Transformer has already been executed. This means that the XML available at this time is the CDF that is used by the matrix and not the original XML (if a different XML was used with an XML Transformer). Note that the rendered content is placed inside a `<div>` element.

Every cell that is painted in a matrix is actually a combination of a `<td>` and a `<div>` tag. The system owns the `<td>` tag and does not expose access except by the various public APIs exposed by the matrix and its columns. However, by using a Value Template, the developer can modify how the `<div>` tag is rendered. By reserving access to the `<td>` tag, the system tries to ensure that developer errors do not corrupt the layout and sizing of the overall matrix, while providing flexibility to the developer.

The larger XSL style sheet that is included with General Interface passes the following additional parameters to the Value Template from the context:

- `jsx_cell_width` represents the width in pixels of the cell that is being painted. It does not include the padding and border widths of the table cell.

- `jsx_row_number` represents the row number that's being painted.

- `jsx_descendant_index` represents the current level of the record being painted.

Value Template is called as the `<div>` is being rendered. Thus, a value template has the capability to add style elements to this `<div>` element. Listing 8.5 shows a sample value template used in the example (oilconsumptions) included with this chapter.

Listing 8.5   A Simple Value Template

```
<xsl:template xmlns:xsl="http://www.w3.org/1999/XSL/Transform">
  <xsl:choose>
    <xsl:when test="@y1966 > @y1965">
      <xsl:attribute name="style">color:red;</xsl:attribute>
    </xsl:when>
    <xsl:otherwise>
      <xsl:attribute name="style">color:green;</xsl:attribute>
    </xsl:otherwise>
  </xsl:choose>
  <xsl:value-of select="{0}"/>
</xsl:template>
```

Note how the value template checks the value in one column (@y1966) with the value in another column (@y1965), and if it is greater, it adds the style to change the color to red; otherwise, it adds the style element with green color.

Also note that at the end, the value template sets the value to `select="{0}"`. This enables default handling by TIBCO General Interface. So, in essence, this value template only added the style to make the color red if the value @y1966 is greater than the value @y1965, or else it made the style green. This is done to display the number in red if it increases over last year, and to show it in green if it decreases over last year. Figure 8.3 shows this example running in a browser.

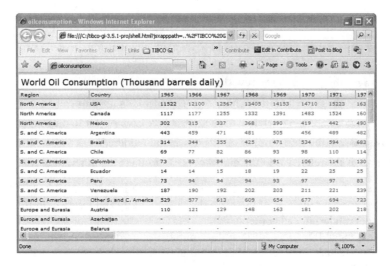

Figure 8.3   World oil consumption project in General
Interface.

General Interface includes some standard value templates that can be used. These value templates are precoded and included with General Interface. You can refer to these templates using their reference names as follows:

- **@image** helps locate image files at runtime. In this case, the **jsximg** attribute of the cell should contain a relative URL of the image that is to be displayed in the cell. The **@image** value template must be used to let TIBCO General Interface know to dynamically change the image path at runtime based on the URL of the page.

- **@unescape** can be used to translate special characters that may be embedded in the CDF attribute—for example, HTML. Use of **@unescape** instructs General Interface to unescape the contents of the attribute and then render it in HTML.

- **@empty** signals to General Interface that the column has no value, but only a special element such as a menu, a select box, or a button.

Using Format Handlers

Another useful property of the matrix column is the format handler. This value contains a reference to a JavaScript method that can be used to format the contents of the cell. The format handler method is called after the data is rendered. Use this feature with extreme caution because when it is placed in the property for a column, this method will be called for every single cell that is rendered in that column. This could make the rendering process very slow.

A format handler function has the following general signature:

```
function(element,cdfkey,matrix,matrixcolumn,rownumber,server)
```

The following parameters are used:

- `element` is the reference to the HTML `<div>` element for the cell content as rendered.
- `cdfkey` is the `jsxid` of the row that the cell belongs to.
- `matrix` is the reference to the Matrix object that contains this cell.
- `matrixcolumn` is the reference to the `Matrix.Column` object that contains this cell.
- `rownumber` is the row number of this row being rendered.
- `server` is the reference to the global controller object for this application.

The `Matrix.Column` class has a method named `setFormatHandler`, which takes a reference to a JavaScript method of the form shown previously and inserts it in the chain to be called after rendering cell contents.

TIBCO General Interface also includes a number of predefined format handlers that can be used to format different types of data onscreen.

Table 8.1 shows predefined format handlers that are available with TIBCO General Interface. Note that there must be no spaces after the comma in the definition of the format handlers.

Table 8.1   **Format Handlers Available in TIBCO General Interface**

Formatter	Description

`@number,integer`
`@number,percent`
`@number,curre-ncy`
	Formats the numeric value in the cell as an integer, percent, or currency. For example, a cell with a value of 25 will be displayed as $25.00 if the column's format handler is `@number,currency`. These format handlers correspond to Excel formats Number, Percent, and Currency, respectively.

`@datetime,short`
`@datetime,medium`
`@datetime,long`
`@datetime,full`
	Formats the value in the cell to a DateTime format. The value in the cell must be the number of milliseconds since January 1, 1970 (same as Java). For example, if the value in the CDF is 1158054271967, the long format is used and the application is localized to the default localization (us_en). The output is the following: September 12, 2006 5:44:31 AM GMT-04:00. The keywords `short`, `medium`, `long`, and `full` define how the date is formatted. Using the `short` modifier results in dates in "9/12/2006 5:44:31"; using the `medium` modifier results in "Sep 12, 2006 5:44:31"; using the `long` format results in "September 12, 2006 5:44:31 AM GMT-04:00"; using the `full` format results in "Tuesday September 12, 2006 5:44:31 AM GMT-04:00".

Table 8.1   **Continued**

Formatter	Description

`@date,short`
`@date,medium`
`@date,long`
`@date,full`
	Similar to the `datetime` format handler, formats and displays only the date part without the time part contained in the value. For example, the value 1158054271967 will be displayed as "September 12, 2006" when this format handler is used.

`@time,short`
`@time,medium`
`@time,long`
`@time,full`
	Converts the time part contained in the value to be displayed as HH:MM:SS. For example, the value 1158054271967 will be displayed as "5:44:31" when this format handler is applied.

`@message,*`	This is a way to display dynamic messages. The CDF must contain a string expression including parameters where various formats can be applied to each parameter, and a new string is constructed to be displayed. Special parameters are denoted using curly braces. See the `jsx3.util.MessageFormat` class in "TIBCO General Interface API Reference" for full details.
`@unescape`	Unescapes any onscreen entities to render the tagged output, not the tags themselves. Use this template if a CDF attribute contains HTML. In Firefox, this is used to disable output escaping, as this function is not available to the embedded TransforMiiX processor. In Internet Explorer, a Value Template by the same name (`@unescape`) is used to facilitate output escaping. Important: For cross-browser support, be sure to set this property for both the format handler and the value template fields.
`@lookup`	Resolves to a lookup value associated with a bound edit mask (select-combo). This allows the human-readable text to display, while storing the actual `jsxid` value in the underlying CDF.

Displaying Controls in Columns

GI Builder's Component Libraries palette shows a large number of components in the Matrix Columns subcategory. Any of these can be dragged and dropped onto a matrix in the canvas. These are instances of `jsx3.gui.Matrix.Column` class preconfigured to display a control in all rows in a column in the matrix.

The control will display in every row in the matrix by default. If you want to hide the control in some rows, you can use the CDF value `jsxnomask` in the corresponding `record` element for the row.

When you insert one of these elements into the Application DOM in TIBCO General Interface, you will notice a new child element of the column. The child element is called the edit mask. In TIBCO General Interface, a column can contain any other object that implements the `jsx3.gui.Form` interface. So a custom class may be developed to display any other custom control in the matrix column. General Interface already includes a number of controls that implement this interface and therefore can be included in a matrix. Additional custom controls can be developed as needed.

The important thing to note about these Column types is that they are all preconfigured instances of the `jsx3.gui.Matrix.Column` class. The control that is contained within the column implements the `jsx3.gui.Matrix.EditMask` interface. At runtime, General Interface creates only a single instance of this control in a floating `<div>`. Clients may retrieve the value of the instance that is currently being edited using the methods provided by the `jsx3.gui.Matrix.EditMask` interface (`emGetSession()` and others).

Some types of edit masks are always displayed, whereas others are displayed only when the target cell in the matrix receives focus. For example, a TextBox edit mask displays only when a given cell is clicked. However, edit masks such as Button and CheckBox are shown in every cell in the column. By using the `jsxnomask` property, developers can control which of the "always displayed" mask types actually get hidden.

Available Controls in Matrix Columns

Following is a discussion of the controls that can be used in matrix columns.

Button

This column displays a simple command button in each row of the matrix. The command button can be used to take action on the row of the matrix. In GI Builder, select the `buttonMask` element in the component hierarchy, and then select the Event Handler palette to set up event handlers for this button. Because this is an instance of the `jsx3.gui.Button` class, it supports all the events that are supported by the standard Form Button object—that is, Execute, Menu, and Destroy.

Button—Delete

Using this column displays a predefined Delete button in every row. The button displays an "X" image and has a predefined event handler for Execute, which deletes the current row from the matrix. This is a special instance of ImageButton, described next.

Button—ImageButton

This column is preconfigured with an image button in it. The difference between a simple button and an ImageButton is that an ImageButton has different images associated with it for its various states—on, down, mouseover, and disabled. Each of those images are properties of ImageButton, and custom images can be used instead of the default images supplied by General Interface. ImageButton raises four events: Execute, Toggle, Menu, and Destroy. The default control in GI Builder is preset with a tiny script in its Execute event handler, which simply logs a line of text.

Button—ToolbarButton

The ToolbarButton column is similar to the ImageButton except that it behaves like a toolbar button. When you mouse over an ImageButton, it highlights if no other toolbar button in the group is selected. Clicking a toolbar button changes its state to "on". Clicking it again changes its state back to "off".

Checkbox

This column type renders a check box in the column. A check box in every row can be used for visually displaying multiple selections in a grid. Clicking a check box checks it, and clicking it again unchecks it. Using the following simple script for the Toggle event of a check box will automatically select the row in which the check box is clicked:

```
this.getParent().getParent().selectRecord
    (this.emGetSession().recordId);
```

Note that all edit mask controls implement the `jsx3.gui.Matrix.EditMask` interface and have a method `emGetSession`, which can be used to get the state of the current edit session. The state contains the following keys:

- `matrix` — `jsx3.gui.Matrix`—Reference to the matrix object where the editing is occurring.
- `column` — `jsx3.gui.Matrix.Column`—The column that's being edited.
- `recordId` — `String`—jsxid of the row that is being edited.
- `td` — `HTML Element`—Reference to the HTML element that's being edited.
- `value` — `String`—The current value.

Date

This column is preconfigured to display formatted date values onscreen. Values are converted using a default `@date` format handler. The title of the column is preset to Date. By default this will display the `date` CDF attribute formatted as a date.

This column does not have an edit mask associated with it and cannot be used to allow user input. Use the DatePicker column if you need to accept user input.

Date Picker

Using this column displays a DatePicker object in each cell in the column when the user clicks in it. Nothing will display initially if the column does not have any value. If it has a value, it is formatted as Date and displayed; a tiny calendar icon appears next to the date, which can be used to bring up a mini calendar control. After a selection is made in the calendar control, it is updated.

Image

This column displays an image in each row. The CDF attribute `jsximg` must be the URL of an image. The column is preset with a value template of `@image` to automatically convert the relative URL to a full URL at runtime.

Mask—Block

Any custom block can be displayed when the user clicks a cell that contains a BlockMask. This column contains a block. Because a block is a container, it can in turn contain other General Interface components, such as check boxes, radio buttons, buttons, and so on. By default, the block contains a slider that can be used to set a value for the cell. Any custom controls can also be added to this block. This type of column can be used whenever there is a complex set of numbers or items behind a final value. Insert a BlockMask column and add all the user interaction elements that define the final value on the block so that whenever a user clicks on the final value, the block is displayed, allowing the user to view or edit the values behind.

Mask—Dialog

Similar to Mask—Block, this component hides a dialog in every cell. When the user clicks a cell with this component, a dialog is displayed. Whenever a click is received in any other part of the application, the dialog is hidden by General Interface. Similar to DatePicker, only one dialog is ever painted. This single instance is moved around the screen when necessary to target a given cell.

Menu

This column displays an action menu in each cell. All the events that are supported by the Menu class are also supported by the Menu mask. The Execute event of the menu can be used to call custom action scripts. The default script put in by GI Builder is

```
jsx3.log('Executed menu item ' + strRECORDID +
    ' in row ' + this.emGetSession().recordId + '.');
```

This logs a message when a user clicks this cell and selects a menu item. Also note that the code to retrieve the current `recordId` where the click was received is identical to the code we used previously for Checkbox. Because this is an edit mask, it too implements the interface `jsx3.gui.Matrix.EditMask` and therefore has a method `emGetSession()` to retrieve the current edit session.

Radio Button

This type of column displays a radio button in every cell. An instance of the `jsx3.gui.RadioButton` class is placed in an edit mask for the column. Clicking a radio button automatically deselects radio buttons in other rows. `RadioButton` supports two events: `select` and `destroy`.

Select

Using a Select column displays a Select control in every cell when the user clicks it. After the user makes a selection, the associated text value is displayed using the format handler `@lookup` (as discussed in the section "Using Format Handlers"). A typical use of this might be to create a grid where users can input multiple rows of data in a single batch and some of that data involves picking from a menu (for example, States, Countries, and so on). The Select component fires the following events: before select, select, key down, key up, and destroy. Similar to Mask Dialog and TextBox, only a single Select control is painted. It is positioned and displayed over a target matrix cell as and when needed.

As with other columns, a Select column is able to retrieve the context using the `emGetSession()` method of the EditMask interface.

Select—Combo

Select—Combo adds the capability to type in text that is not in the original Select box. When the user presses the Enter key, the text is automatically inserted in the grid. The application can then retrieve the values input by the user by reading the XML data backing the matrix.

Text

This is the basic content column for a matrix that displays text. This is preconfigured to use no format handlers and no default value template. It is the most basic column in a matrix. Note that this column is not an edit mask because it does not allow any inline editing of text. Use Text Field if you want to allow inline editing of data.

Text—HTML

This is similar to the Text column and has all the basic settings for a default column, except that it uses `@unescape` for both value template and format handler properties. Recall that the value template `@unescape` and format handler `@unescape` allow the display of HTML content in the cell.

Use this type of column to insert any HTML fragment into cells. Note that this column is not an edit mask because it does not allow any inline editing of text. Use Text Field if you want to allow inline editing of data. You can still use appropriate format handlers to format the input from the user after the user presses Enter.

Text—Number

The Text—Number column is preconfigured to work for displaying numeric values in data cells. This column is preconfigured with a value template of `@empty` and a format handler of `@number,integer`. Note that the `@empty` value template ensures that the text is displayed only after it has been formatted by the format handler. If you need to show the raw number as the grid is rendered, make sure you remove the `@empty` value template from this column.

Note that this column is not an edit mask because it does not allow any inline editing of data in the column. Use Text Field if you want to allow inline editing of data. You can still use appropriate format handlers to format the input from the user after the user presses Enter.

Text Area

The Text Area column functions like the Text Field column, except that it has a bigger text input area like the `<textarea>` tag in HTML. When the user clicks a cell, a text area opens up and allows the user to input long text. After the user presses Enter, the text is inserted into the matrix. Text Area allows for multiline content.

Text Field

The Text Field column can be inserted in the matrix to allow user input in a text box field. This is similar to having an `<input type=text>` tag in each cell for accepting input. However, unlike the `input` tag, having a Text Column becomes active only when a user clicks in the cell. When the user finishes typing and presses the Enter key, the text is entered into the matrix's backing CDF.

A basic spreadsheet with a fixed number of columns can be easily created by using columns of this type. If all columns were of type Text, a user will be able to type into any column and input text. The columns also have other standard features of the Matrix class—the columns can be reordered, resized, and sorted with the data that's in it.

An application can provide other controls (for example, a Submit button) in the panel to allow users to invoke an action that can save the contents of this mini spreadsheet.

Time

This column is preconfigured to display formatted time values onscreen. Values are converted using a default `@time` format handler. The title of the column is preset to Time. By default this will display the `time` CDF attribute formatted as a date.

This column does not have an edit mask associated with it and cannot be used to allow user input. Use the TimePicker column if you need to accept user input.

Time Picker

Using this column displays a TimePicker object in each cell in the column when the user clicks in it. Nothing will display initially if the column does not have any value. If it has a value, it is formatted as Time and displayed. When the user clicks in a cell, it displays a small control where time can be edited (or entered) using up- and down-arrow icons on the right in a standard format. The new time is entered into the matrix when the user clicks somewhere else on the window.

Manipulating Data Dynamically

The Matrix class in General Interface provides a very rich interface to enable dynamic updates of any element within it. The sample program `watchlist` included at the end of this chapter demonstrates the use of these APIs to dynamically update contents of a matrix cell.

Commonly Used Methods of the Matrix Class

The Matrix class in TIBCO General Interface is rich with numerous fields and methods. General Interface includes good API documentation with the product. The following sections provide additional details about some of the more commonly used methods of the `jsx3.api.Matrix` class.

getRecord

This method is inherited from the `jsx3.xml.CDF` class but can be used to retrieve the contents of any row of a matrix. What's more is that the returned result can be treated as a native JavaScript object to enable code such as `record.symbol` to refer to the symbol attribute within this record element in the backing XML CDF.

It takes one argument—`jsxid`—of the record to be retrieved. Notice how it is used in the `addSymbol` method of the `watchlist` application at the end of this chapter.

getContentElement

This method returns the HTML element associated with a specific cell. This makes it very convenient to update the contents of a matrix cell. It takes two arguments—`jsxid` and `attribute name`—and returns the cell that's at the intersection of the two.

This can be used to directly access the native HTML element in a matrix at runtime. Note how this method is used in the example.

getValue

If the selection model of a matrix is set to Single Selection, the method `getValue` returns the `jsxid` of the currently selected row. If the selection model is Multiple Selections, a list of `jsxids` of all the selected rows is returned.

redrawCell

This method can be used to redraw a single cell individually. It takes three arguments— `jsxid` of the row, a reference to the `jsx3.gui.Matrix.Column` object that represents the cell, and a Boolean—to indicate whether to suppress triggers. Recall that in a Matrix column, you can provide a comma-separated list of columns in its Triggers property of all the columns that must be repainted if this column changes. The last Boolean parameter effectively turns off those triggers, and General Interface does not repaint the other cells if you supply a value of `false` for it.

redrawRecord

Similar to `redrawCell`, this method allows you to repaint a single row in the matrix. This method takes the `jsxid` of the record to redraw and an argument to indicate whether this is a newly inserted record or if it's being deleted.

repaint

This method repaints the entire matrix again. This method should be used very carefully because rendering is the most time-consuming operation in JavaScript. Multiple calls to this method are unnecessary and must be avoided. For example, if you are adding columns to a matrix using JavaScript APIs, you will get much better performance if you add all the columns and then repaint only once when you are done.

repaintData

This call is very useful if you know that the structure of your matrix has not changed and only new data is to be painted. This repaints only the data in cells and performs much better than repainting the entire matrix. Call this method if the data (rows) have changed but the columns have not.

selectRecord

This method can be used to select a specific row in a matrix. This can be used by JavaScript to select any row. The only argument it requires is `jsxid` of the row to be selected. If the Selection model of the matrix is multiselect, it adds to the currently selected rows.

setValue

This method can be used to select a single row or multiple rows in a matrix. The only argument it requires is an array of `jsxid` of the rows to be selected. Use `selectRecord()` when you need to add to the current selection and `setValue()` when you want to replace the current selection with your own.

insertRecord

This method is inherited from the `jsx3.xml.CDF` class but can be used to insert a new row into the matrix. It can be passed a native JavaScript object containing name-value pairs for all the CDF attributes, including `jsxid`.

　　Note how it is used in the `watchlist` sample application. The following code line inserts a new record with three attributes—`jsxid`, `price`, and `direction`:

```
mat.insertRecord({jsxid: symbolBox.getValue(),
                  price: priceBox.getValue(),
                  direction: '-'}, true);
```

Sample Applications

Two sample applications are included with this chapter. The application named `oilconsumption` demonstrates the use of value templates and XML Transformers, and the application named `watchlist` demonstrates how to dynamically manipulate the contents of a matrix. Complete source code for the applications is included in the `examples` folder on the CD-ROM. HTML files that can be used to launch the application in the browser are also included. Open the file `oilconsumption.html` to launch the `oilconsumption` application, and launch the file `watchlist.html` to see a dynamically updating `watchlist`.

The `watchlist` application uses a `window.setTimeout` function to update the prices on the client side. The purpose of this application is to demonstrate the APIs that are available in General Interface to update the contents of a matrix. For a real-world application, the data will be served from the back-end applications. In the following chapters, we will discuss how to integrate General Interface applications to server-side technologies, including Java Messaging Service.

9

Integrating with Web Services

One of the major strengths of the TIBCO General Interface product is its ability to work with web services. The framework includes classes and interfaces to call a web service and retrieve the response. General Interface Builder includes a tool to develop a front end for web services. You simply supply the URL for a Web Service Description Language (WSDL) and the wizard retrieves all available operations and requests. You can develop client code with just a few clicks.

Web service is a vast topic encompassing many standards, protocols, and technologies. In this chapter we will take a brief look at what web services are and how to integrate a web service with TIBCO General Interface.

General Interface clients can be integrated with either Java or .NET web services. In this chapter we will first build a web service. Both Java and .NET versions of the same service are included on the companion CD-ROM. You need only one of them to work with the General Interface sample application included in this chapter that demonstrates how to integrate a General Interface application with a web service.

Web Services Related Standards

Web service is a standard for communicating between programs running on different machines. Many aspects of the web service specification exist, as standardized by W3C. Most commonly, however, the term refers to client and servers communicating using XML messages that follow the Simple Object Access Protocol (SOAP) standard.

The web services specification defines a mechanism for systems that provide services to define and register permitted operations, including request and response message formats. Requesters or client programs can then easily discover and make use of the services offered by the provider.

Services offered by a provider are defined using Web Service Description Language (WSDL)—an XML format that can be easily parsed by programs on machines of any underlying architecture and running any operating system. Web services architecture includes a centralized repository of WSDLs from providers and an interface to register and retrieve WSDLs.

Universal Description Discovery and Integration, or UDDI, specification defines a collection of nodes that provide a standard interface to register web services as well as client-side interfaces to discover such providers and the operations and messages they support.

Many related standards support or augment the web service architecture. WS-Security standard deals with security and authentication issues related to web services. WS-ReliableMesssaging is a specification to define how to send and receive messages in a reliable way between clients and servers of web servers. WS-Addressing defines a way to describe the address elements of messages to and from service providers, and the WS-Transaction standard addresses how to handle transactions in the context of web services.

General Interface and Web Services

Although General Interface is a great tool to build web service clients, some limitations exist to using the browser as a web service client. TIBCO General Interface's framework uses JavaScript to make web service calls, and all JavaScript on a web page is subject to the browser's security constraints.

General Interface can only make web service calls over HTTP because the browser only supports making HTTP requests. So unlike a fat client, General Interface cannot make a web service call using any protocol other than HTTP. Often, General Interface applications are used to augment server-side web-based applications (.NET or J2EE), so if necessary, a back-end adapter can be easily built to enable General Interface to make web service calls using protocols other than HTTP.

The GI Builder IDE that's included with TIBCO General Interface includes a wizard-based tool that makes it very easy to create web service clients that can send requests to a web service, receive a response from it, and display the results in any of General Interface's data consuming controls—for example, Matrix.

Building a Web Service

First we will need a back-end web service that General Interface can communicate with. Web services may be built using Java or .NET. Subsections that follow provide step-by-step instructions on how to build a web service using Java and .NET. You need only one of them to work on the General Interface client. Files for both projects are included on the CD-ROM.

Using Java

Several Java frameworks are available that enable quick web service development and deployment. Apache Axis2 (http://ws.apache.org/axis2/) is an open-source web service engine that can be deployed under Tomcat to host web services developed in Java.

Details of installing Axis 2 and building a web service are also included in this section.

Please note that the suggested directory paths are for the Windows platform. If you are using Linux or Macintosh for these examples, you will need to use directory paths appropriate for your environment.

Installing Axis2

Installation of Axis2 is very easy if you have already installed Tomcat (refer to the section "Deploying the Application Under Tomcat" in Chapter 3, "Quick Start TIBCO General Interface," if you have not installed Tomcat).

Axis2 is distributed in several forms. A binary distribution includes a standalone web server to host web services. There is also a war distribution that includes a web application archive file that can be deployed to Tomcat. At the time of this writing, the latest version is 1.4; Figure 9.1 shows the contents of the war distribution file—`axis2-1.4-war.zip`.

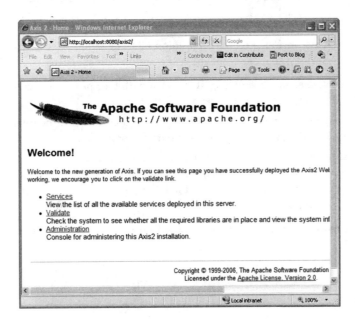

Figure 9.1   Default Axis2 home page.

1. After Tomcat is installed, download the zip file containing the latest binary release from http://ws.apache.org/axis2/download.cgi and extract its contents.

2. File `axis2.war` contains the web service engine that needs to be deployed to Tomcat. Copy this file `axis2.war` to Tomcat's `webapps` folder—for example, `C:\tomcat55\webapps`.

3. Start Tomcat by running the `startup.bat` file in the bin subdirectory (for example, `C:\tomcat55\bin\startup`).

4. Open an Internet browser and navigate to the URL http://localhost:8080/axis2/ to view the default Axis2 home page as shown in Figure 9.1.

After we develop the code for our service, we will deploy it (in the section "Deploying Under Axis2 in Tomcat").

Developing the Web Service Code in Java

Although you can build this sample without Apache Ant, it will make the process of building code a lot quicker and easier. Installing Ant is very easy. Download the latest binary version of Apache Ant from http://ant.apache.org/bindownload.cgi (or use the package provided on the companion CD) and extract its contents to your hard disk (C:\) and rename the folder to ant (`C:\ant`) and add the bin (`C:\ant\bin`) directory into the `PATH` environment variable.

Axis2 is able to present any plain old Java Object (POJO) as a web service to clients. A sample web service is included on the companion CD. The sample web service is developed using three classes: `SongBean`, `SongLibrary`, and `MiTunesService`.

- The class `SongBean` is a simple JavaBean class with four properties (artist, title, album, and price), each with a getter and setter function.

- Class `SongLibrary` represents a Singleton that is used to cache the song entries in memory, including methods to add and retrieve song titles.

- Class `MiTunesService` is the basic interface of the web service. It has three main operations: `getSongList`, `addSong`, and `getSongListByArtist`. Method `getSongList` returns all the songs in the library, `addSong` adds a given song to the library, and `getSongListByArtist` returns all songs by a specified artist.

To build the web service that will be deployed, create the directory structure as shown in Figure 9.2

Figure 9.2   Directory structure
for `MiTunesService` in Java.

Create the file SongBean.java from Listing 9.1, SongLibrary.java from Listing 9.2, and MiTunesService.java from Listing 9.3. (Files are also included on the companion CD under the examples/chapter9 folder.)

Listing 9.1   Java Source File—SongBean.java

```java
/* File: SongBean.java
 * Description: JavaBean for Song data.
 * Author: Anil Gurnani
 */

package com.tibcobooks.gi.chapter9;

import java.util.*;


public class SongBean implements Cloneable {
  private String artist;
  private String title;
  private String album;
  private double price;

  public SongBean() { }
  public SongBean(String ar, String t, String al, double p) {
    this.artist = ar;
    this.title = t;
    this.album = al;
    this.price = p;
  }

  public SongBean clone() {
    SongBean ab = new SongBean();

    try {
      ab = (SongBean)super.clone();
    } catch( Exception ex ) {
      // we just log it and return an empty object
      ex.printStackTrace();
    }
    return ab;
  }

  public String getArtist() { return artist; }
  public String getTitle() { return title; }
```

```java
    public String getAlbum() { return album; }
    public double getPrice() { return price; }

    public void setArtist(String a) { this.artist = a; }
    public void setTitle(String t) { this.title = t; }
    public void setAlbum(String a) { this.album = a; }
    public void setPrice(double p) { this.price = p; }
    public String toString() {
      return "[" + this.artist + "," + this.title + ","
             + this.album + "," + "," + this.price + "]";
    }

    public static void main(String args[]) {
      SongBean a1 = new SongBean();
      a1.setArtist("Fergie");
      a1.setTitle("Big Girls Dont Cry");
      a1.setAlbum("The Dutchess");
      a1.setPrice(1.99);

      SongBean a2 = new SongBean();
      a2.setArtist("Nickelback");
      a2.setTitle("Savin Me");
      a2.setAlbum("All The Right Reasons");
      a2.setPrice(1.49);

      System.out.println("SongBean a1="+a1);
      System.out.println("SongBean a2="+a2);
    }
}
```

Listing 9.2   Java Source File—`SongLibrary.java`

```java
/* File: SongLibrary.java
 * Description: Caches Song data
 *      This class is a thread safe singleton. Clients must use the getInstance()
 *      method to obtain a reference to an instance.
 *      artist:title:album:price
 * Author: Anil Gurnani
 */

package com.tibcobooks.gi.chapter9;

import java.util.*;
import java.io.*;
import java.util.concurrent.locks.*;
```

```java
public class SongLibrary {
  private static SongLibrary instance;
  private SortedMap<String,List<SongBean>> songLibrary;
  private ReadWriteLock rwlock = new ReentrantReadWriteLock();

  private String songs[] = {
      "Fergie:Big Girls Dont Cry:The Dutches:0.99",
      "Fergie:Fergalicious:The Dutches:0.99",
      "Fergie:Glamorous:The Dutches:0.99",
      "Rihanna:Dont Stop The Music:Good girl gone bad:0.99",
      "Chris Brown:With You:Exclusive:0.99",
      "Fall Out Boy:This aint a scene:Infinity on High:0.99",
      "Nickelback:Savin Me:All the Right Reasons:0.99"
  };

  public static SongLibrary getInstance() {
    if( instance == null ) {
      instance = SongLibrary.createInstance();
    }
    return instance;
  }

  public List<SongBean> getSongListByArtist(String a) {
    Lock rlock = rwlock.readLock();
    rlock.lock();
    List<SongBean> sl = null;
    try {
      sl = songLibrary.get(a);
    } catch(Exception ex) {
      ex.printStackTrace();
    } finally {
      rlock.unlock();
    }
    return sl;
  }

  public List<SongBean> getSongList() {
    Lock rlock = rwlock.readLock();
    rlock.lock();
    List<SongBean> sl = new LinkedList<SongBean>();
    try {
      Set<Map.Entry<String,List<SongBean>>>
          ss = songLibrary.entrySet();
      Iterator<Map.Entry<String,List<SongBean>>>
          iter = ss.iterator();
      while( iter.hasNext() ) {
```

```java
        Map.Entry<String,List<SongBean>> m = iter.next();
        if( m != null ) {
          sl.addAll(m.getValue());
        }
      }
    } catch(Exception ex) {
      ex.printStackTrace();
    } finally {
      rlock.unlock();
    }
    return sl;
  }

  public void addSong(SongBean sb)
  {
    Lock wlock = rwlock.writeLock();
    wlock.lock();
    try {
      List<SongBean> sl =
            songLibrary.get(sb.getArtist());
      if( sl == null ) {
        sl = new LinkedList<SongBean>();
        songLibrary.put(sb.getArtist(),sl);
      }

      //System.out.println("ading "+SongBean);
      sl.add(sb);  // add the song to the list
    } catch ( Exception ex ) {
      ex.printStackTrace();
    } finally {
      wlock.unlock();
    }
  }

  private SongLibrary() {
    songLibrary = new TreeMap<String,List<SongBean>>();
  }

  private static synchronized
  SongLibrary createInstance() {
    if( instance == null ) {
      instance = new SongLibrary();
      // initializes the map with static data
      instance.loaddata();
    }
    return instance;
```

```java
  }

  private void loaddata()
  {
    try
    {
      for( int i =0; i < songs.length; i++ ) {
        addSong(songs[i]);
      }
    }
    catch ( Exception ex )
    {
      ex.printStackTrace();
    }

  }

  private void addSong(String songData) {
    try {
      String[] tokens = songData.split(":");
      if( tokens.length < 4 ) {
        System.out.println("Invalid line format");
        return;
      }
      double price = 0.0;
      try {
        price = Double.parseDouble(tokens[3]);
      } catch ( Exception e ) {
        System.out.println("Invalid price format");
      }
      SongBean songBean = new SongBean
            ( tokens[0],tokens[1],tokens[2], price);
      addSong(songBean);
    } catch ( Exception ex ) {
      ex.printStackTrace();
    }
  }
}
```

Listing 9.3   Java Source File—`MiTunesService.java`

```java
/* File: MiTunesService.java
 * Description: Provides methods to retrieve song data
 *      This class implements service methods to retrieve
 *      song data for clients.
 * Author: Anil Gurnani
```

```
*/

package com.tibcobooks.gi.chapter9;

import java.util.*;

public class MiTunesService {

  public SongBean[] getSongList() {
    return SongLibrary.getInstance().
      getSongList().toArray(new SongBean[0]);
  }
  public SongBean[] getSongListByArtist(String artist) {
    return SongLibrary.getInstance().
     getSongListByArtist(artist).toArray(new SongBean[0]);
  }
  public void addSong(SongBean sb) {
    SongLibrary.getInstance().addSong(sb);
  }
}
```

Note that `MiTunesService` has methods that return composite objects. The Axis2 framework automatically generates code for handling marshaling and unmarshaling between the web service and the client. Method `getAlbumList` returns an array of `AlbumBean` objects and the method `getAlbumListByArtist` also returns a similar array of `AlbumBean` objects. In General Interface, these will be displayed in a Matrix component.

After writing the code for the web service, create a `build.xml` file to build your application into a deployment unit (`.aar` file) that can be deployed under Axis2.

Create a `build.xml` file as shown in Listing 9.4 in the project top-level directory—`MiTunesService`.

Listing 9.4   `Build.xml` for `MiTunesService` Web Service

```
<project name="MiTunesService" basedir="."
        default="generate.service">

    <property environment="env"/>
    <property name="AXIS2_HOME"
        value="C:/downloads/axis2-1.3"/>

    <property name="build.dir" value="build"/>

    <path id="axis2.classpath">
        <fileset dir="${AXIS2_HOME}/lib">
            <include name="*.jar"/>
        </fileset>
```

```
    </path>

    <target name="compile.service">
        <mkdir dir="${build.dir}"/>
        <mkdir dir="${build.dir}/classes"/>

        <!--First let's compile the classes-->
        <javac debug="on"
               fork="true"
               destdir="${build.dir}/classes"
               srcdir="${basedir}/src"
               classpathref="axis2.classpath">
        </javac>
    </target>

    <target name="generate.wsdl"
        depends="compile.service">
        <taskdef name="java2wsdl"
         classname="org.apache.ws.java2wsdl.Java2WSDLTask"
         classpathref="axis2.classpath"/>
        <java2wsdl className =
          "com.tibcobooks.gi.chapter9.MiTunesService"
          outputLocation="${build.dir}"
          targetNamespace=http://com.tibcobooks.gi.chapter9/
          schemaTargetNamespace =
          "http://com.tibcobooks.gi.chapter9.MiTunesService/xsd">
            <classpath>
                <pathelement path="${axis2.classpath}"/>
                <pathelement location="${build.dir}/classes"/>
            </classpath>
        </java2wsdl>
    </target>

    <target name="generate.service" depends="compile.service">
        <!--aar them up -->
        <copy toDir="${build.dir}/classes" failonerror="false">
            <fileset dir="${basedir}/resources">
                <include name="**/*.xml"/>
            </fileset>
        </copy>
        <jar destfile="${build.dir}/MiTunesService.aar">
            <fileset excludes="**/Test.class" dir="${build.dir}/classes"/>
        </jar>
    </target>

    <target name="clean">
```

```
            <delete dir="${build.dir}"/>
        </target>
</project>
```

We need to build one last file that defines the web service for Axis2—`service.xml`—as shown in Listing 9.5.

Listing 9.5   Service Description File `service.xml`

```
<service name="MiTunesService" scope="application"
 targetNamespace="http://com.tibcobooks.gi.chapter9/">
    <description>
        Mi Tunes Service
    </description>
    <messageReceivers>
        <messageReceiver
          mep=http://www.w3.org/2004/08/wsdl/in-only
          class=
    "org.apache.axis2.rpc.receivers.RPCInOnlyMessageReceiver"/>
        <messageReceiver
          mep=http://www.w3.org/2004/08/wsdl/in-out
          class =
        "org.apache.axis2.rpc.receivers.RPCMessageReceiver"/>
    </messageReceivers>
    <schema schemaNamespace =
        "http://com.tibcobooks.gi.chapter9.MiTunesService/xsd"/>
    <parameter name = "ServiceClass">
        com.tibcobooks.gi.chapter9.MiTunesService
    </parameter>
</service>
```

Note that this `service.xml` file is in a directory META-INF inside the resources folder, and `build.xml` adds it to the deployment archive file `MiTunesService.aar`. This file contains information about the service, including description and input and output messages for Axis2.

After creating the files, open a DOS command window and change the current working directory to the top-level folder for our web service—`C:\Projects\chapter9\MiTunesService`—and run the command

```
C:>ant
```

This will produce a deployable web service package, `MiTunesService.aar`, inside the build directory. We will deploy this file to Axis2 (in the section "Deploying a Web Service") later in this chapter.

Using .NET

Microsoft's Internet Information Service (IIS) includes support for web services and does not require any additional components. However, you must install the .NET Framework 2.0 to use the sample included here. Download and install .NET Framework 2.0 (or higher) from Microsoft's website (http://msdn.microsoft.com/en-us/netframework) and install it by launching the downloaded installer package.

Although it is possible to code the .NET web services outside the Visual Studio environment, this section provides steps to build it using Visual Studio.

Developing the Sample Web Service in C# Using Visual Studio .NET

Before launching Visual Studio, create a folder to store all your Visual Studio projects (`C:\DotNetProjects`).

To develop the sample web service for this chapter in C#, launch Visual Studio and select File, New, Project to bring up the New Project dialog. Select Web under Visual C# in the Project Type area and select ASP.NET Web Service Application from the Visual Studio Installed Templates, as shown in Figure 9.3.

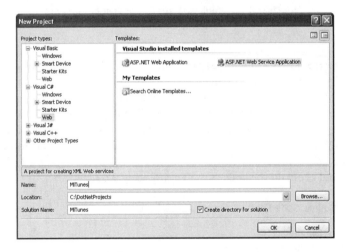

Figure 9.3   Creating a new web service in
Visual Studio.

Enter the name of the project (MiTunes) and Visual Studio will automatically supply the name of the solution. Make sure the check box that says Create a Directory for Solution is checked, and click OK to create the project. Visual Studio creates the default files for the web service and names the service `Service1.asmx` by default, as shown in Figure 9.4.

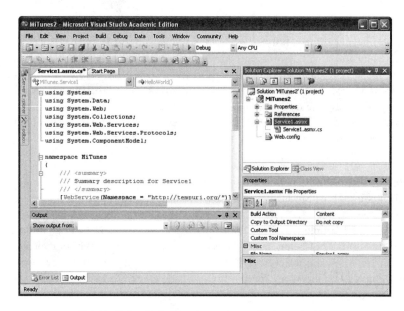

Figure 9.4   Default web service project created by
Visual Studio.

Rename `Service1.asmx` to `MiTunesService.asmx` by right-clicking `Service1.asmx` in
the Solution Explorer and selecting the Rename option from the menu. Also change the
name of the class from `Service1` to `MiTunesService` in the source code of the file. You also
need to change the reference class name in the text file `MiTunesService.asmx`. To do this,
you click the right mouse button on the name of the file (`MiTunesService.asmx`) and select the Open With menu option; then select Source Code (Text) Editor from the dialog
and click OK.

The file should contain the code as shown in Listing 9.6.

Listing 9.6   Source Code File—`MiTunesService.asmx`

```
<%@ WebService Language="C#"
    CodeBehind="MiTunesService.asmx.cs"
    Class="MiTunes.MiTunesService" %>
```

Edit the contents of the `MiTunesService.asmx.cs` file to add the interface methods as
shown in Listing 9.7. Note the three main interface methods: `getSongList`,
`getSongListByArtist`, and `addSong` in our web service.

Listing 9.7   Source Code File—`MiTunesService.asmx.cs`

```
using System;
using System.Data;
```

```
using System.Web;
using System.Collections;
using System.Web.Services;
using System.Web.Services.Protocols;
using System.ComponentModel;

namespace MiTunes
{
  /// <summary>
  /// Provides methods to retrieve song data
  /// This class implements service methods to retrieve
  /// song data for clients.
  /// Author: Anil Gurnani
  /// </summary>
  [WebService(Namespace = "http://www.tibcobooks.com/gi/")]
  [WebServiceBinding(ConformsTo = WsiProfiles.BasicProfile1_1)]
  [ToolboxItem(false)]
  public class MiTunesService : System.Web.Services.WebService
  {
    [WebMethod]
    public SongBean[] getSongList()
    {
      return SongLibrary.getInstance().
        getSongList().ToArray();
    }
    [WebMethod]
    public SongBean[] getSongListByArtist(String artist)
    {
      return SongLibrary.getInstance().
        getSongListByArtist(artist).ToArray();
    }
    [WebMethod]
    public void addSong(SongBean sb)
    {
      SongLibrary.getInstance().addSong(sb);
    }
  }
}
```

Create two new classes, SongBean and SongLibrary, from Listings 9.8 and 9.9, respectively. To add a new class in Visual Studio, select Add Class from the Project menu, choose Class from Visual Studio Installed Templates, and supply the appropriate name for each class.

Listing 9.8   Source Code for SongBean.cs

```
using System;
```

```csharp
using System.Data;
using System.Configuration;
using System.Web;
using System.Web.Security;
using System.Web.UI;
using System.Web.UI.WebControls;
using System.Web.UI.WebControls.WebParts;
using System.Web.UI.HtmlControls;

namespace MiTunes
{
  public class SongBean
  {
    private String artist;
    private String album;
    private String title;
    private double price;
    public String Artist
    {
      get { return this.artist; }
      set { this.artist = value; }
    }
    public String Title
    {
      get { return this.title; }
      set { this.title = value; }
    }
    public String Album
    {
      get { return this.album; }
      set { this.album = value; }
    }
    public double Price
    {
      get { return this.price; }
      set { this.price = value; }
    }
    public SongBean(String a, String t, String b, double p)
    {
      this.artist = a;
      this.album = b;
      this.title = t;
      this.price = p;
    }
    public SongBean() { }
  }
}
```

Listing 9.9   Source Code for `SongLibrary.cs`

```
using System;
using System.Data;
using System.Collections.Generic;
using System.Configuration;
using System.Web;
using System.Web.Security;
using System.Web.UI;
using System.Web.UI.WebControls;
using System.Web.UI.WebControls.WebParts;
using System.Web.UI.HtmlControls;

namespace MiTunes
{
  public class SongLibrary
  {
    private static SongLibrary instance = null;
    private SortedDictionary<String,List<SongBean>> songLibrary;

    private String[] songs = {
      "Fergie:Big Girls Dont Cry:The Dutches:0.99",
      "Fergie:Fergalicious:The Dutches:0.99",
      "Fergie:Glamorous:The Dutches:0.99",
      "Rihanna:Dont Stop The Music:Good girl gone bad:0.99",
      "Chris Brown:With You:Exclusive:0.99",
      "Fall Out Boy:This aint a scene:Infinity on High:0.99",
      "Nickelback:Savin Me:All the Right Reasons:0.99"
    };

    public static SongLibrary getInstance() {
      if( instance == null ) {
        instance = SongLibrary.createInstance();
      }
      return instance;
    }

    public List<SongBean> getSongListByArtist(String a) {
      List<SongBean> sl = null;
      try {
        sl = songLibrary[a];
      } catch(Exception ex) {
        Console.WriteLine(ex.Message);
      }
```

```
      return sl;
    }

    public List<SongBean> getSongList() {
      List<SongBean> sl = new List<SongBean>();
      try {
          foreach( KeyValuePair<String, List<SongBean>> kvp in songLibrary ) {
              foreach ( SongBean sb in kvp.Value ) {
                sl.Add(sb);
            }
          }
      } catch(Exception ex) {
        Console.WriteLine(ex.Message);
      }
      return sl;
    }

    public void addSong(SongBean sb)
    {
      List<SongBean> sl = null;
      try {
        sl = songLibrary[sb.Artist];
      }
      catch ( KeyNotFoundException kex)
      {
          sl = new List<SongBean>();
      }
      //System.out.println("ading "+SongBean);
      sl.Add(sb);  // add the song to the list
      songLibrary[sb.Artist] = sl;
    }

    private SongLibrary() {
      songLibrary = new SortedDictionary<String,List<SongBean>>();
    }

    private static
    SongLibrary createInstance() {
      if( instance == null ) {
        instance = new SongLibrary();
        // initializes the map with static data
        instance.loaddata();
      }
      return instance;
    }
```

```
private void loaddata()
{
  try
  {
    for( int i =0; i < songs.Length; i++ ) {
      addSong(songs[i]);
    }
  }
  catch ( Exception ex )
  {
    Console.WriteLine(ex.Message);
  }
}

private void addSong(String songData) {
  try {
      Char[] delimiters = { ':' };
    String[] tokens = songData.Split(delimiters);
    if( tokens.Length < 4 ) {
      Console.WriteLine("Invalid line format");
      return;
    }
    double price = 0.0;
    try {
      price = Double.Parse(tokens[3]);
    } catch ( Exception e ) {
      Console.WriteLine("Invalid price format");
    }
    SongBean songBean = new SongBean
        ( tokens[0],tokens[1],tokens[2], price);
    addSong(songBean);
  } catch ( Exception ex ) {
    Console.WriteLine(ex.Message);
  }
}
}
}
```

Now we are ready to build our solution and deploy it. From the Build menu, select the Build Solution option to build the web service classes. We will deploy it in the next section.

Deploying a Web Service

A web service has several common functions that it must perform, including setting up a listener for requests, parsing the request parameters and converting them to native language objects, and then packaging the return value from the service into XML response format. Standards make it possible to build this code external to the business logic for the operations.

Containers such as IIS or Tomcat with Axis2 provide the capabilities to expose methods provided by any class as a web service using these standards.

Deploying Under Axis2 in Tomcat

Deploying a web service under Axis2 is a matter of copying the output from the previous `ant` command in the section "Developing a Web Service Using Java." The deployment package is inside the build folder and is named `MiTunesService.aar`. Copy it to the services directory inside the `axis2` deployment directory in the folder `WEB-INF` under the folder `axis2`, which is deployed in the `webapps` directory under the `tomcat` directory. The complete directory hierarchy is shown in Figure 9.5.

Figure 9.5   Web service deployment directory for Apache Axis2.

After deploying the service, make sure Tomcat is running, and open up a browser and navigate to the URL http://localhost:8080/axis2/services/listServices. You should see MiTunesService listed as one of the deployed services, as shown in Figure 9.6.

You can call the operation getSongListByArtist along with the artist parameter of Fergie to get a list of all songs by Fergie using the URL http://localhost:8080/axis2/services/ MiTunesService/getSongListByArtist?artist=Fergie.

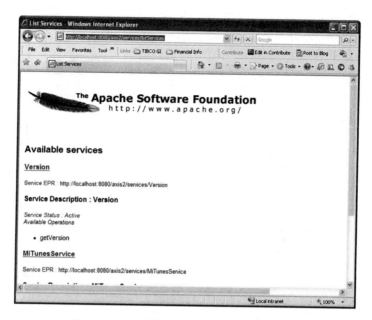

Figure 9.6   MiTunesService deployed under
Apache Axis2.

You will see a page as shown in Figure 9.7.

Deploying Under IIS

There are a couple of ways to deploy under IIS. Visual Studio includes wizards and templates to build your own installer project, which can create a single deployment unit that will be installed using Microsoft Installer on any Windows server running IIS.

For this exercise, you can deploy using Visual Studio directly to a folder under the C:\InetPub\wwwroot folder on your local IIS installation. To do this, select Publish MiTunes from the Build menu and provide the full path of the directory where to deploy this service (C:\InetPub\wwwroot\MiTunes), as shown in Figure 9.8.

There is one more step before this web service can be used. Click Start, select Control Panel, and then click Open Internet Information Server Administration Control Panel by navigating to the item Internet Information Services in the Administrator Tools subfolder inside Control Panels. When you expand the Web Sites node, you will see the MiTunes application depicted by a simple folder icon, as shown in Figure 9.9.

Right-click this folder and select Properties. The Application Name in the Properties dialog will be grayed out, as shown in Figure 9.10. Click the Create button next to the application name and click OK to install this new web service as an application.

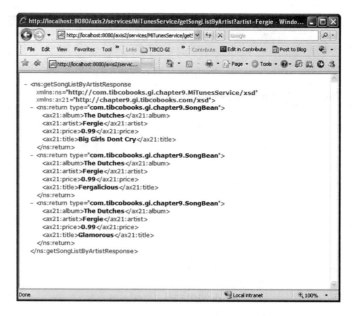

Figure 9.7   Results of operation
getSongListByArtist from MiTunesService.

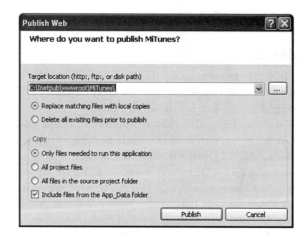

Figure 9.8   Publishing MiTunes
web service.

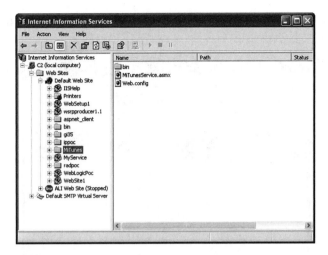

Figure 9.9   MiTunes folder in IIS Admin
console.

Figure 9.10   The MiTunes
Properties dialog.

Now your web service is deployed under IIS. Go to the URL http://localhost/
MiTunes/MiTunesService.asmx. You should see the MiTunesService page as shown in

Figure 9.11. Note that by default, .NET Framework gives you some pages to test the operations in your web service.

Figure 9.11   The MiTunesService
home page under IIS.

Developing a Web Service Client Using General Interface

Now we are ready to develop a client using General Interface, which will allow us to list songs in the library and to add songs to our library. The complete application is included on the companion CD. I describe some key parts of the application in the following section.

Building GUI Screens for the Sample General Interface Client

Three tabs in the application correspond to each operation of the web service. The first tab, labeled All Songs, contains a single button to fetch all the songs in the library using the web service operation getSongList. The second tab, labeled By Artist, contains a text box to take a parameter to call the operation getSongListByArtist, and it populates the matrix below with the results. The third tab, Add Song, contains four text fields and a button to provide the capability to add a new song to the library.

1. Launch GI Builder and create a new project named **MiTunesClient**.

2. Drag and drop a Tabbed Pane container from the Components Library palette onto the drawing canvas, and GI Builder will create three tabbed panes by default. Change the Caption property of the tabs to All Songs, By Artist, and Add Song, respectively. Also change the Name property to AllSongs, ByArtist, and AddSong, respectively.

3. Drag and drop a Layout—Top/Over component onto the pane in the first tab and adjust its Rows Array property to 30,*.

4. Drag and drop a button in the top panel and a Grid control in the bottom panel, and update the properties as follows.

5. Change the Name property of the Button to getAllSongsButton and the Text/HTML property to Get All Songs. Also change its Relative X/Y property to Absolute and adjust it onscreen as shown in Figure 9.12.

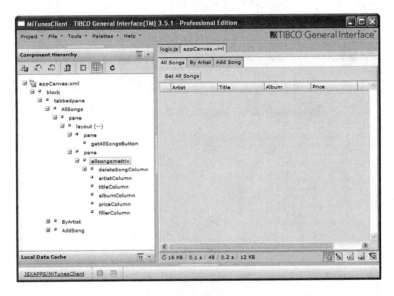

Figure 9.12   The All Songs tab of the MiTunesClient
project.

6. Change the Name property of the Grid to allsongsmatrix and delete the two default columns mc1 and mc2 from it. Also clear out the XML String property by right-clicking the name and selecting Reset/Clear from the menu. Add a Button—Delete column, three Text columns, a Text—Number column, and finally, an empty Text column (to act as filler) to the Matrix component allsongsmatrix. Also set the XML Cache Id property to allsongs; memorize this name because it will be needed

when you build the mapping from the web service call using the XML Mapping Utility.

7. Update the properties of the columns to match the names and column headers as shown in Figure 9.12. It's important to remember to set the Att Name property of corresponding columns correctly (artist for artistColumn, title for titleColumn, album for albumColumn, and price for priceColumn). The return document from the web service call will map column data to these CDF attributes.

8. Open up the XML Mapping Utility by selecting it from the Tools menu to begin creating a mapping rule.

9. In the XML Mapping Tool window, enter the URL of the WSDL of the web service: http://localhost:8080/axis2/services/MiTunesService?wsdl. (Note that the URL will be different if you are using the .NET version of the web service for this sample.) Click the Parse Document button. GI Builder will parse the WSDL and show you the operations and their input and output, as in Figure 9.13.

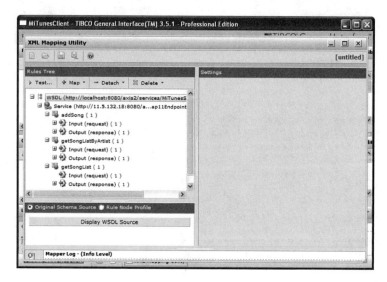

Figure 9.13   The XML Mapping Utility after parsing WSDL.

10. The getSongList operation does not require any input mappings because it does not take any parameters. To map the output message to CDF elements, expand the node Output (response)(1) in the tool by clicking the plus sign. The number in parentheses shows whether it's a repeating element or just a single one. In this case,

the number 1 indicates that there is going to be only one such node in the response document. A new child node named getSongListResponse will appear.

11. Double-click the mouse on this node to further expand it to show another child node named `return[SongBean](0-unbounded)`. Note that the numbers in parentheses show that this is a repeating sequence of records. Double-click again to expand it to show individual attributes, as in Figure 9.14.

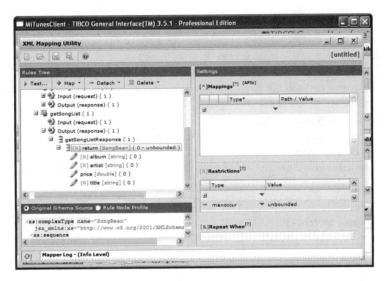

Figure 9.14   XML Mapping Utility showing individual elements of getSongList response.

Mapping the Response to CDF Document

What needs to be done is to map each element of the return record into a CDF attribute and the entire response into a CDF document.

1. To map the elements of the record to CDF attributes, select each element (by clicking it) and then select Map, CDF Attribute from the menu. You will see the mapping appear in the Settings section on the right side under Mappings.

2. To map the CDF document, select the node `getSongListResponse` and click the menu handle in the Type column in the first (empty) row in the Mappings area within Settings on the right side of the window, and select CDF Document from the menu. Type the value **allsongs** in the Path/Value field for this mapping row. Recall that the name of the cache to which our allsongsmatrix is bound is also **allsongs**. Whenever this mapping rule is invoked, the contents of the cache **allsongs** will be updated based on the response from the web service call.

3. Click the disk icon in the toolbar at the top to save this mapping rule. Save this rule in the rules folder as `getsonglist.xml`.

4. General Interface includes a feature to generate code to invoke the web service for which the mapping rule is created. Select the menu item based on the name of the operation from the Generate menu to let General Interface generate the JavaScript code. GI Builder will place the code on the Clipboard, from where it may be pasted into a JavaScript file. Although the generated code can be directly used in simple applications, it is necessary to build custom JavaScript code.

The sample application includes code to invoke each of the operations. The design of the sample application includes three classes—`GetSongHandler`, `GetSongListByArtistHandler`, and `AddSongHandler`—each of which has the code to subscribe to events and call the appropriate mapping rule upon receiving that event. The events are published by buttons on the panes.

The file `logic.js` has a single method `main` that creates an instance each of the three handler classes. The constructor of each class subscribes to events and responds to events as they are raised by users' button clicks.

Listing 9.11 shows the entire JavaScript source code for the `GetSongHandler` class.

Listing 9.11   Source Code—`GetSongHandler.js`

```
jsx3.lang.Class.defineClass(
  "com.tibcobooks.gi.chapter9.GetSongHandler",
  null,
  null,
  function(GetSongHandler) {

    GetSongHandler.prototype.init = function() {
        var app = MiTunesClient.getServer();
        app.subscribe('GET_SONG_LIST', this, this.callgetSongList);
    }

    GetSongHandler.prototype.callgetSongList = function() {
      var objService = MiTunesClient.loadResource("getsonglist_xml");
      objService.setOperation("getSongList");

      //subscribe
      objService.subscribe(jsx3.net.Service.ON_SUCCESS,
        this.ongetSongListSuccess);
      objService.subscribe(jsx3.net.Service.ON_ERROR, this.ongetSongListError);
      objService.subscribe(jsx3.net.Service.ON_INVALID,
        this.ongetSongListInvalid);

      //PERFORMANCE ENHANCEMENT: uncomment the following line of code to use
      XSLT to convert the server response to CDF (refer to the API docs for
      jsx3.net.Service.compile for implementation details)
```

```
    //objService.compile();

    //call the service
    objService.doCall();
  };


  GetSongHandler.prototype.ongetSongListSuccess = function(objEvent) {
    //var responseXML = objEvent.target.getInboundDocument();
    var mat = MiTunesClient.getJSXByName("allsongsmatrix");
    mat.repaint();
  };


  GetSongHandler.prototype.ongetSongListError = function(objEvent) {
    var myStatus = objEvent.target.getRequest().getStatus();
    objEvent.target.getServer().alert("Error","The service call failed.
    The HTTP Status code is: " + myStatus);
  };


  GetSongHandler.prototype.ongetSongListInvalid =
          function(objEvent) {

        objEvent.target.getServer().alert("Invalid",
        "The following message node just failed validation:\n\n"
        + objEvent.message);
  };


  }
);
```

Note the use of the function `loadResource`. This method in the API allows you to
load any resource from the server on demand. The rules file is not loaded on the client
side until it is needed. This mechanism can also be used to load XML components on demand.

Also note that the method to invoke the web service sets up functions to be called in
the event of success, failure, and invalid request; it sets up the operation and calls the
method `doCall` to invoke the web service.

Mapping Input Fields to Request Messages

Creating mappings for Input parameters is also very easy with this XML Mapping Utility.
The tool even generates the appropriate fields and adds them to the canvas, which can be
used to accept data from the user.

Follow these steps to bind an input parameter to the operation getSongListByArtist:

1. Create the user interface elements as shown in Figure 9.15. Note that you can
    clone the matrix from the All Songs pane and move it to this pane.

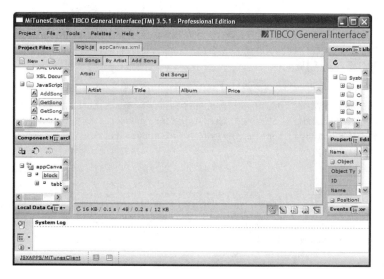

Figure 9.15   The user interface for the
getSongListByArtist operation.

2. Be sure to change the Name and XML Cache ID properties of this matrix to
   `songsbyartistmatrix` and `allsongsbyartist`, respectively.

3. Name the text field `artistTextBox` because it will be used to map the input parameter for the web service call.

4. Close the XML Mapping Utility if it is still open, and open another clean instance
   of it. Then type the URL of the WSDL again and click Parse Document. Click the
   plus sign next to the Input node under the `getSongListByArtist` node to reveal
   the only parameter required—`artist`. Select it and click the menu handle in the
   empty row in the Settings area under Mappings, toward the right side of the mapping tool window. Select DOM from the menu and type the name of the text field
   that contains what you want to send to the web service. In this case, it is
   `artistTextBox`.

5. Map the output response to CDF Record and CDF Attributes and CDF Document as before, except name the CDF Document **songsbyartist** this time to
   match the value of `XML Cache Id` of the matrix on this tab.

Another powerful feature of the Mapping tool is its capability to generate DOM ele-
ments to accept user data for web service calls. The user interface for the last tab Add
Song in this sample was built using automatic generation of DOM elements from the
Mapping utility.

To generate a Form element to accept user input, select the menu option DOM (map
and create) while having any Input parameter selected in the Mapping utility. Also make

sure a Block element is selected in the General Interface component hierarchy. The tool will automatically create Form elements to accept input with and set up the Name property and create an appropriate binding in the mapping rules so that when the rule is invoked, it will pass the value typed in by the user in the Form field.

Make sure to look at the scriptlets that have been placed in the event handlers for the buttons to follow how this design completely decouples the handlers from the GUI elements. Each button simply publishes an event, and the handlers respond to those events. This design makes it possible to reuse the handlers (and the buttons) in any application, and it makes it very easy to bind any other user events to invoking the web service—for example, using the `HotKey` class to associate a hotkey to invoke the web service `getSongList`.

10

Integrating with Portals

Web portals have evolved considerably in the past several years. Modern enterprise portal software can aggregate static and dynamic content from various back-end technologies and allow business users to create dynamic websites by pulling together from a collection of portlets in a distributed environment running on a combination of UNIX-Linux/Java and Windows .NET platforms. Figure 10.1 shows a high-level architecture for an Enterprise Portal.

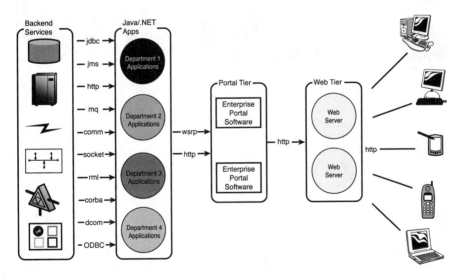

Figure 10.1   High-level portal architecture.

In this chapter, we discuss techniques to integrate TIBCO General Interface applications into a portal.

Anatomy of a Portal

The subject of portal architectures is vast enough to require many books. In this chapter, the focus will be on integrating TIBCO General Interface applications into a portal. Figure 10.2 shows conceptually how a portal page comprises several portlets.

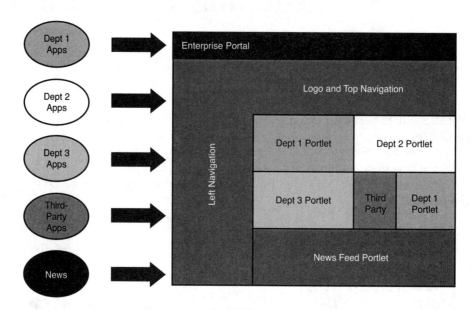

Figure 10.2   Portal as an aggregator.

A portal provides a very rich user experience to its visitors by breaking a web page into smaller components that can be managed individually. A portal page is made up of many small portlets, which can communicate among themselves and with different data sources to present one cohesive view of the underlying data. Portal visitors can also customize their pages by choosing from among a variety of themes, styles, and even other portlets to make their own unique page. Separate components, known as skins, can be layered on top of functional portlets to give the entire portal a consistent look and feel, with all the content blending into a single portal to present a rich user experience.

A portal is built in a highly modular fashion to allow flexibility in terms of presenting content to end users. A collection of portlets is available to portal content administrators and end users to put together the layout of pages per their needs and requirements. Portlets expose certain key properties that can be customized to create custom instances of portlets. For example, the portal builder (administrator) may set up a default ZIP code for a weather portlet so that whenever the portlet is first added to a page, it always shows the weather for New York City. However, a customer who lives in Los Angeles can then customize it and change the ZIP code so that whenever she loads the page with the weather portlet, it will show weather for Los Angeles.

A portal page is built using a number of building blocks that include Desktop, Books, Pages, and Portlets. Developers build portlets, and business owners can use these portlets to put together Pages, Books, and Desktops. A page may contain any number of disparate portlets, and a book may contain any number of pages from any source. A page may contain other books or pages. The look and feel in a portal is controlled via themes and skins. Users are able to pick from a number of available themes and choose a look and feel.

Portlets that make up the portal page can be built using `<iframe>` tags, `<div>` or `<span>` tags, or using the JSR 168 standard. JSR 168 is a Java standard that defines the presentation and interaction models associated with these parts of a page called portlets. Currently the JSR community is working on an upgraded portlet specification, JSR 286. The new specification is going to draw upon the previous specification and add several capabilities to it, including modern AJAX interactions.

There is also another standard for web services running remotely to provide HTML fragments to the portal. This protocol (Web Services for Remote Portlets) provides the capability to present HTML fragments via standard web services calls. All required data and parameters are passed to the web service, which can then respond with an HTML fragment. As of April 1, 2008, WSRP version 2.0 has been approved. WSRP 2.0 allows remote portlets to carry out complex AJAX interactions with the client as though they were running natively in the web server (or the portal tier). Many vendors have already started delivering support for WSRP 2.0 in their portal software products.

Portal Value Proposition

An Enterprise Portal has many advantages. Following are some of the key benefits to all participants and to the end users of enterprise applications.

Aggregation of Content from Various Applications and Sources

An Enterprise Portal consisting of applications from all lines of business will result in a unique user experience for clients. Users will not have to navigate to different websites or pages to see different content of interest to them. They will not be limited to seeing only one application content per page. End users will be able to put together a page with the portlets they use for their daily work. Business owners will gain tremendous flexibility and time to market for new product development and service innovations. The Enterprise Portal will empower business groups to put together new products and services that use existing portlets like building blocks. Because a portal is built using small components, incremental components are quick and inexpensive to build and deploy. This allows tremendous flexibility in information architecture and speedy product development, and it accelerates service innovation.

Federated Search Across All Data Sources

When end users are looking for something on the Enterprise Portal, they will not need to search for it on multiple Enterprise websites or applications. Instead, they will be able to search across all content exposed via any business line that is relevant for their search. An Enterprise Portal makes it possible to have a single search portlet return results by referencing a combined index of all business applications and content.

Entitlements

Entitlements can be used in a portal to create different tiers or segments of end users. Policies can be created to allow access to only certain portlets for users in a specific tier. Additionally, each application can define a set of roles that are required to access certain portlets. For example, a trade processing application might allow everyone to view the trades, but might not allow everyone to edit trades. This can be accomplished easily by setting entitlements on a View Trade portlet and Edit Trade portlets. Users can be granted roles based on attributes defined by LOB application groups. Administration of such entitlements is delegated and is completely controlled by the application groups.

Private Labeling and Branding

Enterprise Portal treats presentation styles separately from functional portlets. So, it is possible to create a new brand using a different look and feel only by creating the style components such as themes and skins. The newly branded application can draw upon content from various available sources as discussed previously in the section "Aggregation of Content from Various Applications and Sources" and can be made available to a specific group of users by way of creating access control policies as discussed in the preceding "Entitlements" section.

Personalization

Content selectors and campaigns enable marketing groups to push specific content to targeted audiences. A portal inherently supports the capability to create user segments dynamically, which makes it possible to show specific messages to a selected community of users. For example, announcements about a new high-value product could be shown to all users who reach a target of $100 million in net worth.

Common Infrastructure

Multiple applications will be able to share a common infrastructure, resulting in cost advantages for the business groups. Platform engineering resources can focus on enhancing the underlying infrastructure that will benefit all portal participants.

Global Reach

An instance of the portal will be available in each region. Any application that goes on the portal can take advantage of this to present its content to users across the globe by deploying only in their local region. Federation capabilities of Enterprise Portal make it possible to access applications from another region and cache their content for high performance in any region.

High Availability

Portal is built with extremely high availability in mind. Multiple redundant servers exist within each data center. It is possible to failover from one data center to another for any tier within each region. Furthermore, it will be possible to failover from one region to another completely by simply logging in to the portal again.

Support, Operations, and Monitoring

Applications can take advantage of highly automated support, operations, and monitoring infrastructure of Enterprise Portal, allowing application teams to be alerted before end users begin to call with issues.

Architectural Considerations

TIBCO General Interface is a client-side technology and therefore is able to integrate with any back-end technology. It is possible to use General Interface applications in portals built using any technology. However, as discussed in the following sections, there are some specific considerations when you use multiple General Interface applications on a single page.

Use of General Interface Framework

Because General Interface framework is mainly composed of JavaScript files, it is important to ensure that only one copy of the source files be loaded in browser memory to preserve precious memory inside the browser. This is especially important when you consider that many applications may compete for the same memory space.

GI Cache Utilization

Each application that has a potential to be loaded with other applications must use only the bare minimum set of resources because it might be sharing that space with multiple applications. JavaScript has a garbage collection mechanism similar to that of Java; however, applications must utilize memory carefully because excessive use of memory could result in browsers freezing or crashing.

Namespaces

Another common issue is when the same application is included twice in the same page. This can cause namespace clashes when the application is referenced by name. This can be avoided by using a `jsxappns` attribute in the main script tag that is used to bootstrap the General Interface application. Use a unique value for each inclusion of the same application. Also make sure to not refer to the namespace by name in the code; instead, always use the APIs provided by General Interface, such as `this.getServer()` to obtain a reference to the application server object.

Entering and Leaving the Page

Applications must be aware of entry and exit from the page to ensure that they properly initialize and release resources. Each application may provide methods to initialize and destroy, which may be called via `onLoad` and `onUnload` methods in the browser page to ensure best performance. General Interface applications may also have a state that they need to save and restore at these two points.

Minimizing Asynchronous Calls

This might seem contradictory at first, because AJAX calls are always asynchronous. But every asynchronous call creates a new thread in the browser, and unless controlled properly, these threads could cause the browser to crash or become unresponsive. Special attention must be paid to avoid race conditions in the code. This is important even when there is only one application in a page, but it becomes even more important when there is more than one application in a single page.

Versions of General Interface

Only a single version of the framework file `JSX30.js` can be referenced on a single page. Therefore, when you include multiple General Interface applications on the same page, make sure that all applications use the same version of General Interface. Because General Interface versions are backward compatible, it is sufficient to make sure the latest version is what is loaded. However, it is best to include applications built using the same version.

Using `<iframe>` Tags

One way to achieve an aggregated experience is to use `<iframe>` tags. Browsers support an `<iframe>` tag that can be used to divide the available screen area into smaller rectangular parts. Each iFrame can then present a different web application. This approach can be achieved very easily without using any special container or application server.

However, many drawbacks exist to this approach. Pages with several `<iframe>` tags can be slow to render. There is no direct way to control the look and feel of each component. Each application that is referenced in the `<iframe>` must provide a consistent look and feel across the portal page. Also, no opportunities exist to share the look and feel components directly.

From TIBCO General Interface's perspective, it is easiest to integrate applications in an iFrame because each iFrame behaves like a different browser window. Therefore, there is no extra code or change required to a General Interface application to run it inside an iFrame. Simply set the `src` attribute of the `<iframe>` tag to point to the HTML page that launches the General Interface application.

When a browser includes two or more iFrames that contain a General Interface application, the General Interface boot loader will be run multiple times, and the TIBCO splash screen will appear once for each iFrame that has a General Interface application. JavaScript files will also be loaded once for each iFrame that contains the General Interface application. This could result in significant memory overhead for the browser, depending on how the applications are written.

Using `<div>` and `<span>` Tags

It is possible to create a page consisting of multiple `<div>` and `<span>` elements and have a General Interface application reside within each `<div>` or `<span>` tag. The deployment utility included with TIBCO GI Builder can be used to generate a script fragment for an inline `<div>`. This scriptlet can then be pasted inside each `<div>` and `<span>` tag.

If the same General Interface application is loaded multiple times on the same page, it is important to note that application code must not reference the server by application name. Instead, all code must obtain the instance of the server class to use by using the JavaScript APIs provided by General Interface (such as `this.getServer()`, or by using the context parameters for events).

Listing 10.1 shows a simple HTML page that includes two General Interface applications in the same page.

Listing 10.1   Two General Interface Apps in a Single Page

```
<html>
<head>
<title>two GI apps on a page</title>
</head>
<body bgcolor=white>
<div style="width:400px;height:160px;" id="ratesportlet">
   <script type="text/javascript" src="JSX/js/JSX30.js"
     jsxapppath="JSXAPPS/ratesportlet"
     jsxapploader="1" >
   </script>
</div>
<p>
<div style="width:400px;height:160px;" id="newsportlet">
   <script type="text/javascript" src="JSX/js/JSX30.js"
     jsxapppath="JSXAPPS/newsportlet"
     jsxapploader="1" >
```

```
    </script>
  </div>
  </body>
  </html>
```

Using JSR 168

The JSR 168 standard defines a portlet as a web component managed by a portlet container that provides the environment in which a portlet executes. The portlet container also manages the portlet life cycle and provides persistent storage for portlet preferences. Requests from user interactions are received by the portlet container and in turn are routed to the appropriate portlet.

Portlets are similar to Servlets in that they both service web requests and are both managed by their respective containers. They have many similarities with Servlets, yet they differ from Servlets in some respects. Similarities include the fact that they are both Java based, generate dynamic content, and interact with clients using a request/response paradigm. Differences include the fact that portlets generate only fragments of an HTML page, and they are not bound to a URL.

Portlets are deployed in web applications with deployment and assembly descriptors as defined by portlet containers.

A complete portlet project for JBoss is included on the book's CD to demonstrate how to build JSR 168–based portlets containing TIBCO General Interface applications. It is best to include all your TIBCO General Interface application-based portlets into a single web application because that will make it easy to reference the TIBCO General Interface runtime libraries. Follow the steps in the next section to build a JBoss portal with JSR 168 portlets that include TIBCO General Interface applications on a portal page.

Installing JBoss Portal

Download the latest binary distribution from the JBoss website at http://www.jboss.org/ jbossportal/download/index.html. Download the package JBoss Portal + JBoss AS (at the time of this writing, the latest version is JBoss Portal + JBoss AS 4.2.2 portal version 2.6.5SP1). Extract the contents of the zip file to the directory of your choice (c:\).

The only requirement for running JBoss Portal on your machine is JDK 1.5 or later. If you do not already have a JDK installed, download the installer from http://java.sun.com and install it before proceeding.

Open a DOS command prompt and make sure the JAVA_HOME variable is set to point to the location of your JDK, and launch JBoss Portal using the run command in the bin folder.

```
C:>cd C:\jboss-portal-2.6.5.SP1
C:\jboss-portal-2.6.5.SP1>set JAVA_HOME=C:\jdk1.5.0_15
C: \jboss-portal-2.6.5.SP1>run
```

You will see some log messages scroll by until you see the message that reads `Started` in `2m:2s:813ms` (of course, the time may be different on your machine). Figure 10.3 shows the screen after starting JBoss.

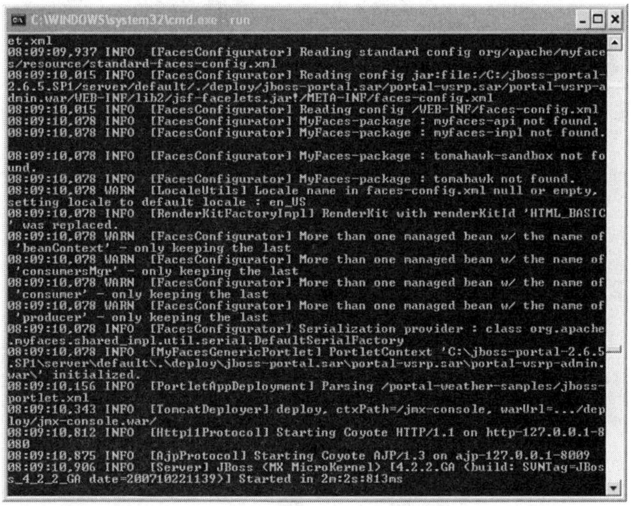

Figure 10.3   Running JBoss.

Open up a browser and navigate to the URL http://localhost:8080/portal. You will see the default JBoss portal screen as shown in Figure 10.4.

Deploying GI Portlets to JBoss Portal

Deploy the `giportlets.war` application included on the companion CD by copying it to the location `C:\jboss-portal-2.6.5.SP1\server\default\deploy`. You will see messages in the DOS window to indicate that the new application was deployed. After the application is deployed, refresh the portal page (by selecting the Refresh icon on IE7) to view the newly added page GI Portlets. When you click the GI Portlets tab, you will see the page with two GI portlets, as shown in Figure 10.5.

All project files, including the `ant` build script, are included on the companion CD-ROM. The overall solution includes three key components for each portlet: a Portlet Java class file, a JSP file that launches the TIBCO General Interface application inside the portlet, and the General Interface application files. The portlets are defined using two Java source code files, `GINewsPortlet.java` and `GIRatesPortlet.java`. Listing 10.2 shows `GINewsPortlet.java`

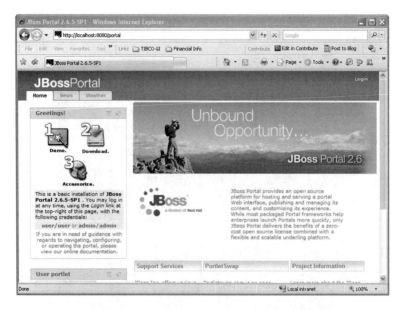

Figure 10.4   The default JBoss Portal page.

Figure 10.5   Two GI portlets on a portal page.

Listing 10.2   Source Code for `GINewsPortlet.java`

```
/* File: GINewsPortlet.java
 * Description: A JSR 168 portlet that displays interest
 *              rates using a TIBCO GI widget
 * Author: Anil Gurnani
 */


package com.tibcobooks.gi.chapter10;


import javax.portlet.ActionRequest;
import javax.portlet.ActionResponse;
import javax.portlet.GenericPortlet;
import javax.portlet.PortletException;
import javax.portlet.PortletRequestDispatcher;
import javax.portlet.RenderRequest;
import javax.portlet.RenderResponse;
import javax.portlet.UnavailableException;
import java.io.IOException;

public class GINewsPortlet extends GenericPortlet
{
    protected void doView(RenderRequest rRequest,
      RenderResponse rResponse)
    throws PortletException, IOException, UnavailableException
    {
        rResponse.setContentType("text/html");
        PortletRequestDispatcher prd =
          getPortletContext().getRequestDispatcher(
          "/WEB-INF/jsp/ginewsportlet.jsp");
        prd.include(rRequest, rResponse);
    }

    public void processAction(ActionRequest aRequest,
      ActionResponse aResponse)
    throws PortletException, IOException, UnavailableException
    {
    }

    protected void doHelp(RenderRequest rRequest,
      RenderResponse rResponse)
    throws PortletException, IOException, UnavailableException
    {
        rResponse.setContentType("text/html");
        PortletRequestDispatcher prd =
          getPortletContext().getRequestDispatcher(
```

```
      "/WEB-INF/jsp/help.jsp");
      prd.include(rRequest, rResponse);
   }


   protected void doEdit(RenderRequest rRequest,
      RenderResponse rResponse)
   throws PortletException, IOException, UnavailableException
   {
      rResponse.setContentType("text/html");
      PortletRequestDispatcher prd =
        getPortletContext().getRequestDispatcher(
      "/WEB-INF/jsp/edit.jsp");
      prd.include(rRequest, rResponse);
   }
}
```

The bold line in Listing 10.2 shows how to load the JSP page that launches the GI portlet. Listing 10.3 shows the JSP page source code.

Listing 10.3   Source Code for `ginewsportlet.jsp`

```
<%@ taglib
  uri="http://java.sun.com/portlet" prefix="portlet" %>
<portlet:defineObjects/>

<div style="width:100%;height:160px;"
   id="newsportlet">
   <script type="text/javascript"
     src="<%=renderResponse.encodeURL(
       renderRequest.getContextPath()
       +"/JSX/js/JSX30.js")%>"
    jsxapppath="<%=renderResponse.encodeURL(
      renderRequest.getContextPath()
      +"/JSXAPPS/newsportlet")%>"
    jsxapploader="1" >
   </script>
</div>
```

The key thing in the JSP page is the call to encodeURL. This ensures that the URLs for the resources will be properly mangled by the portal and thus will work even when the portlet is remotely accessed using the WSRP.

11

Integrating with Databases

JavaScript was designed as a scripting language for browsers. TIBCO General Interface applications, like other browser-based applications, can communicate with server-side applications using the HTTP protocol. General Interface applications can directly communicate with any database that supports the HTTP interface. General Interface's strong XML processing capabilities can be used to work with databases that support XML resultsets. However, the more common scenario is to have some middle-tier components (Servlets or web services) connect to the database and provide state management, caching, and marshaling/unmarshaling of data.

In this chapter we discuss how to access and display data using TIBCO General Interface applications. First we explore a simple client using the lightweight control—Table. Then we hook it up to a Java/J2EE back end using a Servlet. Then we connect up the same client to the database using an ADO.NET client.

Finally, we build a simple application that uses server-side pagination for fast performance when the complete data set is too large to be downloaded to the client.

Building the Client

Whereas the Matrix widget requires columns to be defined during design time, the Table widget that was introduced in version 3.5 of TIBCO General Interface supports a dynamic column set. Columns for a Table widget can be easily changed using the JavaScript method `setColumnProfile()` in the `jsx3.gui.Table` class.

The user interface for this simple example consists of two panes. The top pane is for user input and the bottom pane displays the results. Users can enter a SQL query in the input pane and click Submit. The application then runs the query on the database using a middle-tier component (such as a Java Servlet or an aspx page) and displays the top 100 rows of the resultset in a Table widget in the pane below.

1. To build the sample client, launch GI Builder and create a new project named **gisql**.

2. Drag and drop a Layout—Top/Over component into `appCanvas.xml` and set its **Rows Array** property to 40,*.

3. Drag and drop a Table widget in the lower pane and set its **Name** property to
   datagrid. Note that the Table widget is not in the System-Matrix category. It is in
   the System-Miscellaneous category of components in the Component Libraries
   palette.

4. Drag and drop a Text Box widget from the Form Elements category in the Component Libraries palette into the top pane.

5. Set its Name property to query, the Relative XY property to Absolute, the Left
   property to 10, the Top property to 8, and the Width property to 320.

6. Drag and drop a Button widget from the Form Elements category in the Component Libraries palette into the top pane.

7. Set its Name property to execute, the Relative XY property to Absolute, the Left
   property to 339, the Top property to 8, and the Text/HTML property to Execute.

The project in GI Builder will look like Figure 11.1.

Figure 11.1   Layout of elements for the `gisql`
project.

We need to define the interaction between the client and the back-end component.
The client will make an HTTP call with one parameter named query, which contains the
SQL query. The middle-tier component then executes that query and returns an XML

document that has two major elements—one for resultset metadata and another one for resultset data.

The code behind the Execute button will parse the output from the call and use XSL style sheets to parse the response document. The metadata element is used to dynamically set up columns using the method `setColumnProfile()` in the `jsx3.gui.Table` class. The data element is used to update the table data using the method `setSourceXML()`.

A sample data file is shown in Listing 11.1. Use the File, New XML Document option to create a new XML document and enter the XML data shown in Listing 11.1 as sample data for this application. Save this document in the `xml` folder under the root application folder.

Listing 11.1   Sample Response Containing Metadata and Data for Table

```xml
<?xml version="1.0" encoding="utf-8" ?>
<resultset>
<metadata>
  <record jsxid="a5" jsxwidth="100"
    jsxtext="&lt;div style='padding:8px;
    border-right:solid 1px gray;
    border-bottom:solid 1px gray;
    white-space:nowrap;'&gt;Col 1&lt;/div&gt;"
    jsxpath="jsxtext"/>
  <record jsxid="a1" jsxwidth="100"
    jsxtext="&lt;div style='padding:8px;
    border-right:solid 1px gray;
    border-bottom:solid 1px gray;
    white-space:nowrap;'&gt;Col 2&lt;/div&gt;"
    jsxpath="jsxtext"/>
  <record jsxid="a7" jsxwidth="100"
    jsxtext="&lt;div style='padding:8px;
    border-right:solid 1px gray;
    border-bottom:solid 1px gray;
    white-space:nowrap;'&gt;Col 3&lt;/div&gt;"
    jsxpath="jsxtext"/>
  <record jsxid="a8" jsxwidth="100"
    jsxtext="&lt;div style='padding:8px;
    border-right:solid 1px gray;
    border-bottom:solid 1px gray;
    white-space:nowrap;'&gt;Col 4&lt;/div&gt;"
    jsxpath="jsxtext"/>
</metadata>
<data>
  <record jsxid="1" jsxtext="Afghanistan"/>
  <record jsxid="2" jsxtext="Albania"/>
  <record jsxid="3" jsxtext="Algeria"/>
  <record jsxid="4" jsxtext="American Samoa"/>
```

```
    <record jsxid="5" jsxtext="Andorra"/>
    <record jsxid="6" jsxtext="Angola"/>
    <record jsxid="7" jsxtext="Anguilla"/>
  </data>
</resultset>
```

As discussed previously, we need two XSL style sheets—one to extract the metadata part from the response and convert to CDF for consumption by General Interface and the second one to parse and convert the data portion of the document to CDF format for display in the Table component.

Listings 11.2 and 11.3 contain the simple XSL documents that will be used to convert the response. Select File, New XSL Document twice to create XSL documents. Save these XSL documents in the xsl folder under the root application folder as rsdata.xsl (Listing 11.2) and as rsmetadata.xsl (Listing 11.3). Note that both style sheets differ only in the value of the match attribute in the <xsl:template> tag.

Note that the only difference in the XSL styles sheets in Listings 11.2 and 11.3 is the portion of the response XML they process. Listing 11.2 processes the element /resultset/data and Listing 11.3 processes /resultset/metadata in the response.

Listing 11.2   XSL Style Sheet to Convert Response Data to CDF

```
<?xml version="1.0"?>
<xsl:stylesheet
  xmlns:xsl="http://www.w3.org/1999/XSL/Transform" version="1.0">
  <xsl:output method="xml" indent="yes"/>

  <xsl:template match="/resultset/data">
    <data jsxid="jsxroot">
      <xsl:for-each select="record">
        <xsl:copy>
          <xsl:for-each select="./@*">
            <xsl:copy/>
          </xsl:for-each>
        </xsl:copy>
      </xsl:for-each>
    </data>
  </xsl:template>
</xsl:stylesheet>
```

Listing 11.3   XSL Style Sheet to Convert Response Metadata to CDF

```
<?xml version="1.0"?>
<xsl:stylesheet
  xmlns:xsl="http://www.w3.org/1999/XSL/Transform" version="1.0">
  <xsl:output method="xml" indent="yes"/>
```

```
<xsl:template match="/resultset/metadatadata">
  <data jsxid="jsxroot">
    <xsl:for-each select="record">
      <xsl:copy>
        <xsl:for-each select="./@*">
          <xsl:copy/>
        </xsl:for-each>
      </xsl:copy>
    </xsl:for-each>
  </data>
</xsl:template>
</xsl:stylesheet>
```

Now we need some JavaScript code to send the SQL query to the server and retrieve the resultset in XML. We can use General Interface's framework classes to develop the code quickly and test it using the integrated JavaScript Test tool. Click the `logic.js` tab and enter the code from Listing 11.4, or copy and paste it. Note that this file and the complete project is included on the companion CD-ROM. The value of variable `url` will depend on the web server you are using. The value in the listing is, for example, using IIS where the data file `testdata.xml` has been placed in the default website folder `C:\InetPub\wwwroot`.

Listing 11.4   JavaScript Method to Retrieve the Resultset

```
function getResultSet()
{
  var url = 'http://localhost/testdata.xml';
  var dt = new Date();
  var req = new jsx3.net.Request();
  var method = "GET";
  url += '?requestid='+dt.getTime();
  req.open(method, url, false);
  req.send();
  if( req.getStatus() == 200 ) {
    var responseDoc = req.getResponseXML();
    var table = gisql.getJSXByName('datagrid');
    var template = new jsx3.xml.XslDocument();
    template.load("JSXAPPS/gisql/xsl/rsmetadata.xsl");
    var cpdoc = template.transformToObject(responseDoc);
    template = new jsx3.xml.XslDocument();
    template.load("JSXAPPS/gisql/xsl/rsdata.xsl");
    var datadoc = template.transformToObject(responseDoc);
    table.setColumnProfile(cpdoc);
    table.setSourceXML(datadoc);
    table.repaint();
  } else {
```

```
      gisql.alert('Error', 'Call failed');
  }
}
```

GI Builder includes a JavaScript test utility that can be used to test this method. Select the option JavaScript Test Utility from the Tools menu to bring up the window as shown in Figure 11.2. Type the method name into the window and click the Execute button to test the method. If everything went well, the table display will change to display four fixed-width columns.

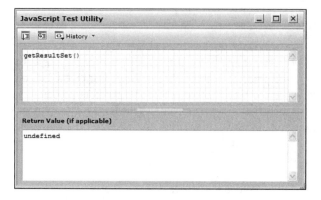

Figure 11.2   JavaScript Test Utility integrated in GI Builder.

The following sections describe connecting this client application to a middle-tier back end.

Setting Up the Database

The samples in this chapter use Microsoft SQL Server Express database with the AdventureWorks sample database. Download the SQL Server Express edition from the Microsoft website at www.microsoft.com/sql/editions/express/default.mspx and install it on your machine. The connection string used in the example assumes that the SQL Server is installed to use Mixed Mode authentication. Also download the AdventureWorks sample database from http://codeplex.com/SqlServerSamples and install it using the instructions provided. After running the installer, you must attach the database files using the script in Listing 11.5.

Listing 11.5   Script to Attach AdventureWorks Database After Installing It

```
exec sp_attach_db @dbname = N'AdventureWorks',
 @filename1 = N'C:\Program Files\Microsoft SQL
```

```
Server\MSSQL.1\MSSQL\Data\AdventureWorks_Data.mdf',
@filename2 = N'C:\Program Files\Microsoft SQL
Server\MSSQL.1\MSSQL\Data\AdventureWorks_log.ldf'
```

Integrating Using .NET

The most appropriate web component on the .NET platform for this example is an HttpHandler. The complete Visual Studio 2005 solution is included on the CD-ROM.

To build the application in Visual Studio 2005, create a new website project using the File, New, Web Site menu option. Provide a path (c:\InetPub\wwwroot\gisql) to create the initial folder structure for the website. Note that there is another folder named gisql that was created earlier by TIBCO General Interface for the client part of the same project. We will copy files from General Interface's project folder inside Visual Studio 2005 to integrate the client with the middle-tier components.

After the initial project is created in Visual Studio 2005, integrate General Interface resources by copying the folder JSX (in the TIBCO General Interface installation directory) and JSXAPPS\gisql (in the GI Workspace directory) and the file logger.xml (also in TIBCO General Interface installation directory) into the c:\InetPub\wwwroot\gisql directory using Windows Explorer.

After copying TIBCO General Interface resources into the project, you need to refresh the Visual Studio 2005 solution to reflect the changes on the file system. In the Solution Explorer, click the right mouse button over the folder name (c:\InetPub\wwwroot\gisql) and select Refresh Folder from the context menu.

Use the deployment utility in TIBCO General Interface to generate the code to insert into the Default.aspx. Listing 11.6 shows the integrated Default.aspx page.

Listing 11.6   Default.aspx Page for the gisql Project

```
<%@ Page Language="VB" AutoEventWireup="false"
 CodeFile="Default.aspx.vb" Inherits="_Default" %>

<!DOCTYPE html PUBLIC "-//W3C//DTD XHTML 1.0 Transitional//EN"
 "http://www.w3.org/TR/xhtml1/DTD/xhtml1-transitional.dtd">

<html xmlns="http://www.w3.org/1999/xhtml">
<head runat="server">
    <title>Database Example</title>
</head>
<body>
<div style="width:100%;height:400px;">
<script type="text/javascript"
  src="JSX/js/JSX30.js"
  jsxapppath="gisql">
</script>
</div>
```

```
</body>
</html>
```

Now add an HttpHandler to the project. Click the right mouse button on the folder name in Solution Explorer and select Add New Item from the menu to bring up Visual Studio's Add New Item dialog as shown in Figure 11.3. Select Generic Handler from the list of items and enter a name for the handler—**GetResultSet.ashx**.

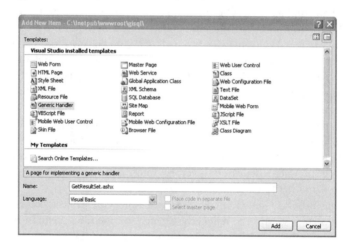

Figure 11.3   The Visual Studio 2005 Add
New Item dialog.

The `GetResultSet.ashx` handler executes the query using ADO.NET and prepares the CDF response as shown in Listing 11.7.

Listing 11.7   Complete Code for `GetResultSet.ashx` Handler

```
<%@ WebHandler Language="VB" Class="GetResultSet" %>


Imports System
Imports System.Web
Imports System.Data
Imports System.Data.SqlClient

Public Class GetResultSet : Implements IHttpHandler

Public Sub ProcessRequest(ByVal context As HttpContext) Implements
 IHttpHandler.ProcessRequest
    context.Response.ContentType = "text/xml"
    context.Response.Write("<?xml version=""1.0""?>")
    context.Response.Write("<resultset>")
```

```
   Dim connectionString As String = "Data Source=C2\SQLEXPRESS;Initial
Catalog=AdventureWorks;" _
      & "Integrated Security=SSPI;"
   Dim query As String = context.Request.QueryString.Get("query")

   Using connection As New SqlConnection(connectionString)
     Dim command As SqlCommand = connection.CreateCommand()
     command.CommandText = query
     Try
       connection.Open()
       Dim dataReader As SqlDataReader = _
         command.ExecuteReader()
       context.Response.Write("<metadata>")
       Dim i As Integer
       For i = 1 To dataReader.FieldCount
         Dim fieldName As String = dataReader.GetName(i - 1)
         context.Response.Write("<record jsxid="""
         + i.ToString + """ jsxwidth=""100""
         jsxtext=""&lt;div style='padding:8px;border-right:
         solid 1px gray;border-bottom:solid 1px gray;
         white-space:nowrap;'&gt;" + fieldName +
         "&lt;/div&gt;"" jsxpath=""" + fieldName + """/>")
       Next
       context.Response.Write("</metadata>")
       context.Response.Write("<data>")
       Dim rownumber As Integer = 1
       Do While dataReader.Read() And rownumber < 500
         context.Response.Write("<record jsxid="""
           + rownumber.ToString + """ ")
         For i = 1 To dataReader.FieldCount
           Dim fieldName As String = dataReader.GetName(i - 1)
           Dim fieldValue As String = dataReader(i - 1).ToString
           context.Response.Write(fieldName + "="""
           + fieldValue + """ ")
         Next
         context.Response.Write("/>")
         rownumber = rownumber + 1
       Loop
       context.Response.Write("</data>")
       dataReader.Close()
     Catch ex As Exception
       Console.WriteLine(ex.Message)

     End Try

   End Using
```

```
    context.Response.Write("</resultset>")
  End Sub

  Public ReadOnly Property IsReusable()
          As Boolean Implements IHttpHandler.IsReusable
    Get
      Return True
    End Get
  End Property

End Class
```

To integrate the General Interface client-side application with this back end, a small change is required to the `logic.js` file of the TIBCO General Interface client application. The value of the `url` parameter should be changed now to point to this handler—`GetResultSet.ashx`. This will ensure that the General Interface client will call the middle-tier component to retrieve the dynamic data set instead of using a static results file that we used for testing our prototype.

Integrating Using J2EE

The common middle-tier component for a J2EE web application is a Servlet. This section describes how to build a Servlet using Eclipse and integrate it with the General Interface client built in the previous section.

The sample Servlet to connect to SQL Server 2005 Express uses the JDBC driver provided by Microsoft at http://msdn.microsoft.com/en-us/data/aa937724.aspx. Run the file after downloading it to extract its contents to another folder. Copy the `sqljdbc_auth.dll` file from the folder `<extract root>\sqljdbc_1.2\enu\auth\x86` to your `C:\WINDOWS\System32` directory, and then start Tomcat (installed in `c:\tomcat55`). This DLL is required to use Integrated Authentication for SQL Server.

One limitation of using the SQL JDBC driver with this authentication mechanism is that whenever you redeploy the application that uses integrated authentication, you will need to shut down and restart Tomcat.

The Servlet shown in Listing 11.8 uses JDBC to retrieve the data and converts it to CDF as needed by TIBCO General Interface.

Listing 11.8   Java Source Code for Servlet `GetResultSetServlet`

```
package com.tibcobooks.gi.chapter11;


import java.io.*;
import javax.servlet.http.*;
import javax.servlet.*;
import java.sql.*;
```

```java
public class GetResultSetServlet extends HttpServlet {
  public void doGet(HttpServletRequest req,
                    HttpServletResponse res)
    throws ServletException, IOException
  {
    String query = req.getParameter("query");
    PrintWriter out = res.getWriter();
    res.setContentType("text/xml");
    out.println("<?xml version=\"1.0\"?>");
    out.println("<resultset>");

    // Create a variable for the connection string.
    String connectionUrl = "jdbc:sqlserver://localhost:1433;" +
      "databaseName=AdventureWorks;integratedSecurity=true;";

    // Declare the JDBC objects.
    Connection con = null;
    Statement stmt = null;
    ResultSet rs = null;

    try {
      // Establish the connection.
      Class.forName("com.microsoft.sqlserver.jdbc.SQLServerDriver");
      con = DriverManager.getConnection(connectionUrl);

      // Create and execute an SQL statement that returns a
      // set of data and then display it.
      stmt = con.createStatement();
      rs = stmt.executeQuery(query);
      ResultSetMetaData rsmd = rs.getMetaData();
      out.println("<metadata>");
      for( int i = 1; i < rsmd.getColumnCount()+1 ; i++ )
      {
         String fieldName = rsmd.getColumnName(i);
         out.println("<record jsxid=\"" +
           Integer.toString(i) +
           "\" jsxwidth=\"100\" jsxtext=\"&lt;div
           style='padding: 8px;border-right:solid
           1px gray;border-bottom:solid 1px gray;
           white-space:nowrap;'&gt;" + fieldName
           + "&lt;/div&gt;\" jsxpath=\""
           + fieldName + "\"/>");
      }
      out.println("</metadata>");
      out.println("<data>");
```

```
    int rownumber = 1;
    while (rs.next()) {
      out.println("<record jsxid=\"" +
       Integer.toString(rownumber) + "\" ");
      for( int i = 1; i < rsmd.getColumnCount()+1; i++ )
      {
        String fieldName = rsmd.getColumnLabel(i);
        String fieldValue = "(null)";
        Object fieldObject = rs.getObject(i);
        if( fieldObject != null)
          fieldValue = fieldObject.toString();
        out.println(fieldName + "=\"" + fieldValue + "\" ");
      }
      out.println("/>");
      rownumber = rownumber + 1;
    }
    out.println("</data>");
  }

  // Handle any errors that may have occurred.
  catch (Exception e) {
    e.printStackTrace();
  }

  finally {
    if (rs != null)
      try { rs.close(); } catch(Exception e) {}
    if (stmt != null)
      try { stmt.close(); } catch(Exception e) {}
    if (con != null)
      try { con.close(); } catch(Exception e) {}
    out.println("</resultset>");
  }
  out.close();
  }
}
```

You'll find the complete sample project on the CD-ROM, including the `build.xml` and `build.properties` files to build and deploy the complete application using `ant`. If you have installed SQL Server Express, AdventureWorks, SQL JDBC Authentication Library, and Tomcat, you can drag the `gisql.war` file into the Tomcat's `webapps` folder to run the application. Figure 11.4 shows the sample `gisql` application running in the browser. The figure shows the result of running the following query:

```
SELECT  e.EmployeeID, c.FirstName, c.LastName, e.Title
FROM    HumanResources.Employee e, Person.Contact c
WHERE   e.ContactID = c.ContactID
```

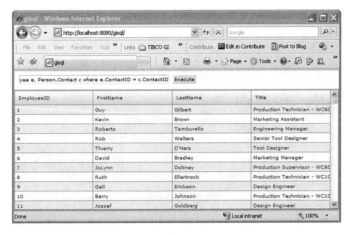

Figure 11.4   Sample application `gisql` running in the browser.

Building a Master/Detail Sample Application

Master Detail is a very common pattern when you work with databases. In a Master Detail pattern there is a Master table with summary rows and a related Detail table that contains the details. For example, for an order the Master record may contain the customer name, shipping method, and total cost and the Detail records may contain the individual items in the order with their corresponding quantities, prices etc. General Interface's design makes it very easy to implement a Master Detail application. This simple example shows how to build Master Detail applications using General Interface. All the files necessary to build the example are included on the CD-ROM, along with a ReadMe file that describes how to build and deploy the application.

First, build the General Interface user interface by dragging and dropping components to make the GUI look like Figure 11.5. Note that a Layout Top/Over component exists at the root level. In its top pane is a Label component with text, a Date Picker component, and a Button component. In the second pane is another Layout Top/Over component with two panes. The top pane of the second Layout component has the grid that shows order headers, and the bottom pane has the grid that shows order details.

One main controller class handles user events and communicates with the back end. The default file `logic.js` contains the main method, which is called when the application is first loaded into the browser. Listing 11.9 shows the source for `logic.js`. The `main()` method loads the `MasterDetail` class, creates an instance of it, and initializes it.

Listing 11.9   File `logic.js` Contains the `main()` Method That Is Called on Application Load

```
function main()
{
    jsx3.require('com.tibcobooks.gi.chapter11.MasterDetail');
```

```
var md = new com.tibcobooks.gi.chapter11.MasterDetail(MasterDetail);
md.initialize();
}
```

Figure 11.5   GUI for the Master Detail example.

The controller `MasterDetail.js` contains the initialize method, which subscribes to events generated by user-interface components. As shown in Listing 11.10, it also contains methods to interact with the back end. Note that this design with General Interface event handlers completely decouples the event handlers from the GUI controls and makes the code extremely flexible and easy to maintain. The events published by the controls contain all the information necessary to process the event, and the event handler sends a request to the back end to retrieve the data and populates the model. Note that this design results in automatically caching the responses from each call to the middle tier because the browser will cache returned XML documents. If you want to force an explicit call to the back end each time, add an extra parameter (for example, `requestid` equal to the current time in milliseconds).

Listing 11.10   Source Code for `MasterDetail.js`

```
/*
 * This is the main controller class for
 * MasterDetail application. Create a single
 * instance of it in main by calling init only once.
 *
 * @author Anil Gurnani
```

```
 *
 */

jsx3.lang.Class.defineClass (
"com.tibcobooks.gi.chapter11.MasterDetail",
null,
null,
function(MasterDetail)
{
  MasterDetail.instance = null;
  MasterDetail.prototype.server = null;

  MasterDetail.prototype.getServer = function() {
    return this.server;
  }

  MasterDetail.prototype.init = function(serverobj)
  {
    this.server = serverobj;
  }

  // create exactly one instance and call this method
  // only once.
  // reason why initialize is not done in init is
  // to avoid subscribing by every instance
  // (in case multiple instances are created by mistake)
  MasterDetail.prototype.initialize = function()
  {
    // subscribe to GET_ORDER_HEADERS event
    this.getServer().
       subscribe('GET_ORDER_HEADERS', this, 'onGetOrderHeaders');
    // subscribe to GET_ORDER_DETAILS event
    this.getServer().
       subscribe('GET_ORDER_DETAILS', this, 'onGetOrderDetails');
  }

  MasterDetail.prototype.sendRequest = function(url)
  {
    var req = new jsx3.net.Request();
    var method = "GET";
    req.open(method, url, false);
    req.send();
    var responseDoc = null;
    if( req.getStatus() == 200 ) {
    responseDoc = req.getResponseXML();
    } else {
```

```
      this.getServer().alert('Error', 'Call failed');
      }
      return responseDoc;
    }

  MasterDetail.prototype.onGetOrderHeaders = function(objEvent)
  {
    var responseDoc = this.sendRequest
      ('GetOrderHeaders?OrderDate='+escape(objEvent.orderdate));
    if( responseDoc != null ) {
      var headertable = this.getServer().getJSXByName('OrderHeaders');
      headertable.setSourceXML(responseDoc);
      headertable.repaint();
    }
  }

  MasterDetail.prototype.onGetOrderDetails = function(objEvent)
  {
    var responseDoc = this.sendRequest
      ('GetOrderDetails?OrderID='+escape(objEvent.orderid));
    if( responseDoc != null ) {
      var headertable = this.getServer().getJSXByName('OrderDetails');
      headertable.setSourceXML(responseDoc);
      headertable.repaint();
    }
  }
}
);
```

With the MasterDetail event handler as defined in Listing 11.10, the GUI controls can have embedded scripts to publish the appropriate event. Listing 11.11 shows the scriptlet for the Go button, and Listing 11.12 shows the scriptlet for the Execute event on the headers grid.

Listing 11.11   Scriptlet to Publish the Event to Get Orders for a Given Date

```
this.getServer().publish({id: 'GET_ORDER_HEADERS',
   subject:'GET_ORDER_HEADERS',
   orderdate:this.getServer()
    .getJSXByName('OrderDatePicker').getValue()})
```

Listing 11.12   Scriptlet to Publish the Event to Get the Details of an Order

```
this.getServer().publish({id: 'GET_ORDER_DETAILS',
    subject:'GET_ORDER_DETAILS',
    orderid:this.getRecord(strRECORDID).SalesOrderID})
```

Remember to set the `classpath` by going to the Project Settings dialog as shown in Figure 11.6 to tell General Interface where to find the class definition for the class Master-Detail.

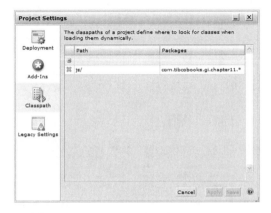

Figure 11.6   Setting `classpath` for the
MasterDetail application.

Two Java Servlets support this front end: `GetOrderHeadersServlet.java` and `GetOrderDetailsServlet.java`. The included file **web.xml** contains deployment descriptors for the two Servlets. All the files necessary to build the example are included on the CD-ROM, along with a ReadMe file that describes how to build and deploy the application.

Building a Paginated Grid Example

Often, there is a need to display large databases to the user where it is not possible to download the contents of the entire table to the client. The Matrix component is great for manipulating rows after the data has been downloaded into the browser cache. General Interface's rich set of interfaces and events, however, makes it very easy to build highly flexible server-side paging components, such as the ASP.NET 2.0 AJAX Grid component. A full sample project including `ant` build scripts and General Interface project files is included on the CD-ROM.

This sample shows a small application that includes a handler you can use to build an independent pagination component that allows a user to navigate through a large table using a single Servlet (or HttpHandler in Windows) component in the middle tier. State is maintained by the middle-tier components, and the General Interface client sends in parameters to request specific pages. Upon receiving the response, the General Interface client displays the grid and updates the navigation links at the bottom.

Figure 11.7 shows the sample running in the browser, and Listings 11.13 and 11.14 show key implementation files—`PaginatedGrid.js` and `GetPageServlet.java`.

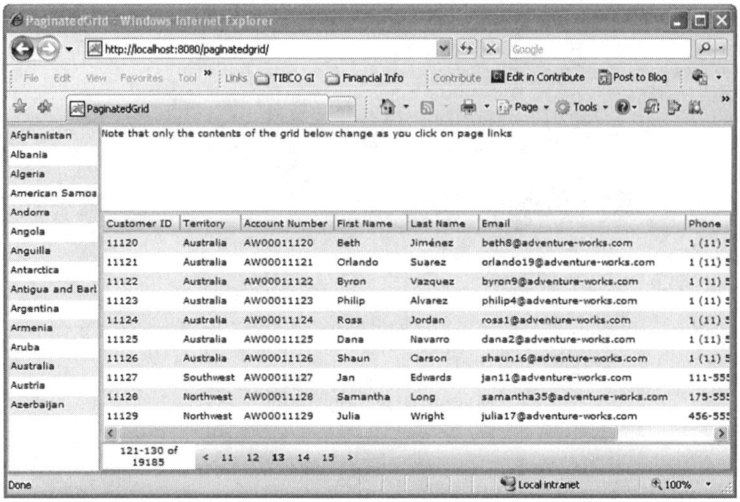

Figure 11.7   The sample PaginatedGrid shows server-side paging with TIBCO General Interface.

Note that the paging logic is implemented in the `GetPageServlet.java` with the help of SQL Server 2005's `ROW_NUMBER()` function. If you are using MySQL database, the query for paging will involve the use of `LIMIT` and `OFFSET` keywords instead.

The example sorts only the rows that are displayed on the client. If the requirement is to sort the entire resultset by the column, a custom handler can be developed in General Interface to be called before the sorting to retrieve data sorted by the column clicked.

Listing 11.13   File `PaginatedGrid.js`

```
/*
 * This is the main controller class for
 * PaginatedGrid application. Create a single
 * instance of it in main by calling init only once.
 *
 * @author Anil Gurnani
 *
 */


jsx3.lang.Class.defineClass (
```

```
"com.tibcobooks.gi.chapter11.PaginatedGrid",
null,
null,
function(PaginatedGrid)
{
  PaginatedGrid.instance = null;
  PaginatedGrid.prototype.server = null;

  PaginatedGrid.prototype.getServer = function() {
    return this.server;
  }

  PaginatedGrid.prototype.init = function(serverobj)
  {
    this.server = serverobj;
  }

  // create exactly one instance and call this method
  // only once.
  // reason why initialize is not done in init is
  // to avoid subscribing by every instance
  // (in case multiple instances are created by mistake)
  PaginatedGrid.prototype.initialize = function()
  {
    // subscribe to GET_PAGE event
    this.getServer().
       subscribe('GET_PAGE', this, 'onGetPage');
    // get first page and populate the grid
    this.onGetPage({id:'GET_PAGE',subject:'GET_PAGE',pageid:'1'});
  }

  PaginatedGrid.prototype.sendRequest = function(url)
  {
    var dt = new Date();
    url += '&requestid='+escape(dt.getTime());
    var req = new jsx3.net.Request();
    var method = "GET";
    req.open(method, url, false);
    req.send();
    var responseDoc = null;
    if( req.getStatus() == 200 ) {
    responseDoc = req.getResponseXML();
    } else {
    this.getServer().alert('Error', 'Call failed');
    }
    return responseDoc;
```

```
    }

    PaginatedGrid.prototype.onGetPage = function(objEvent)
    {
      jsx3.log('onGetPage pageid='+objEvent.pageid);
      var url = 'GetPage?pageid='+escape(objEvent.pageid);
      var dt = new Date();
      var responseDoc = this.sendRequest(url);

      if( responseDoc != null )
      {
        var mat = this.getServer().getJSXByName('pagedata');
        mat.setSourceXML(responseDoc);
        this.updateNavigation(responseDoc);
      }
    }


    PaginatedGrid.prototype.setToolbarButton = function(tbbutton, tbtext)
    {
      jsx3.log('tbtext='+tbtext);
      jsx3.log('tbbutton='+tbbutton);
      if( tbtext != null )
      {
        tbbutton.setText(tbtext);
        tbbutton.setEnabled(true, false);
      }
      else
      {
        tbbutton.setText('');
        tbbutton.setEnabled(false, false);
      }
    }

    PaginatedGrid.prototype.updateNavigation = function(responseDoc)
    {
      jsx3.log('updateNavigation start');
      var navigationNode = responseDoc.selectSingleNode('/getPageResponse/
        navigation');
      jsx3.log('navigationNode='+navigationNode);
      // update text ( e.g. 1-10 of 63)
      var pagecountbox = this.getServer().getJSXByName('pagecount');
      jsx3.log('pagecountbox='+pagecountbox);
      pagecountbox.setText(navigationNode.getAttribute('pagecount'));
      jsx3.log('pagecount done');
```

```
    // set text and enable/disable page links
    var previouslink = this.getServer().getJSXByName('previouslink');
    jsx3.log('previous link ='+previouslink);
    this.setToolbarButton(previouslink, navigationNode.getAttribute('previ-
      ouslink'));
    jsx3.log('previous link done');

    var page1link = this.getServer().getJSXByName('page1link')
    this.setToolbarButton(page1link, navigationNode.getAttribute('page1link'));
    jsx3.log('page1link done');

    var page2link = this.getServer().getJSXByName('page2link')
    this.setToolbarButton(page2link, navigationNode.getAttribute('page2link'));
    jsx3.log('page2link done');

    var page3link = this.getServer().getJSXByName('page3link')
    this.setToolbarButton(page3link, navigationNode.getAttribute('page3link'));
    jsx3.log('page3link done');

    jsx3.log('navigationNode='+navigationNode);
    var page4link = this.getServer().getJSXByName('page4link')
    this.setToolbarButton(page4link, navigationNode.getAttribute('page4link'));
    jsx3.log('page4link done');

    var page5link = this.getServer().getJSXByName('page5link')
    this.setToolbarButton(page5link, navigationNode.getAttribute('page5link'));
    jsx3.log('page5link done');

    var nextlink = this.getServer().getJSXByName('nextlink')
    this.setToolbarButton(nextlink, navigationNode.getAttribute('nextlink'));

    // repaint the whole thing
    var gridcontrol = this.getServer().getJSXByName('gridcontrol');
    gridcontrol.repaint();
  }

}
);
```

Listing 11.14   File `GetPageServlet.java`

```java
package com.tibcobooks.gi.chapter11;

import java.io.*;

import javax.servlet.http.*;
import javax.servlet.*;
```

```java
import java.sql.*;

public class GetPageServlet extends HttpServlet {
  public void doGet(HttpServletRequest req,
          HttpServletResponse res)
  throws ServletException, IOException
  {
    // pass more of these as a parameter for dynamic paging.
    int pagelinksinpanel = 5;
    int pagesize = 10;
    int pagenumber = 1;
    int startRow = 1;
    int endRow = startRow + pagesize - 1;
    int rowCount = 0;
    String pageid = req.getParameter("pageid");
    if( pageid == null ) pageid = "1";
    if( pageid.equals("<") ) {
      // go to previous page
      pagenumber = getCurrentPageNumber(req) - 1;
    } else if( pageid.equals(">") ) {
      // go to next page
      pagenumber = getCurrentPageNumber(req) + 1;
    } else {
      // go to numbered page
      try {
        pagenumber = Integer.parseInt(pageid);
      } catch (Exception ex) {
        // not a number - stay at current
        pagenumber = getCurrentPageNumber(req);
      }
    }
    if( pagenumber <= 0 ) pagenumber = 1;

    PrintWriter out = res.getWriter();
    res.setContentType("text/xml");
    out.println("<?xml version=\"1.0\"?>");
    out.println("<getPageResponse>");

    // Create a variable for the connection string.
    String connectionUrl = "jdbc:sqlserver://localhost:1433;" +
      "databaseName=AdventureWorks;integratedSecurity=true;";

    String countQuery = "SELECT COUNT(CustomerID) FROM Sales.Customer";

    String query =
```

```
"SELECT * FROM "
+ "(SELECT ROW_NUMBER() OVER (ORDER BY cust.CustomerID) as RowNumber,"
    +" cust.CustomerID,"
    +" terr.Name AS Territory,"
    +" cust.AccountNumber,"
    +" cont.FirstName,"
    +" cont.LastName,"
    +" cont.EmailAddress,"
    +" cont.Phone"
+" FROM    Sales.Customer cust,"
    +" Sales.SalesTerritory terr,"
    +" Sales.Individual indi,"
    +" Person.Contact cont"
+" WHERE   cust.TerritoryID = terr.TerritoryID"
+" AND   cust.CustomerID = indi.CustomerID"
+" AND   cont.ContactID = indi.ContactID ) AS Customers "
+" WHERE   RowNumber >= ?"
+" AND   RowNumber <= ?";


// Declare the JDBC objects.
Connection con = null;
Statement stmt = null;
ResultSet rs = null;
ResultSet crs = null;
PreparedStatement pstmt = null;

out.println("<pagedata>");
try {
 // Establish the connection.
 Class.forName("com.microsoft.sqlserver.jdbc.SQLServerDriver");
 con = DriverManager.getConnection(connectionUrl);
 // get the count first
 stmt = con.createStatement();
 crs = stmt.executeQuery(countQuery);
 crs.next();
 rowCount = crs.getInt(1);
 // now determine start row based on pagenumber
 startRow = pagesize * (pagenumber - 1) + 1;
 endRow = startRow + pagesize -1;

 pstmt = con.prepareStatement(query);
 pstmt.setInt(1,startRow);
 pstmt.setInt(2,endRow);
 rs = pstmt.executeQuery();
 ResultSetMetaData rsmd = rs.getMetaData();
```

```
 int rownumber = 1;
 while (rs.next()) {
  out.println("<record jsxid=\"" + Integer.toString(rownumber) + "\" ");
  for( int i = 1; i < rsmd.getColumnCount()+1; i++ )
  {
String fieldName = rsmd.getColumnLabel(i);
String fieldValue = "null";
Object fieldObject = rs.getObject(i);
if( fieldObject != null)
  fieldValue = fieldObject.toString();
    out.println(fieldName + "=\"" + fieldValue + "\" ");
}
  out.println("/>");
  rownumber = rownumber + 1;
 }
}

// Handle any errors that may have occurred.
catch (Exception e) {
 e.printStackTrace();
}

finally {
 if (rs != null) try { rs.close(); } catch(Exception e) {}
 if (stmt != null) try { stmt.close(); } catch(Exception e) {}
 if (con != null) try { con.close(); } catch(Exception e) {}
 out.println("</pagedata>");
 out.println("<navigation ");
 out.println(" pagecount=\""+startRow+"-"+endRow+" of "+rowCount+"\"");
 if( pagenumber > 5 ) {
   out.println(" previouslink=\"&lt;\"");
 }
 int linknumber = (pagenumber-1)/pagelinksinpanel * pagelinksinpanel + 1;
 for( int i = 1; i <= pagelinksinpanel; i++,linknumber++)
 {
   if( linknumber == pagenumber ) {
     out.println(" page"+i+"link=\"&lt;b&gt;"+linknumber+"&lt;/b&gt;\"");
   } else {
     out.println(" page"+i+"link=\""+linknumber+"\"");
   }
 }
 if( pagenumber < rowCount/pagesize )
 {
   out.println(" nextlink=\"&gt;\"");
 }
 out.println("/>");
```

```
    out.println("</getPageResponse>");
      setCurrentPageNumber(req,pagenumber);
      out.close();
    }
  }

  private int getCurrentPageNumber(HttpServletRequest req)
  {
    Integer pageNumber = null;
    HttpSession sess = req.getSession(true);
    if( sess != null )
      pageNumber = (Integer)sess.getAttribute("pageid");
    if( pageNumber == null )
      pageNumber = new Integer(1);
    return pageNumber.intValue();
  }

  private void setCurrentPageNumber(HttpServletRequest req, int pagenumber)
  {
    Integer pageNumber = new Integer(pagenumber);
    HttpSession sess = req.getSession(true);
    sess.setAttribute("pageid",pageNumber);
  }
}
```

Integrating with Messaging Systems

Enterprise infrastructures always include a messaging backbone such as IBM MQ or TIBCO EMS. JavaScript classes included with General Interface make it easy to build AJAX-enabled applications that can receive a message asynchronously and display it in the browser window. This chapter discusses issues that occur when integrating with a back-end messaging system, and it provides best practices and samples to integrate General Interface with the open source messaging system Apache Active MQ.

The example presented in this chapter uses JMS, so it should be easy to replace Apache Active MQ with any messaging broker that supports JMS API.

Participants in a messaging system are completely decoupled. Any number of senders may send a message to a queue at any time. Because HTTP is a simple request/response protocol, it's a challenge to integrate any web-based client to such a system.

Additionally, because of security concerns, it is very important to have internal systems behind one or more firewalls, depending on the security requirements and network architecture. Therefore, it is a challenge to contact a web-based client to deliver a message asynchronously.

Architectural Considerations

This section discusses several architectural considerations and issues that occur when integrating a General Interface application with a messaging system.

Browser Resources

First, the browser resources must be preserved. Because the browser can run on any platform, it is important for the solution to use minimum memory and as few threads as possible. Ideally, the program must not consume any threads. If each request to the back end blocks a thread, the browser might become unresponsive on some platforms.

Number of Pending Requests

It is important to channel all requests through a single pipeline to ensure that only a small number of requests are pending. Each pending request consumes a socket, which is another precious resource on most platforms. If the number of asynchronous requests is not controlled, the browser may deplete its available sockets and might not be able to make any outgoing requests for any other requests and might appear frozen.

Push Versus Pull

Messaging systems usually "push" a message to the listeners. In overly simplified terms, a messaging system makes available some named destinations known as topics and queues. Clients interested in sending messages can connect and deliver a message to a destination. Programs interested in listening to all messages addressed to a specific topic or queue register themselves as subscribers. The messaging broker then notifies them when a new message is available at the destination of their interest.

Pull, on the other hand, refers to the client checking periodically to see whether a message is available. Traditionally, browsers could do pull only by periodically calling a service to check whether a message is available. If the rate of messages is slow, many pull requests would return empty handed. This is a drain on resources, including network bandwidth.

Server-Side Thread

Java Servlet specification and other web component specifications require that the entire request must be completed on a single thread. When a web request is received, a new thread is created, and the response must be returned within the context of this thread. Thus, the request thread will be blocked until a response is returned.

This is a challenge if a synchronous client is used to retrieve messages from a broker. Although it is not a problem for a desktop application, this is a major problem for a web-based application. Desktop applications are typically used by only one user at any one time, whereas a web application can have hundreds or even thousands of simultaneous users. Modern systems are quite powerful but are not yet able to sustain many thousand sockets and threads at the same time.

Server-Side State

Clients of a messaging system must also maintain state with regard to their communications with the message broker. Most web platforms include some mechanism to maintain the state of an application. However, the web model makes it difficult to know when a client is no longer required and can be freed.

For example, if a user opens a browser-based client and connects to establish a session, and then immediately exits the browser application, the component that is maintaining state in the middle tier would not know to immediately release resources.

Message Transformation

Often you can use a common canonical form of XML messages that can be used by all applications within the Enterprise. XML messages can be easily transformed using XSLT in TIBCO General Interface. As discussed in Chapter 8, "Advanced Features of Matrix," the Matrix component in General Interface supports a property called XML Transformer. This feature can be used to transform any XML message format into a CDF format that can be consumed by General Interface's Grid view for display onscreen.

Message Filtering

Enterprise Messaging infrastructures are built for very high volumes and performance. A common pattern seen in messaging systems is the use of a message filter to remove unwanted messages from a stream of messages. Each client is usually interested in only a subset of messages.

For example, a department store might have different departments to process different types of items. Each department is interested only in the orders it needs to process. A message filter can be used to display only orders for shoes on the screen of the shoe department's computer.

It is best to filter messages as close to the source as possible. With TIBCO General Interface, the filter criteria must be sent to the middle tier to reduce the extra network traffic that will be required to receive all messages in the browser and then apply filtering criteria. Particularly if the volume of messages is very high, the browser will not be able to handle them gracefully.

AJAX-Based Solution Using TIBCO General Interface

AJAX provides an elegant solution for receiving messages asynchronously over HTTP. TIBCO General Interface's framework enhances that capability and allows developers to build client-side applications that can subscribe to messages using a middle-tier component such as a Servlet.

Examples in this chapter use TIBCO General Interface's `jsx3.net.Request` class to send an asynchronous request to the server. The Servlets in the middle tier manage the communication with the message broker, send the message or retrieve the next available message, and return to the request handler on the browser. Figure 12.1 shows the high-level architecture for this approach.

Installing ActiveMQ

To build and run the example in this chapter, you need to install Apache ActiveMQ. Download the latest binary package from http://activemq.apache.org/download.html and extract its contents to your hard drive (`c:\`). Figure 12.2 shows the contents of the resulting folder. Open the `bin` folder and double-click the file `activemq.bat` to launch the ActiveMQ daemon process.

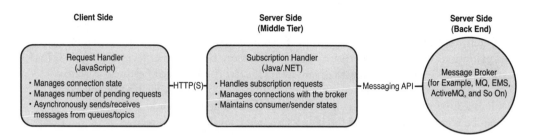

Figure 12.1   Messaging solution architecture.

Figure 12.2   Contents of the Apache
ActiveMQ folder.

After starting ActiveMQ, launch a browser and enter the default location of the ActiveMQ administration console—http://localhost:8161/admin. Figure 12.3 shows the console home page.

Click Queues in the navigation bar and create a queue for the RollingGrid demo named **QUEUE.RollingGridDemo** as shown in Figure 12.4.

Rolling Grid Example

This example shows how to asynchronously receive messages and update a view using TIBCO General Interface's framework components. Complete project files are included on the companion CD-ROM.

Figure 12.3   Apache ActiveMQ
Console home page.

Figure 12.4   Creating a new queue in ActiveMQ.

A Matrix component displays incoming messages. A JavaScript controller component asynchronously receives messages and injects them into the matrix at runtime. Similar to the examples in Chapter 11, "Integrating with Databases," a `main()` method is used to initialize the controller and kick off the sequence of AJAX calls to receive the next message.

The `sendRequest()` method is used to make an asynchronous call to a middle-tier component `GetMessageServlet,` which retrieves the message and returns as XML data in response to the AJAX call. Note that the sample gets messages by sending a new request for every message retrieved. The General Interface client also sends a new request on successfully receiving a message or after a timeout. This ensures that only one request is pending for a message at any one time.

Building the Client

Use GI Builder to create the user interface screens for this example, as shown in Figure 12.5.

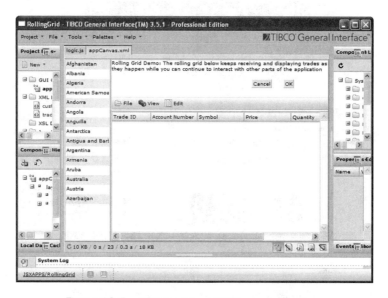

Figure 12.5   GUI client for AJAX Message Receiver.

To build the application as shown in Figure 12.5, create a new project named **RollingGrid** and drag and drop a Layout—Side/Side component into the `appCanvas.xml`. Drag and drop a default List component into the left pane and delete its first column. While keeping the List selected, bring up the Events Editor palette and enter a null statement (a single semicolon) for the `Spyglass` event property. This will underline the items in the list when the mouse hovers over them.

Create an HTML file as shown in Listing 12.1. This will be used to send some test messages to the message queue. Create a new folder named `html` to save this file. Name this file **sendtestmessages.html** and save it in the folder named `html`.

Listing 12.1   Source Code File `sendtestmessages.html`

```html
<html>
<a href="http://localhost:8080/rollinggrid/SendTestMessages">
Send Test Messages</a>
</html>
```

Add a Layout—Top/Over component to the pane on the right and create some content items in the top pane, including a toolbar with some toolbar buttons. Add a third pane to this Layout—Top/Over component and set its `Rows Array` property to `*,80,270` to divide the display area into three parts. Add an iFrame component in the middle pane and set its Source URL property to `sendtestmessages.html`.

Add a Grid component to the bottom pane. Name this Grid component `tradesgrid` and add seven text columns with Name, Att Name, and Caption properties of TradeID, AccountNumber, Symbol, Price, Quantity, NetMoney and Filler, respectively.

Make sure the `XML Cache ID` property of the grid is set to `tradescache`.

Now create the `logic.js` and `RollingGrid.js` files as shown in Listings 12.2 and 12.3, respectively. Much of this code is similar to the controllers used in the previous chapter examples, except the method `sendRequest()`, which is different for this example. In the `sendRequest()` method, the third parameter to the `open()` call is now `true`. This is to tell General Interface to make the request asynchronously and deliver the results to the event handler that is registered using the `subscribe()` method earlier in the same method.

Listing 12.2   File `logic.js`

```javascript
/* place JavaScript code here */
function main()
{
   jsx3.log('main');
   jsx3.require('com.tibcobooks.gi.chapter12.RollingGrid');
   var rg = new com.tibcobooks.gi.chapter12.RollingGrid(RollingGrid);
   rg.initialize();
   com.tibcobooks.gi.chapter12.RollingGrid.instance = rg;
}
```

Listing 12.3   File `RollingGrid.js`

```javascript
/*
 * This is the main controller class for RollingGrid application.
 * Create a single instance of it in main by calling init only once.
```

```
   * @author Anil Gurnani
   *
   */

jsx3.lang.Class.defineClass (
"com.tibcobooks.gi.chapter12.RollingGrid",
null,
null,
function(RollingGrid)
{
  RollingGrid.instance = null;
  RollingGrid.prototype.server = null;

  RollingGrid.prototype.getServer = function() {
    return this.server;
  }

  RollingGrid.prototype.init = function(serverobj)
  {
    this.server = serverobj;
  }


  // create exactly one instance and call this method only once
  // reason why initialize is not done in init is to avoid
  // subscribing by every instance (just in case other instances
  // are created)
  RollingGrid.prototype.initialize = function()
  {
    // send subscription request
    // in this example first request
    // to get the next message
    // automatically subscribes
    // create empty doc and cache it
    var xmlDoc = new jsx3.xml.Document();
    xmlDoc.loadXML("<?xml version='1.0'?><data jsxid='jsxroot'></data>");
    this.getServer().getCache().setDocument('trades.xml',xmlDoc);
    this.getNextMessage('QUEUE.RollingGridDemo');
  }
  RollingGrid.prototype.getNextMessage = function(queueName)
  {
    this.sendRequest('http://localhost:8080/rollinggrid/GetMessage?QueueName='
        +queueName);
  }


  RollingGrid.prototype.sendRequest = function(url)
```

```
    {
      var dt = new Date();
      url = url + '&requestid='+dt.getTime();

      var req = new jsx3.net.Request();
      req.subscribe(jsx3.net.Request.EVENT_ON_RESPONSE, this, 'onMessage');
      req.subscribe(jsx3.net.Request.EVENT_ON_TIMEOUT, this, 'onTimeout');
      var method = "GET";
      req.open(method, url, true);
      req.send();
    }
    RollingGrid.prototype.onMessage = function(objEvent)
    {
      var req = objEvent.target;
      var reqsponseDoc = null;
      if( req.getStatus() == 200 ) {
        responseDoc = new jsx3.xml.Document();
        var responseText = objEvent.target.getResponseText();
        jsx3.log('responseText='+responseText);
        responseDoc.loadXML( responseText );
        this.insertRecord(responseDoc);
        // post another request
        this.getNextMessage();
      } else {
        this.getServer().alert('Error', 'Call failed');
      }
    }


    RollingGrid.prototype.onTimeout = function(objEvent)
    {
      // post another request
      this.getNextMessage();
    }


    RollingGrid.prototype.insertRecord = function(responseDoc)
    {
      var node = responseDoc.selectSingleNode('/data/record');
      if( node != null )
      {
        var tradesgrid = this.getServer().getJSXByName('tradesgrid');
        tradesgrid.insertRecordNode(node);
        tradesgrid.focusRowById(node.getAttribute("jsxid"));
      }
    }
  }
);
```

Building the Complete Application Using Eclipse

General Interface content can be easily integrated with Eclipse web applications. This section describes the steps necessary to build a new web application named rollinggrid and integrate the General Interface application RollingGrid into it.

Download and install Eclipse (if it is not already installed). Eclipse can be downloaded from www.eclipse.org/downloads/packages/. Select the package titled Eclipse IDE for Java EE Developers to build J2EE applications, including web services and AJAX or TIBCO General Interface web applications.

After you download the Eclipse package, extract its contents to your hard disk (`c:\`). Then, using Windows Explorer, navigate to the `bin` directory and launch `eclipse.exe` by double-clicking it. When you launch Eclipse for the first time, it prompts you for a Workspace directory. Click Browse and select a convenient location (`C:\EclipseWorkspace`) on your hard disk. You can use the Make New Folder button to create a new directory.

When you launch Eclipse for the first time, you will see a Welcome screen with several navigation icons. Click the X next to the Welcome tab to close this screen. You will see the default Eclipse perspective with four primary areas: Project Explorer on the left, an Editor window in the center, an outline view on the top right, and a few tabs at the bottom, including Problems, Tasks, Properties, Servers, Data Source Explorer, and Snippets.

Select New, Project from the File menu and choose Dynamic Web Project after expanding Web by clicking the + sign next to it, as shown in Figure 12.6. Click Next to move to the next step of this wizard, and provide the name of the project, `rollinggrid`, as shown Figure 12.7. You can click Finish at this step, and Eclipse will apply defaults for the remaining steps.

To create the Servlets for the project, click the right mouse button on the `WebContent` folder in the project and select New, Other from the context menu. From the Select a Wizard dialog, expand Web and select Servlet, as shown in Figure 12.8.

Provide the Java Package Name as **com.tibcobooks.com.gi.chapter12** and the class name as **GetMessageServlet** in the Create Servlet dialog box in Eclipse, as shown in Figure 12.9.

In the next step, provide a meaningful description for this Servlet, and edit the URL mapping as shown in Figure 12.10.

To add the Servlets API library to the project, select the project in Project Explorer and select Project, Properties. Click Java Build Path on the left and the Libraries tab on the right in the Properties dialog, as shown in Figure 12.11. Click the Add External Jars button and in the JARS Selection dialog, navigate to the `c:\tomcat55\common\lib` folder in the Look In field at the top of the dialog.

Create another Servlet class named `SendTestMessageServlet` and set its URL mapping name to `SendTestMessages`. Use the contents from Listings 12.4 and 12.5 for the source code of the two Servlets.

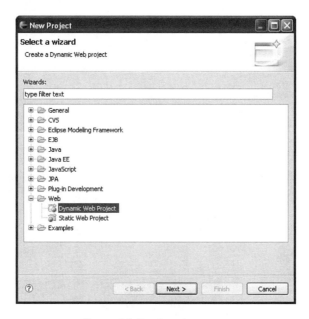

Figure 12.6   Creating a new
Dynamic Web Project in Eclipse.

Figure 12.7   Providing the
project name.

Figure 12.8   Choose Servlet from
the Select a Wizard dialog.

Figure 12.9   Providing the Java
package and class name.

Figure 12.10   Providing a description and editing the URL mapping.

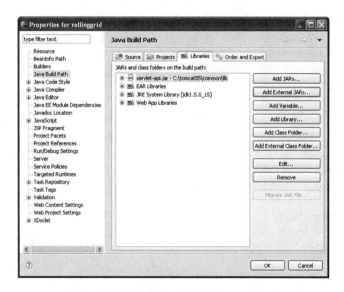

Figure 12.11   Adding Tomcat's `servlet-api.jar` file to the project.

Listing 12.4   File `GetMessageServlet.java`

```java
package com.tibcobooks.gi.chapter12;
import java.io.*;
import javax.servlet.http.*;
import javax.servlet.*;
import java.io.IOException;
import javax.jms.Connection;
import javax.jms.Destination;
import javax.jms.ExceptionListener;
import javax.jms.JMSException;
import javax.jms.Message;
import javax.jms.MessageConsumer;
import javax.jms.Session;
import javax.jms.TextMessage;
import org.apache.activemq.ActiveMQConnection;
import org.apache.activemq.ActiveMQConnectionFactory;

public class GetMessageServlet extends HttpServlet implements ExceptionListener {

private static final long serialVersionUID = 1L;

  private Session session;
  private Destination destination;
  private String subject = "QUEUE.RollingGridDemo";
  private String user = ActiveMQConnection.DEFAULT_USER;
  private String password = ActiveMQConnection.DEFAULT_PASSWORD;
  private String url = ActiveMQConnection.DEFAULT_BROKER_URL;

  public void doGet(HttpServletRequest req,
                    HttpServletResponse res)
    throws ServletException, IOException
  {
    HttpSession sess = req.getSession(true);
    MessageConsumer consumer = (MessageConsumer)sess.getAttribute("consumer");
    if( consumer == null )
        consumer = initConsumer(sess);

    String msg = "";
    if( consumer != null )
       msg = getNextMessage(consumer);

    if( msg == null || msg.length() == 0 )
        msg = "<?xml version=\"1.0\"?><data jsxid=\"jsxroot\"/>";

    res.setContentType("text/xml");
    PrintWriter out = res.getWriter();
    out.println(msg);
```

```java
        out.close();
    }

    public MessageConsumer initConsumer(HttpSession sess)
    {
        MessageConsumer consumer = null;
        try {
        ActiveMQConnectionFactory connectionFactory =
                new ActiveMQConnectionFactory(user, password, url);
        Connection connection = connectionFactory.createConnection();
        connection.setExceptionListener(this);
        connection.start();
        session = connection.createSession(false, Session.AUTO_ACKNOWLEDGE);
        destination = session.createQueue(subject);
        consumer = session.createConsumer(destination);
        sess.setAttribute("consumer", consumer);
      } catch (Exception e) {
        System.out.println("Caught: " + e);
        e.printStackTrace();
      }
      return consumer;
    }

    public String getNextMessage(MessageConsumer consumer) {
        String msg = "";
        try {
            Message message = consumer.receive(2000); // wait for 2 seconds
            if (message != null && message instanceof TextMessage) {
                TextMessage txtMsg = (TextMessage)message;
                msg = txtMsg.getText();
                System.out.println("Received: " + msg);
            }
        } catch (JMSException e) {
            System.out.println("Caught: " + e);
            e.printStackTrace();
        }
        return msg;
    }
    public void onException(JMSException arg0) {
        System.out.println("JMS Exception occurred: "+arg0.getMessage());
    }


}
```

Listing 12.5   File `SendTestMessagesServlet.java`

```
package com.tibcobooks.gi.chapter12;
import java.util.Date;
import java.io.*;
import javax.servlet.http.*;
import javax.servlet.*;
import javax.jms.Connection;
import javax.jms.DeliveryMode;
import javax.jms.Destination;
import javax.jms.MessageProducer;
import javax.jms.Session;
import javax.jms.TextMessage;
import org.apache.activemq.ActiveMQConnection;
import org.apache.activemq.ActiveMQConnectionFactory;

public class SendTestMessagesServlet extends HttpServlet {

  private static final long serialVersionUID = 1L;
  private Destination destination;
  private int messageCount = 25;
  private long timeToLive;
  private String user = ActiveMQConnection.DEFAULT_USER;
  private String password = ActiveMQConnection.DEFAULT_PASSWORD;
  private String url = ActiveMQConnection.DEFAULT_BROKER_URL;
  private String subject = "QUEUE.RollingGridDemo";

  public void doGet(HttpServletRequest req,
                    HttpServletResponse res)
    throws ServletException, IOException
  {
    sendTestMessages();

    PrintWriter out = res.getWriter();
    Date dt = new Date();
    out.println("<html>");
    out.println("<body>");
    out.println("<a
      href=\"http://localhost:8080/rollinggrid/
      SendTestMessages?requestid="+
        dt.getTime()+"\">Send Test Messages</a>");
    out.println("</body>");
    out.println("</html>");
    out.close();
  }

  public void sendTestMessages() {
      Connection connection = null;
```

```java
    try {
        System.out.println("Connecting to URL: " + url);
        if (timeToLive != 0) {
            System.out.println("Messages time to live " + timeToLive + " ms");
        }
        // Create the connection.
        ActiveMQConnectionFactory connectionFactory =
            new ActiveMQConnectionFactory(user, password, url);
        connection = connectionFactory.createConnection();
        connection.start();

        // Create the session
        Session session = connection.createSession(false,
            Session.AUTO_ACKNOWLEDGE);
        destination = session.createQueue(subject);

        // Create the producer.
        MessageProducer producer = session.createProducer(destination);
        producer.setDeliveryMode(DeliveryMode.NON_PERSISTENT);
        if (timeToLive != 0) {
            producer.setTimeToLive(timeToLive);
        }
        // Start sending messages
        sendLoop(session, producer);
        System.out.println("Done.");
    } catch (Exception e) {
        System.out.println("Caught: " + e);
        e.printStackTrace();
    } finally {
        try {
            connection.close();
        } catch (Throwable ignore) {
        }
    }
}

protected void sendLoop(Session session, MessageProducer producer)
        throws Exception {
    for (int i = 0; i < messageCount || messageCount == 0; i++) {
        TextMessage message = session.createTextMessage(createMessageText(i));
        String msg = message.getText();
        System.out.println("Sending message: " + msg);
        producer.send(message);
    }

}
```

```java
private String getAccountNumber()
{
    String[] accountNumbers = {
        "932-23652", "278-43581", "398-17462", "620-89163", "983-28674",
        "932-23652", "278-43581", "398-17462", "620-89163", "983-28674" };
    int index = (int) (Math.random() * 10 % 10);
    return accountNumbers[index];
}

private String getSymbol()
{
    String[] symbols = {
        "IBM", "MSFT", "AAPL", "TIBX", "ORCL",
        "MER", "JPM", "AXP", "LEH", "BAC" };
    int index = (int) (Math.random() * 10 % 10);
    return symbols[index];
}

private double getPrice()
{
    double[] prices = {
        23.87, 41.22, 33.67, 48.72, 14.64,
        25.02, 31.75, 37.86, 13.84, 19.71 };
    int index = (int) (Math.random() * 10 % 10);
    return prices[index];
}

private double getQuantity()
{
    double[] quantities = {
        1000, 2000, 3000, 4000, 5000,
        6000, 7000, 8000, 9000, 10000 };
    int index = (int) (Math.random() * 10 % 10);
    return quantities[index];
}

static int jsxid = 1; // crude way to generate unique ids
private String createMessageText(int index) {
    StringBuffer buffer = new StringBuffer();
    buffer.append("<?xml version=\"1.0\"?>");
    buffer.append("<data jsxid=\"jsxroot\">");
    buffer.append("<record ");
    buffer.append(" jsxid=\""+jsxid+"\" ");
    buffer.append(" TradeID=\""+jsxid+"\" ");
    String an = getAccountNumber();
    String sym = getSymbol();
```

```
    double price = getPrice( );
    double quantity = getQuantity( );
    double netmoney = price * quantity;
    buffer.append(" AccountNumber=\""+an+"\" ");
    buffer.append(" Symbol=\""+sym+"\" ");
    buffer.append(" Price=\""+price+"\" ");
    buffer.append(" Quantity=\""+quantity+"\" ");
    buffer.append(" NetMoney=\""+netmoney+"\" ");
    buffer.append("/>");
    buffer.append("</data>");

    jsxid = jsxid + 1;

    return buffer.toString( );
  }


}
```

Next, import the Apache ActiveMQ library into the project. To do this, first expand the WebContent\WEB-INF\lib folder in the Project Explorer, and then right-click the lib folder and select Import. Then select File from inside the General category to view the File Import dialog, as shown in Figure 12.12, and click Next.

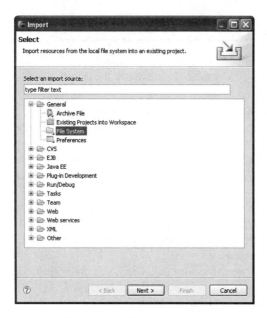

Figure 12.12   Import dialog.

Click the Browse button and navigate to the ActiveMQ installation folder (C:\apache-activemq-5.1.0) and click OK to display its contents in the import dialog. Check the jar file activemq-all-5.1.0.jar as shown in Figure 12.13, and click Finish to import the jar file into the project.

Figure 12.13   Importing the
Active MQ classes into the project.

Use the import dialog to import the JSX folder and logger.xml file into the WebContent folder in the project from the TIBCO General Interface installation directory. Right-click WebContent and select Import. Navigate and select the TIBCO General Interface installation directory on your hard disk (C:\tibco-gi-3.5.1-pro). Open the JSX folder and select the logger.xml file, and then click Finish to import its contents into the project.

Similarly, import the contents of the General Interface project RollingGrid using the File System Import Wizard. Browse to the JSXAPPS folder within GI Builder workspace—C:\TIBCO GI Book\GIWorkspace\JSXAPPS, and then check RollingGrid folder to import it into this project.

Create a new index.html file with the contents as shown in Listing 12.6.

Listing 12.6   File index.html for RollingGrid Project
_____

```
<html>
<head>
```

```
    <title>TIBCO General Interface(TM) - Professional Edition</title>
</head>

<body BGCOLOR="#9898a5" SCROLL="no"
    style="position:absolute;width:100%;height:100%;left:0px;top:0px;
            padding:0px;margin:0px;border:0px;overflow:hidden;">

<div id="jsxmain" style="position:absolute;left:0px;top:0px;width:100%;
            height:100%;">
  <script type="text/javascript" src="JSX/js/JSX30.js"
          jsxapppath="RollingGrid/"
          >
  </script>
</div>

</body>
</html>
```

Now to run and debug this application under Tomcat, you need to add the Tomcat Server. Click the Servers tab in the bottom pane in Eclipse and right-click anywhere in the blank window. Select New, Server to bring up the Define a New Server dialog. Expand Apache and select Tomcat 5.5 in this dialog, as shown in Figure 12.14.

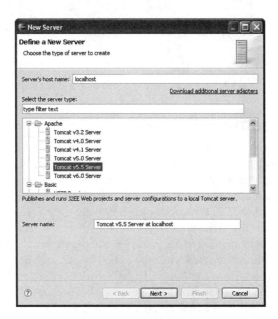

Figure 12.14   Adding a new
Tomcat server to the workspace.

In the screens that follow, navigate to your Tomcat installation folder (`C:\tomcat55`). Add the rollinggrid project to this server and click Finish. Click the right mouse button on the `index.html` file and select Run As, Run on Server from the menu. Select the Tomcat 55 server you defined earlier in this section and click Finish. Eclipse will publish the application to the Tomcat server, launch it, and run the application as shown in Figure 12.15.

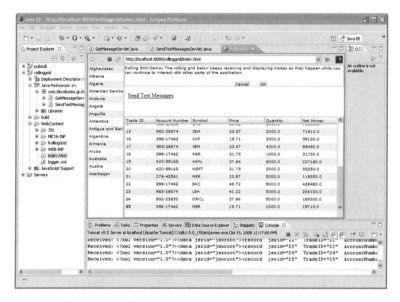

Figure 12.15   Running the application within Eclipse.

Publish Subscribe Example

A common issue when integrating with an asynchronous messaging source is that the AJAX call from the client browser blocks a thread until a response is sent. This causes scalability issues when a large number of connections to the server exist.

The JSR 315 specification for Servlet 3.0 API is currently in progress and provides a mechanism to respond to HTTP requests asynchronously.

Tomcat 6.0 supports the CometProcessor interface where, if a Servlet implements an `event(CometEvent evt)` method its `service()` method is never called. Instead, the Servlet's `event()` method is invoked when the session begins, encounters an error, or ends.

This example shows how to use Tomcat 6.0's CometProcessor interface to implement an asynchronous message service for a large number of connections.

The complete solution is included on the CD-ROM. Listing 12.7 shows the Servlet, which is the key component of this architecture. `GetMessageServlet.java` extends `GenericServlet` (and not `HttpServlet`) and implements the CometProcessor interface.

In its `init()` method it initializes all the JMS objects, subscribes to a JMS topic, and sets up a listener. Then when it gets a Begin Session event, it appends the caller's connection object to an ArrayList, and whenever it receives a message in the `onMessage` method, it delivers it to all the open connections and then closes and ends each response and removes the connections.

The sample code can easily be enhanced to support persistent connections so that a client will need to send an unsubscribe request to be removed from the list. Also, the client can express interest in a limited set of messages upon subscription. The Servlet will then filter messages per client requests.

Listing 12.7   Asynchronous Version of `GetMessageServlet.java` That Implements CometProcessor

```java
package com.tibcobooks.gi.chapter12;

import java.io.*;

import javax.servlet.http.*;
import javax.servlet.*;

import java.io.IOException;
import java.util.ArrayList;
import java.util.Iterator;

import javax.jms.Connection;
import javax.jms.Destination;
import javax.jms.ExceptionListener;
import javax.jms.JMSException;
import javax.jms.Message;
import javax.jms.MessageConsumer;
import javax.jms.MessageListener;
import javax.jms.Session;
import javax.jms.TextMessage;

import org.apache.activemq.ActiveMQConnection;
import org.apache.activemq.ActiveMQConnectionFactory;
import org.apache.catalina.CometEvent;
import org.apache.catalina.CometProcessor;

public class GetMessageServlet extends GenericServlet
   implements MessageListener, ExceptionListener, CometProcessor
   protected ArrayList<HttpServletResponse> connections =
   new ArrayList<HttpServletResponse>();

   private static final long serialVersionUID = 1L;
```

```java
private Session session;
private Destination destination;
private Connection connection;
private MessageConsumer consumer;
private String subject = "TOPIC.PubSubDemo";
private String user = ActiveMQConnection.DEFAULT_USER;
private String password = ActiveMQConnection.DEFAULT_PASSWORD;
private String url = ActiveMQConnection.DEFAULT_BROKER_URL;

@Override
public void destroy() {
  connections.clear();
  try {
  if( consumer != null )
    consumer.close();
  if( session != null )
    session.close();
  if( connection != null )
    connection.close();
  } catch (JMSException e) {
    e.printStackTrace();
  }
}

@Override
public void init() throws ServletException {
  try {
    ActiveMQConnectionFactory connectionFactory =
        new ActiveMQConnectionFactory(user, password, url);
    connection = connectionFactory.createConnection();
    connection.setExceptionListener(this);
    connection.start();
    session = connection.createSession(false, Session.AUTO_ACKNOWLEDGE);
    destination = session.createTopic(subject);
    consumer = session.createConsumer(destination);
    consumer.setMessageListener(this);
  } catch (Exception e) {
    System.out.println("Caught: " + e);
    e.printStackTrace();
  }
}

public void onException(JMSException arg0) {
  System.out.println("JMS Exception occurred: "+arg0.getMessage());
```

```
  }
  public void event(CometEvent event) throws IOException, ServletException {
    HttpServletRequest request = event.getHttpServletRequest();
    HttpServletResponse response = event.getHttpServletResponse();
    if (event.getEventType() == CometEvent.EventType.BEGIN) {
      System.out.println("Begin for session: " +
             request.getSession(true).getId());
      synchronized(connections) {
        connections.add(response);
      }
    } else if (event.getEventType() == CometEvent.EventType.ERROR) {
      System.out.println("Error for session: " +
             request.getSession(true).getId());
      synchronized(connections) {
        connections.remove(response);
      }
      event.close();
    } else if (event.getEventType() == CometEvent.EventType.END) {
      System.out.println("End for session: " + request.getSession(true).getId());
      synchronized(connections) {
        connections.remove(response);
      }
      event.close();
    } else if (event.getEventType() == CometEvent.EventType.READ) {
      System.out.println("Read event received ");
    }
  }

  public void onMessage(Message message) {
    String msg = null;
    if (message != null && message instanceof TextMessage) {
      TextMessage txtMsg = (TextMessage)message;
      try {
        msg = txtMsg.getText();
        // deliver message to all waiting connections
        // filtering could occur here based on
        // the filter set in each session
        // (all sessions will also need to be stored
        // in the ArrayList)
        synchronized(connections)
        {
          Iterator<HttpServletResponse> iter = connections.iterator();
          while( iter.hasNext() )
          {
            HttpServletResponse response = iter.next();
            PrintWriter out = response.getWriter();
```

```
            out.println(msg);

            out.close();
          }
          connections.clear();
        }
      } catch (JMSException e) {
        e.printStackTrace();
      } catch (IOException e) {
        e.printStackTrace();
      }
      System.out.println("Received: " + msg);
    }
  }


  @Override
  public void service(ServletRequest req, ServletResponse res)
      throws ServletException, IOException {
    System.out.println("*?%#*******in service method*******");
      ((HttpServletResponse)res).sendError(400,"Invalid, must use NIO or APR
        connector");
  }
}
```

Tomcat 6.0 is required to run this application. Download the latest version of Tomcat 6.0 (6.0.16 at the time of this writing) and extract its contents to your hard drive (c:\). Make sure the JAVA_HOME variable is set correctly to point to the JDK 5 instance on your machine.

On Windows, you need to place the file tcnative-1.dll anywhere within the PATH directories (for example, c:\Windows\System32) so that Tomcat 6.0 can find it. If Tomcat 6.0 does not find this library, it does not configure the CometProcessor interface and drops back to calling the service() method of the Servlet. So if you see your service() method being called, chances are that you didn't install this tcnative-1.dll, which is required to support native IO in Tomcat 6.0.

On Linux, you will need APR 1.2+ development headers, OpenSSL 0.9.7, JNI headers, and GNU development environment to use this feature. Refer to Tomcat documentation at http://tomcat.apache.org/tomcat-6.0-doc/apr.html for more details on configuring and using native I/O with Tomcat 6.0.

After successfully installing Tomcat with native IO support, you can drag and drop the application war file included on the CD-ROM (pubsub.war), or use the Eclipse project (also included on the CD-ROM) to deploy and test the application. To deploy the war file, copy it to Tomcat's webapps folder.

Make sure Apache ActiveMQ is running when you test this sample application, and be sure that a topic named TOPIC.PubSubDemo has been created using the Admin interface.

When you run this application, any messages you send in one window will be displayed in all the other windows you are currently running. Figure 12.16 shows two windows

running the sample application. Note that you will need to update the ActiveMQ connection URL if you are running the Apache ActiveMQ daemon remotely.

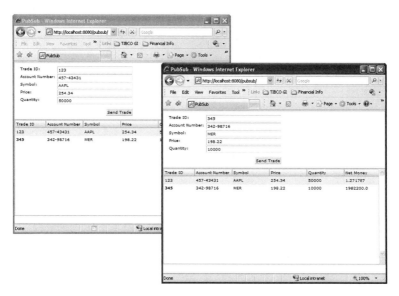

Figure 12.16   Desktop showing two instances of the
sample running.

13

Integrating with SOA and ESBs

An Enterprise Service Bus (ESB) can be used to integrate a large number of applications or services. This chapter briefly discusses various organizations and standards related to the Enterprise Service Bus. It then presents a practical example showing how the TIBCO General Interface application fits into a Service Oriented Architecture communicating with services on the ESB.

Overview of ESB

A Message Bus is an enterprise integration pattern that defines a common data model and a mechanism for exchanging messages between disparate systems. In simple terms, it is a lot like the popular electronic mail system except that the Message Bus is used by software programs and services in an enterprise. TIBCO's Enterprise Message Services (EMS) is an example of a Message Bus.

An ESB adds additional features and functions to a Message Bus. It provides transparent transport bridging and message transformations in addition to the functions of Message Bus to allow integrating a variety of applications and services using different protocols and even different languages. For example, a service that was written to respond to HTTP requests can be invoked using a JMS message via an ESB. The ESB will transparently transform the JMS message into an XML request and make the call using HTTP. It accepts the response from the service, stuffs it back into a JMS message, and responds back to the caller. Note that the calling application is completely unaware that the service it called was an HTTP service.

Even though several books have been written on the subject of ESB, it is very difficult to get a clear definition. Different vendor and community sites and books contain different definitions of an ESB. All of them agree on one thing—that an Enterprise Service Bus provides a common infrastructure for multiple applications and services in an organization to communicate with each other, even if they are using different protocols and platforms; thus, an ESB facilitates Service Oriented Architecture (SOA). Although it is possible to use an ESB for other purposes, its usage is most common in the modern SOA enterprise.

An ESB is the backbone on which an enterprise can build its SOA. It is not necessary for all services to be web services. Any number and types of services can participate in an ESB. Deploying an ESB is the beginning of an SOA. An ESB provides certain core infrastructure services and features that may be used to build and deploy services.

Conceptually, an ESB is similar to the power lines running through your house. You have a number of wall sockets in all rooms, and you can plug in many types of appliances and lights to any of the wall sockets. The power bus at your house is based on well-defined standards; therefore, you are able to buy any electrical appliance with confidence. Figure 13.1 shows this concept.

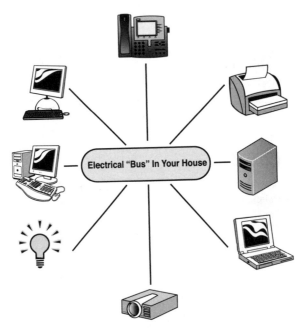

Figure 13.1   Connecting different appliances to the electrical "bus" in your house.

However, when you travel outside the United States, you need an appropriate adapter to connect to the power grid. Similarly, you need adapters to plug your services or applications into an ESB.

An ESB can be thought of as a collection of software components that enables services and applications in an enterprise to communicate and collaborate with each other. It is usually built on top of a messaging backbone such as TIBCO EMS or IBM MQ. Some open source ESBs roll their own messaging layer so you don't need any third-party messaging system to implement their ESB.

Applications and services in an enterprise can be plugged in to the ESB, similar to the way telephones, fax machines, and other devices are plugged in to the telephone network. An ESB provides a mechanism by which services and applications can communicate with each other. Figure 13.2 shows the concept of an ESB.

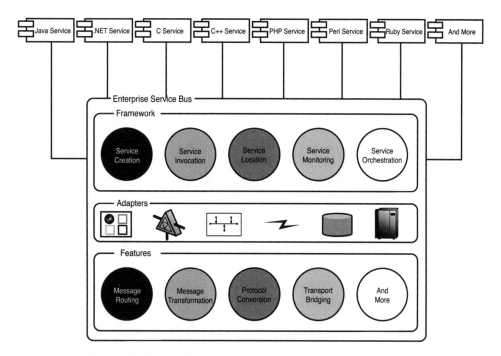

Figure 13.2   An ESB integrating heterogeneous components in an enterprise.

A common goal of all ESBs is to allow services and applications to interchange data in a platform-independent format. Most ESBs, therefore, provide the capability to interact using XML data. TIBCO General Interface's advanced XML capabilities make it easy to build applications that integrate with an ESB. Working examples are included in later sections.

Benefits of an SOA will not be apparent when the first service component goes into production. However, after an organization has deployed a critical set of core infrastructure and business services, it will begin to experience tremendous improvements in its capability to build and deploy new services and applications.

It is useful and important to learn a little bit about the history of the standards and the organizations driving those standards. The Organization for the Advancement of Structured Information Standards (OASIS) and the Open Service Oriented Architecture (OSOA) collaboration are two main organizations involved in evolving standards such as

JBI and SCA that are related to ESBs and SOA. The following sections describe the organizations and their goals and charters in more detail as well as giving some history and the current state and direction of JBI and SCA.

OASIS and OSOA

The Organization for the Advancement of Structured Information Standards (OASIS) is a nonprofit organization focused on defining open standards for the Information Technology industry. Leading IT vendors have representation in OASIS and help drive open standards, which enable interoperability among software and component frameworks as well as business applications and services.

OASIS was founded in 1993 and boasts more than 600 member organizations worldwide in more than 100 countries.

OSOA (www.osoa.org) is an informal group of industry leaders who worked together to define the first draft of the Service Component Architecture and handed it over to OASIS. OSOA still continues as an independent group to define and evolve other related standards.

In April 2007, OASIS formed a new member section called OASIS-Open CSA to further develop and advance the original standard presented by OSOA. OASIS formed several technical committees to address various parts of the Service Component Architecture (SCA) as follows:

- Simplify SOA application development.
- Define an SCA Policy framework for SOA development.
- Standardize bindings for SCA.
- Specify how services can be orchestrated using BPEL. More details about these technical committees can be found online at www.oasis-opencsa.org/committees.

OSOA still participates in the advancement of the SCA standards through participation in the Open CSA committees.

JBI and SCA

Java Business Integration (JBI) and Service Component Architecture (SCA) are two standards that are important when discussing the Enterprise Service Bus. The software community has been working on defining standards for how to build business components effectively. Goals include a very agile, flexible, and nimble organization that is able to quickly respond to changing business requirements, where it does not take weeks or months to change a business process. New services and applications can be quickly built using services that are already deployed in an enterprise, resulting in faster time to market, which promotes service innovations.

JBI and SCA are two separate sets of standards for integrating heterogeneous enterprise systems. Open SOA is an organization composed of industry leaders to collaborate on developing and evolving standards for implementing SOA. Although both SCA and JBI address the common goals of enterprise architecture, they have slightly different areas of focus. JBI focuses on the physical aspects of running services in an ESB, whereas SCA deals with the design of business software components.

JBI is driven by Sun's Java Community Process under Java Specification Request (JSR) 208, which was approved and released in August 2005. SCA, on the other hand, was originally created by a group of vendors, including IBM, BEA, Oracle, SAP and others, to define a general approach to developing business components and guidelines for how they should interact.

SCA was submitted to OASIS (www.oasis-open.org) and the Java Community Process as a proposal for a standard for building components in a heterogeneous environment. JBI is limited to building components in Java language, whereas SCA goes beyond Java to define an architecture for components built using other languages on other platforms.

Several organizations and vendors offer ESB solutions, and many enterprises have rolled their own frameworks to build service components. Some ESB solutions have embraced JBI as the standard, some implement the SCA standard, and still others claim to integrate both SCA and JBI. Even though SCA and JBI appear to be in competition, they are not necessarily mutually exclusive. A framework could support both SCA and JBI.

At the heart of every ESB is a new way of building software for the enterprise. Traditionally, complex software was built as one monolithic application. SOA allows developers to build and deploy smaller, reusable components. Additionally, these components may be dynamically updated, monitored, and even discovered by other services at runtime. Because complete coverage of SCA and JBI is outside the scope of this book, we will limit our discussion to a high-level introduction to various solutions available from the industry today, including open source.

SCA-Based Solutions

TIBCO Active Matrix Service Grid version 2.0 comprises all the necessary components to build SOA solutions based on the SCA standards. TIBCO also markets a subset of the components in the name of Active Matrix Service Bus with all the components except the high-level Registry and Policy components. TIBCO's SCA solution uses its already proven TIBCO Enterprise Messaging Service (EMS) as the underlying transport for the ESB.

Apache Tuscany is an open source solution that is based on the SCA specification. Apache Tuscany is implemented in Java and C++. The Java version is called SCA Java, and the C++ version is called SCA Native. To learn more about Tuscany, visit http://tuscany.apache.org/sca-overview.data/getting_started_Rest_099_07.pdf, which provides step-by-step instructions on how to build a Composite Service Application for an online store.

JBI-Based Solutions

JBI has been out there longer and enjoys a larger number of implementations.

Sun's OpenESB is the reference implementation of JBI specification. It also includes many JBI-compliant components that make it easy to build composite applications using those ready-to-use components. OpenESB is available under the Common Development and Distribution License (CDDL), which is based on the Mozilla license.

Apache ServiceMix is one of the earliest implementations of JBI. ServiceMix also implements another standard originally proposed by Oracle—Event Driven Architecture, or EDA. ServiceMix includes a container to host JBI components. Additionally, ServiceMix provides some useful JBI components for HTTP, JMS, BPEL, Rules, and others.

TIBCO Active Matrix

TIBCO Active Matrix is a suite of products from TIBCO that includes an ESB and a framework for building and managing services in a SOA environment. TIBCO markets two separate suites of software products under the name of Active Matrix. First is an Active Matrix Service Bus that consists of a basic foundation and ESB functionality.

The other version is marketed under the name of Active Matrix Service Grid, which includes all the products in Active Matrix Service Bus and adds two very important components for managing the service providers and consumers in the SOA—a Policy Manager and a Service Registry.

The following sections provide detailed steps on how to install Active Matrix platform and build a simple example with it.

Instaling TIBCO Active Matrix

TIBCO Active Matrix is available for evaluation download from TIBCO. It can be downloaded from www.tibco.com/devnet/activematrix_service_grid/default.jsp. Three packages need to be downloaded to install TIBCO Active Matrix Service Grid:

- `hibernate_3.2.2_win_x86.zip`
- `TIB_amx-servicegrid_2.0.2_win_x86_Evaluation.zip`
- `TIB_emseval-simple_4.4.3_win_x86.zip`

Hibernate needs to be installed first. Extract the contents of the `hibernate_3.2.2_win_x86.zip` archive into a folder (named `hibernate_3.2.2_win_x86`) and open it. Click the TIBCOUniversalInstaller executable to install Hibernate on your machine.

After you accept the license, the installer requires a location to install Hibernate and will ask you whether you want Typical or Custom installation. Accept the default choice presented by the installer (`c:\tibco`) and click Next until you get to the summary screen with the Install button. Click the Install button to begin the installation.

Next, install TIBCO Enterprise Message Service from the `TIB_emseval-simple_4.4.3_win_x86.zip` package. Extract the contents of this package and launch the `TIB_emseval_simple_4.4.3_win_x86` application to install TIBCO EMS on your machine. The Install Shield Wizard walks you through the steps to install TIBCO EMS. Click Next in the opening screen to move forward to the End User License screen. You will not be able to move past this dialog until you scroll all the way down to the last line of the license agreement. Click the I Accept the Terms of the License Agreements option button

and click Next. In the next step of the wizard, accept the default directory proposed
(c:\tibco) and click Next. Choose Typical install at the next step of the wizard and click
Next.

It is best to select Auto for the server startup type, but if you are concerned about usage of system resources, you can pick Manual and start the EMS service only when you
want to work on Active Matrix. If you are installing it on a server, it is best to select Auto
to make sure the services will be running even after a restart. In this step, accept the default for the configuration file location and name and click Next to get to the summary
information screen. Click Next to begin the installation process. Click Finish to exit the
wizard after the installation is complete.

It is useful to go ahead and start the TIBCO EMS service at this point. To start the
service, go to the Services control panel, which is inside the Administrator Tools folder
within Control Panel, and find the TIBCO EMS server. Select it and click Start.

Now you can install the Active Matrix product from the package. Extract the contents
of the archive file named TIB_amx-servicegrid_2..2_win_x86_Evaluation and launch
the TIBCOUniversalInstaller from that folder.

The installation wizard will install TIBCO Active Matrix Foundation, Service Bus, and
the Grid products. Click Next to move to the License screen. Click I Accept the Terms of
the License Agreement and click Next. Accept the default for the directory location of
the installation (c:\tibco) and click Next. Select Typical and click Next. The installation
wizard will take a few minutes to prepare the packages for installation, and then it displays
a summary screen. Click Install to begin the installation process.

After the installation, the wizard gives you options to start the HSQL Database and to
launch the Administrator Server Creation Wizard. Uncheck those boxes for now and click
Next, and then click Finish at the installation summary screen. The summary window
may appear to linger on for a while before it finally closes.

Active Matrix Environment

Before working on an example, we need to set up an Active Matrix environment. An environment is a collection of managed nodes and defines a boundary for components. Additional bindings and references can be configured to allow components in different
environments to communicate and collaborate. We will restrict our discussion and examples to a single Active Matrix environment. More details about Active Matrix and related
concepts can be found at the TIBCO Developer Network at www.tibco.com/devnet/
activematrix_service_grid/.

At least one Administration server must be configured to manage a single Active Matrix environment. Multiple Administration servers can be configured to achieve high
availability and fault tolerance. A database in the environment is used to store persistent
information about the environment.

Each environment may have one or more Active Matrix nodes, which in turn can
house any number of Active Matrix containers. Service providers and consumers run
within an Active Matrix container. Java services run inside the Java container, and .NET

services run inside the .NET container. Similarly, other services run within their corresponding containers. Currently containers exist for Java, C++, .NET, TIBCO Business Works, and TIBCO Adapters. This allows developers to create services in Java, C++, .NET, or TIBCO Business Works. Client applications built using TIBCO General Interface can communicate with any service in the grid, regardless of what language was used to build it.

Figure 13.3 shows a conceptual Active Matrix environment with two nodes and an Administration server.

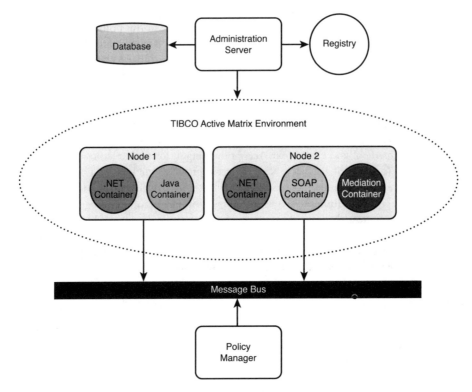

Figure 13.3   Conceptual architecture of an Active Matrix environment.

A TIBCO Active Matrix Registry is the common place where all services within an environment are registered. A consumer communicates with the Registry to find out the provider it needs. For example, a service that requires stock price quotes will ask the Registry for the quote service. Clients built with TIBCO General Interface, however, do not communicate directly with the Registry.

Next, you'll build a sample to get a better understanding of the preceding concepts discussed. To build and run the example, you need an Active Matrix Administrator server.

Follow these steps to configure an Administration Server, which will be used to deploy services that will be used by the TIBCO General Interface client application:

1. Make sure that TIBCO EMS server is running. Open Control Panel, open Administrative Tools, and then open Services to view the status of all running services under Windows. Locate a service named TIBCO EMS Server and make sure it is started. If its status does not show Started, click it, and then click the Start the Service hyperlink to the left of the list of services.

2. Start HSQLDB Server. Click the Start button and select All Programs, TIBCO, Active Matrix 2.0, Start HSQLDB Server. You will see a DOS command window that tells you that the HSQLDB Server has started. Although it does not display it onscreen, note that HSQLDB server listens for requests on port 1234. You will need this when you create the Administration server instance next.

3. Create an Administration Server. Click the Start button and select All Programs, TIBCO, Active Matrix 2.0, Start Administrator Server Wizard. It takes a few minutes for the wizard to initialize when you first launch it, so be patient and wait until the wizard initializes and starts. Click Next on the Welcome Screen to move to the next step to specify configuration details.

4. Accept the defaults—Server Name: AGadmin; Cluster name: AGamx; HTTP Port: 8120; Management Port: 8110; and Authentication Realm: Database Realm. Click Next to move to the Database Realm details screen.

5. Change the string `<portnumber>` in the Database URL field to `1234` because that is the port number the database is listening on. Accept the suggested defaults for all other fields and click Next to move to user credentials section.

6. Specify a username and password here. This is the username and password you will use to log in to the Administration console, from where you can administer various aspects of this Active Matrix environment, including monitoring and deploying new services. Click Next to move to the Active Matrix database details section of the wizard.

7. Note that by default the new Administrator Server uses the same database as the one for the authentication realm. Accept all defaults in this step and click Next to provide information to create a default node. An environment usually consists of one or more nodes. More nodes can be added later, but you need to create at least one node now to deploy your sample Active Matrix services.

8. Enter a name for this new environment (**AGenv**) and a name for this new node (**AGnode1**). Every node must have a management port configured for it; add one for this domain (**3444**). You can accept default settings for the rest of the fields in this step. Click Next to view a summary of the input parameters.

9. Click Next to create the new administrator server. The wizard will take a while to create all the necessary artifacts, and a summary screen at the end will tell you that the environment and node were successfully created. Click Finish to exit the wizard.

TIBCO Active Matrix Administrator server is not automatically started when it is first created. Make sure to close and then reopen the Services control panel. Now you should see an additional service listed named TIBCO ActiveMatrix Administrator Server (AGamx:AGadmin). Select this service and click Start the Service or the Start Service icon in the toolbar below the menu bar. (Make sure that the HSQLDB and TIBCO EMS server are still running. All three services are needed for an environment to function.)

Open up a browser (Internet Explorer) and type the address of the Administrator server into the address bar—**http://localhost:8120**. You should see the Active Matrix admin server login screen.

Enter the username and password that you provided in step 6—admin/admin—to log in and view various management and configuration options for TIBCO Active Matrix.

This version of the Administrator application gives you four perspectives, each filled with functionality. Select Configure an Environment from the Perspective drop-down in the top header to view all the environments that this administrator server is managing.

Because we only have a single environment, it will be automatically selected and will display a status of **installed**. Select this row and click the Start button to start the node. Figure 13.4 shows a screenshot of ActiveMatrix Administrator Server with the node started.

Active Matrix Service Example

In this example, you build a simple Active Matrix SOA Project and create a service that returns a list of books.

The TIBCO Active Matrix suite includes a tool called Business Studio, which can be used to build SOA projects. Visual Studio templates are also available to create individual services for the .NET environment. In this section you use Business Studio to build a SOA project with a single SOAP service and deploy it to the Active Matrix node you created earlier.

Launch TIBCO Business Studio by selecting Start, All Programs, TIBCO, Business Studio 2.1, TIBCO Business Studio. When you launch Business Studio for the first time, it prompts you for a Workspace location. Workspace is where project files are stored. Enter the name of a folder that you want to use as Workspace (**c:\TBSworkspace**). Business Studio opens with a Welcome screen, which has several navigation icons to go to the Overview, Samples, and so on. Close this welcome screen by clicking the X icon in the tab to reveal the default workspace.

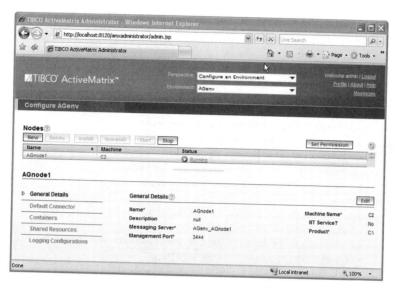

Figure 13.4   TIBCO ActiveMatrix Administrator Server GUI.

To create a new SOA Project select File, New, Active Matrix Resources, and then click the ActiveMatrix SOA project and click Next.

Enter the name of the project. **GetBooks**. in the Project Name field and click Next.

Business Studio gives a list of types of folders required for the project. You will use all of them for this project, so make sure all are checked and click Next.

Business Studio now asks for a physical location of each type of resource in the project. Accept the defaults and click the Next button for each folder until the Next button is grayed out. At this point click Finish to create the default project configuration.

Create a new WSDL for your service, **GetBooks.wsdl**, to begin creating the service. Listing 13.1 shows the GetBooks.wsdl (this file and all files for this project are also included on the companion CD-ROM). Right-click Service Descriptors within the project and select New, WSDL from the menu. Enter the filename **GetBooks.wsdl** and click Next. Make sure the Create WSDL Skeleton is unchecked and accept the defaults and then click Finish. Business Studio creates a blank WSDL document.

TIBCO Business Studio also allows you to build the WSDL for your service visually. For this example click the source tab at the bottom left of the WSDL document just above the Properties area in Business Studio and copy and paste the contents from Listing 13.1.

Listing 13.1   GetBooks.wsdl

```
<?xml version="1.0" encoding="UTF-8"?>
<wsdl:definitions xmlns:wsdl="http://schemas.xmlsoap.org/wsdl/"
```

```
        xmlns:axis2="http://com.tibcobooks.gi.chapter13/"
        xmlns:ns1="http://org.apache.axis2/xsd"
        xmlns:ns="http://com.tibcobooks.gi.chapter13.GetBooksService/xsd"
        xmlns:wsaw="http://www.w3.org/2006/05/addressing/wsdl"
        xmlns:http="http://schemas.xmlsoap.org/wsdl/http/"
        xmlns:ax21="http://chapter13.gi.tibcobooks.com/xsd"
        xmlns:xs="http://www.w3.org/2001/XMLSchema"
        xmlns:mime="http://schemas.xmlsoap.org/wsdl/mime/"
        xmlns:soap="http://schemas.xmlsoap.org/wsdl/soap/"
        xmlns:soap12="http://schemas.xmlsoap.org/wsdl/soap12/"
        targetNamespace="http://com.tibcobooks.gi.chapter13/">
        <wsdl:documentation>GetBooksService</wsdl:documentation>
        <wsdl:types>
            <xs:schema attributeFormDefault="qualified"
                elementFormDefault="qualified"
                targetNamespace="http://chapter13.gi.tibcobooks.com/xsd">
                <xs:complexType name="BookDetails">
                    <xs:sequence>
                        <xs:element minOccurs="0"
                            name="publisher" nillable="true"
                            type="xs:string"/>
                        <xs:element minOccurs="0" name="title"
                            nillable="true" type="xs:string"/>
                    </xs:sequence>
                </xs:complexType>
            </xs:schema>
            <xs:schema xmlns:ax22="http://chapter13.gi.tibcobooks.com/xsd"
                attributeFormDefault="qualified" elementFormDefault="qualified"
                \targetNamespace=
                "http://com.tibcobooks.gi.chapter13.GetBooksService/xsd">
                <xs:import namespace="http://chapter13.gi.tibcobooks.com/xsd"/>
                <xs:element name="getBooksResponse">
                    <xs:complexType>
                        <xs:sequence>
                            <xs:element maxOccurs="unbounded" minOccurs="0"
                                name="return" nillable="true" type="ax22:BookDetails"/>
                        </xs:sequence>
                    </xs:complexType>
                </xs:element>
            </xs:schema>
        </wsdl:types>
        <wsdl:message name="getBooksRequest"/>
        <wsdl:message name="getBooksResponse">
            <wsdl:part name="parameters" element="ns:getBooksResponse"/>
        </wsdl:message>
        <wsdl:portType name="GetBooksServicePortType">
```

```
        <wsdl:operation name="getBooks">
            <wsdl:input message="axis2:getBooksRequest"
                wsaw:Action="urn:getBooks"/>
            <wsdl:output message="axis2:getBooksResponse"
    wsaw:Action="urn:getBooksResponse"/>
        </wsdl:operation>
    </wsdl:portType>
</wsdl:definitions>
```

Next we will create the GetBooks Java component. Expand the Composites in Get-Books project and double-click GetBooks.composite to open up the composite designer. Click Java in the Components section in the palette on the right and make sure it is selected. Then click in the Components area within the designer to create a new component. Enter the name **GetBooksComponent**.

With the GetBooksComponent still selected, click the Service icon in the palette and then click the mouse over the newly created Java component, GetBooksComponent, to bring up the Resource Picker dialog. Expand and select GetBooksPortType in the dialog and click OK to bring up the Java Implementation dialog as shown in Figure 13.5. Enter the project and package name for the new class (**com.tibcobooks.gi.chapter13**) and let Business Studio generate the skeleton for you. Click the disk icon to save the Composite.

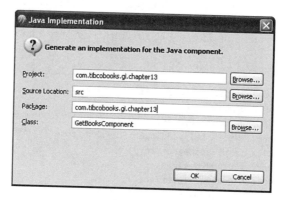

Figure 13.5   Creating a Java implementation for the GetBooksComponent.

Next we will implement the logic for the Java component. First create a new class in the project com.tibcobooks.gi.chapter13. Click the right mouse button on the package named com.tibcobooks.gi.chapter13 and select New, Class. We also have a project by that name, so be sure not to click the right mouse button over the project name. Name this class **BookDetail** and let Business Studio generate the class definition. Edit the code to make it as shown in Listing 13.2.

Listing 13.2   `BookDetail.java`

```java
package com.tibcobooks.gi.chapter13;


public class BookDetail {
 private String publisher;
 private String title;
public String getPublisher() {
    return publisher;
}
public void setPublisher(String publisher) {
    this.publisher = publisher;
}
public String getTitle() {
    return title;
}
public void setTitle(String title) {
    this.title = title;
}

}
```

Double-click the component GetBooksComponent to open up the corresponding Java class. Business Studio will show a default implementation of the service method `getBooks`. Copy the code from Listing 13.3 to return a list of two books.

Listing 13.3   Code for Method `getBooks`

```java
public GetBooksResponseDocument getBooks() {
    GetBooksResponseDocument resp =
        GetBooksResponseDocument.Factory.newInstance();
    GetBooksResponse resp1 = resp.addNewGetBooksResponse();
    BookDetails bd1 = resp1.addNewReturn();
    bd1.setPublisher("Addison Wesley");
    bd1.setTitle("TIBCO General Interface");
    BookDetails bd2 = resp1.addNewReturn();
    bd2.setPublisher("Prentice Hall");
    bd2.setTitle("TIBCO Active Matrix");
    return resp;
}
```

Our ActiveMatrix service is almost ready to be deployed. We need to create a resource and attach a SOAP Service endpoint and bind them before packaging and deploying it.

We need to create an HTTP Server resource for our service. Click the right mouse button on Shared Resource in GetBook project and select New, HTTP Server. Enter the name **GetBooksSharedResource** and click Finish to display the HTTP Server Shared Resource Editor as shown in Figure 13.6.

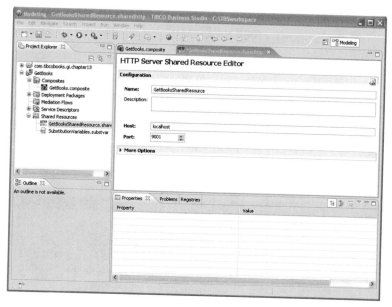

Figure 13.6   Creating an HTTP Shared Resource.

Enter the name of the resource, **GetBooksSharedResource**, and a port number (**9001**) to which the service will bind.

Click the Components canvas again to activate the Composite. Then click the Shared Resource Profile tab to bind the profile to the actual resource. Type the name of the profile (**GetBooksResourceProfile**) and select the type of the profile as HTTP. Then click in the Target column and click the ellipses button there. Select the shared resource you defined earlier (**GetBooksSharedResource.sharedhttp**) to bind to it.

Click the Save icon to save your project so far.

Now we need to add a service endpoint to allow clients to call this service. TIBCO Business Studio provides several options to expose the functionality of a component, including SOAP and JMS. We will use a SOAP service endpoint for our project.

Click the SOAP icon under Services in the palette on the right and drop it in the Services area within the main design canvas in Business Studio. While the SOAP Service icon is selected, click the General tab and click the Browse button next to the Port Type field. Select the only Port Type listed in the dialog—**GetBooksPortType**—and click OK.

Then click the Binding tab in the bottom pane and make sure that the correct resource profile shows up in the Transport Configuration section.

In the same screen, click the Generate WSDL button in the Bindings tab and save the output to a file—**GetBooksWSDL.wsdl**. We will use this .wsdl file later to implement our SOAP client in General Interface.

Click the SOAP service and drag the holder in front of it to draw a connection to the Service icon attached to the Java component GetBooksComponent. This binds the SOAP service to our Java class.

Now we need to update the Service assembly file and prepare it for creating the deployment package. Expand the Deployment Packages folder in the GetBooks project and double-click the Service Assembly file (`GetBooks.saf`) to open up the Service Assembly Editor as shown in Figure 13.7. Click the Refresh button on the top right and save by clicking the disk icon on the top left. Then click the Create Service Assembly Archive button on the top right to build the `GetBooks.zip` file that can be deployed to an ActiveMatrix node.

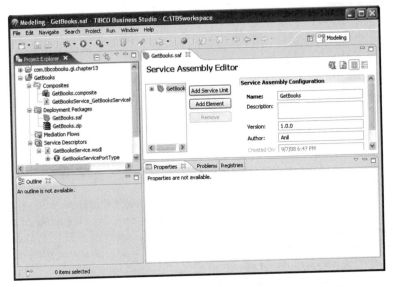

Figure 13.7   The Service Assembly Editor in Business Studio.

After building the deployment unit, log in to the TIBCO Active Matrix Administrator server and deploy the unit.

Open up an Internet Browser, go to http://localhost:8120/, and log in with your username and password that you chose during the setup process.

After logging in, select the perspective Deploy to an Environment. Unless you created multiple environments, the only configured environment will be selected and any service units deployed in it will be displayed.

Click the Upload Service Assembly button and browse to pick the `GetBooks.zip` file from the TIBCO Business Studio's workspace in the GetBooks project folder. You will find the `GetBooks.zip` file inside the Deployment Packages folder.

First you need to tell ActiveMatrix where to deploy your service units. Select the Get-Books assembly and click the Service Units tab below the list of service assemblies. Two service units will be displayed—SOAP and Java—corresponding to our SOAP service endpoint and the Java component that provides the service. Select each one in turn and click Edit on the right pane and map the service to the only available node that was created in the sections above (AGnode1).

After binding both service units to a node, we need to install the HTTP shared resource that we created for our service—GetBooksSharedResource.

Switch to the Configure an Environment perspective by selecting it from the pull-down menu in the top bar and select the only available node—AGnode1.

From the tabs, select Shared Resources and select the GetBooksShardResource. Click the Edit button and click the Yes option button to enable this shared resource. Click Save to save the current state, and then click the Install button above the list of shared resources while GetBooksSharedResource is selected to install it to the selected node.

Switch back to the Deploy to an Environment perspective in the Administrator Server. The GetBooks assembly should now be deployable. Select it and click the Deploy button to deploy the service to Active Matrix node—AGnode1.

After successfully deploying it, you will need to start it before you can connect to it from a General Interface client. Click the Start button to start the service. Its status will change to Running.

At this point your ActiveMatrix service is deployed and running.

Consuming the Response from an AMX Service in General Interface

Now you'll build a General Interface client application that consumes the response produced by the component that was built in the preceding sections.

Launch TIBCO GI Builder and start a new project—GetBooksClient. Drag and drop a Layout—Top/Over component onto the canvas. Drop a button in the top pane and change its Text property to **Get Books**.

Drag and drop a List component into the lower pane. This Matrix will display the results of the call to GetBooks service. Delete both columns mc1 and mc2 and add two Text columns. Clear the XML String contents by selecting Reset/Clear from the menu that comes up when you click the right mouse button on the name of the property. Set the name of this matrix to **booklist** and the XML Cache Id to **booklistcache**. We will bind the response from the SOAP service to this cache document later.

Create a new XML file and copy the contents of the GetBooksWSDL.wsdl file that was generated by TIBCO Business Studio in the previous section. Save this as **GetBooksPT.wsdl** in the XML folder within the folder hierarchy of the General Interface project. We will use this WSDL as the input for the XML Mapping utility.

Start the XML Mapping utility by selecting Tools, XML Mapping Utility from the menu in GI Builder.

Select the WSDL option button and click the Browse button next to the URL field. Browse to the newly created WSDL file and select Open.

Click Parse Document to parse this WSDL file in the XML Mapping utility.

GI Builder parses the document and shows a visual hierarchy of the SOAP service operations and input and output, as shown in Figure 13.8. Double-click getBooksResponse and the return nodes to expand them all.

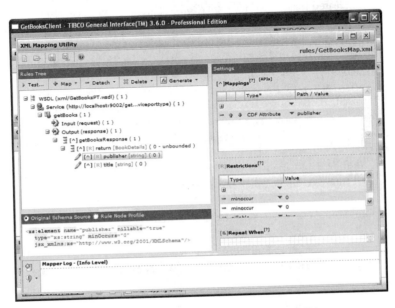

Figure 13.8   The XML Mapping Utility in GI Builder.

Select getBooksResponse in the Rules Tree and select CDF Document in the Settings pane under the Type menu. Enter the name for this document: **booklistcache**.

Select the return node in the Rules Tree panel and select CDF Record in the Settings panel under the Type menu. Do not enter anything for the Path/Value field. Every record is named "record" by default in CDF.

Select the publisher node in the Rules Tree panel and select CDF Attribute in the Settings panel under the Type menu. Enter the name **publisher** for this attribute.

Select the title node in the Rules Tree panel and select CDF Attribute in the Settings panel under the Type menu. Enter the name **title** for this attribute.

You may test your mappings by clicking the Test button in the Rules Tree. After the test is successful, click the disk icon to save the rules in the rules folder and name it **GetBooksMap.xml**. After saving the rules, you can generate the JavaScript code by clicking the Generate button in the XML Mapping Utility. The utility generates the code and places it on the Clipboard.

Close the XML Mapping Utility. Click `logic.js` in the Canvas and paste the code into it.

Only one method needs to be changed. By default, the generated code displays an alert informing you that the call was successful. Instead, we want to repaint the Matrix component with the new data. So change the method `service.ongetBooksSuccess` to match the code in Listing 13.4.

Listing 13.4   JavaScript Method `ongetBooksSuccess`

```
service.ongetBooksSuccess = function(objEvent) {
  //var responseXML = objEvent.target.getInboundDocument();
  var mat = GetBooksClient.getJSXByName("booklist");
  mat.repaintData();
};
```

GI Builder creates a method named `eg.service.callgetBooks` that calls the mapping rule we created using the mapping utility. This method needs to be invoked when the Get Books button is clicked.

In the Component Hierarchy palette in GI Builder, select the button in the top pane and click Events Editor to bring up the Events Editor pane. Enter the method call for the Execute event—`eg.service.callgetBooks();`—which will call the SOAP service and update the response.

You can use the deployment utility to create the `GetBooks.html` file and launch it using Internet Explorer to view the completed application as shown in Figure 13.9.

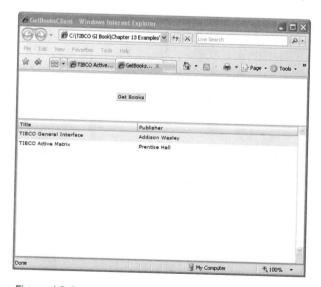

Figure 13.9   The completed General Interface application communicating with ActiveMatrix service.

14

Creating Charts in General Interface

This chapter provides an overview of charting components available with TIBCO General Interface and includes a working example of an application that uses an Area Chart component to represent a stock price. The chart is automatically updated using AJAX every five seconds.

The complete project, including the middle-tier components used to provide data for the chart, is included on the companion CD-ROM.

In addition to having several GUI widgets for use in building interactive web applications, TIBCO General Interface includes a complete set of chart components to build attractive, dynamic visual representations of data using AJAX.

TIBCO General Interface includes building blocks to create all major types of charts, including Area, Bar, Column, Line, Pie, and Bubble Plot and Point plot charts for use in your applications. The Component Guide documentation that ships with the product covers various components and properties in detail.

Charting Components in General Interface

TIBCO General Interface divides the available TIBCO General Interface components into three major groups:

- **Components subcategory**—This includes Axis for various charts, chart labels, grid lines, and legend.

- **Series subcategory**—This includes a series object for various chart types available with General Interface.

- **Individual Chart components**—These combine a predefined set of elements to create a single chart onscreen.

Each Chart component comprises several chart elements. Additional elements can be added to a chart and unwanted elements can be deleted from it as needed.

When you place a Chart component into a block, GI Builder creates the default set of elements for the chart. To customize the chart, you can manipulate the elements and their properties. For example, if you do not want a legend for the chart, click the legend element in the Component Hierarchy palette, and click the Trash icon to delete the legend element from the chart.

All chart-related classes are in the `jsx3.chart` package. All chart-related classes derive from two main base classes: `jsx3.chart.Chart` and `jsx3.chart.ChartComponent`. Figure 14.1 shows the hierarchy of `Chart` subclasses, and Figure 14.2 shows the hierarchy of `ChartComponent` subclasses.

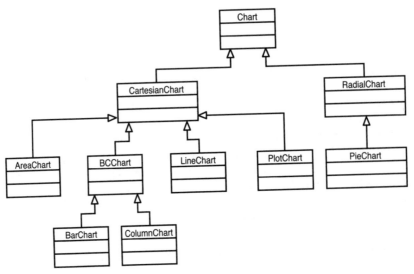

Figure 14.1   Chart subclasses.

Following are some common classes in the TIBCO General Interface Chart library:

- **jsx3.chart.AreaChart**—The main class that represents an area chart. Contains API methods to view and manipulate the area chart onscreen.
- **jsx3.chart.AreaSeries**—Represents a data series for an area chart.
- **jsx3.chart.Axis**—Base class for all types of axis.
- **jsx3.chart.BCChart**—Serves as the base class of bar and column charts. `BarChart` and `ColumnChart` inherit all methods and properties of this class.
- **jsx3.chart.BCSeries**—Base class of `BarSeries` and `ColumnSeries` contains common functionality of the two `Series` classes.
- **jsx3.chart.BarChart**—Represents a bar chart onscreen.

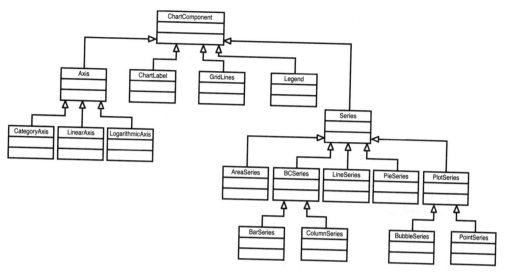

Figure 14.2   ChartComponent subclasses.

- **jsx3.chart.BarSeries**—Data series type for a jsx3.chart.BarChart; a subclass of BCSeries implements methods and properties specific to the series of a bar chart.

- **jsx3.chart.BubbleSeries**—Data series used for a jsx3.chart.BubbleChart; a subclass of PlotSeries implements functionality specific to a bubble plot series.

- **jsx3.chart.CartesianChart**—Base class for charts that are rendered with X and Y coordinates that represent a relationship between data points, such as stock price over time.

- **jsx3.chart.CategoryAxis**—Axis type that displays a set of discrete values on the X axis of a typical chart.

- **jsx3.chart.Chart**—Base class for all charts in this package. Contains methods and properties that are common to all charts—for example, a method to get the Series elements. See the class hierarchy in Figure 14.1.

- **jsx3.chart.ChartComponent**—Base class for other logical components of a chart—for example Axis, Legend, and so on. (See the class hierarchy in Figure 14.2.)

- **jsx3.chart.ChartLabel**—Displays a chart label in the chart.

- **jsx3.chart.ColumnChart**—Implements functionality for a column chart.

- **jsx3.chart.ColumnSeries**—Data series type for a ColumnChart instance. Series elements of ColumnChart are of this type.

- **jsx3.chart.GridLines**—A chart component that renders a grid of lines and fills aligned with an X and Y axis.

- **jsx3.chart.Legend**—Renders a simple legend.
- **jsx3.chart.LineChart**—A class to implement a line chart.
- **jsx3.chart.LineSeries**—Data series for a line chart.
- **jsx3.chart.LinearAxis**—A type of axis that displays a linear range of values with equal distance between any two points.
- **jsx3.chart.LogarithmicAxis**—An axis that displays a range of values logarithmically. Ticks on the axis represent a logarithmic scale.
- **jsx3.chart.PieChart**—A class for a pie chart.
- **jsx3.chart.PieSeries**—Data series for a pie chart.
- **jsx3.chart.PlotChart**—A class for a plot chart. Has common functionality for Bubble and Plot charts.
- **jsx3.chart.PlotSeries**—Base class for Point and Bubble series classes implements behavior shared by PointSeries and BubbleSeries.
- **jsx3.chart.PointSeries**—Data series used for a jsx3.chart.PointChart.
- **jsx3.chart.RadialChart**—Designed as a base class for radial charts. Pie chart is the only subclass implemented so far.
- **jsx3.chart.Series**—Base class for all data series classes.

Building the StockPrice Example

Begin by creating a new project in GI Builder. Name the new project **StockPrice** and use the steps that follow to construct the GUI for the client. Charting components are built as an add-in for TIBCO General Interface. This is to ensure that the charting component will be loaded only by applications that use them. To build the example for this chapter, add charting components to the project using the following steps:

1. Select Project Settings from the Project menu to bring up the project settings dialog as shown in Figure 14.3.

2. Click Add-Ins on the left navigation bar and click the Charting Add-In check box to enable it for this project.

3. Click the Save button in the Project Settings dialog to save your selection. GI Builder displays a message telling you that GI Builder needs to be restarted for this change to take effect.

4. Click the OK button in the alert. Restart GI Builder by closing it and then restarting it. This time GI Builder loads the Charting add-in and shows you the charting components in the Component Libraries palette, as in Figure 14.4.

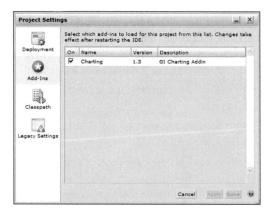

Figure 14.3   Enabling the
Charting Add-In.

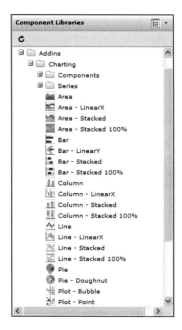

Figure 14.4   Charting components in TIBCO General
Interface.

Create the screen layout for the charting application using the following steps:

1. Drag and drop an AreaChart component onto the application canvas in GI Builder. The default area chart contains a title, an X axis, a Y axis, grid lines, two series of data, and a legend. GI Builder names it areaChart by default.

2. In the Component Hierarchy palette, select series2 (under areaChart) and delete it by clicking the Trash icon.

3. Also delete the legend by selecting the legend element and clicking the Trash icon in the Component Hierarchy palette.

4. Click the right mouse button on appCanvas.xml and select Save and Reload from the menu to see the effects of your changes so far. You will see that the legend is completely gone and that only a single line exists now instead of the two lines in the default chart.

5. Change the Text property of the title element to **Stock Price**.

6. Create a new XML file by selecting File, New, XML Document, and copy and paste the contents from Listing 14.1. (This file is also available on the companion CD-ROM.)

Listing 14.1   File stockprice.xml

```
<data jsxid="jsxroot">
<record time="9:30"  price="30.95"/>
<record time="9:40"  price="31.34"/>
<record time="9:50"  price="31.34"/>
<record time="10:00" price="33.36"/>
<record time="10:10" price="33.56"/>
<record time="10:20" price="33.26"/>
<record time="10:30" price="32.23"/>
<record time="10:40" price="33.43"/>
<record time="10:50" price="33.54"/>
<record time="11:00" price="33.23"/>
<record time="11:10" price="33.56"/>
<record time="11:20" price="33.84"/>
<record time="11:30" price="32.45"/>
<record time="11:40" price="33.43"/>
<record time="11:50" price="33.91"/>
<record time="12:00" price="33.83"/>
<record time="12:10" price="33.46"/>
<record time="12:20" price="33.39"/>
<record time="12:30" price="32.43"/>
<record time="12:40" price="33.11"/>
<record time="12:50" price="33.37"/>
<record time="13:00" price="42.29"/>
<record time="13:00" price="33.49"/>
<record time="13:10" price="33.51"/>
<record time="13:20" price="33.39"/>
<record time="13:30" price="32.30"/>
<record time="13:40" price="33.60"/>
<record time="13:50" price="33.84"/>
```

```
<record time="14:00" price="33.42"/>
<record time="14:10" price="33.56"/>
<record time="14:20" price="33.63"/>
<record time="14:30" price="32.23"/>
<record time="14:40" price="33.64"/>
<record time="14:50" price="33.85"/>
<record time="15:00" price="42.19"/>
</data>
```

7. Select File, Save from the menu, save the file in the XML folder, and name it **stockprice.xml**.

8. Close the XML file by selecting File, Close from the menu.

9. Clear the contents of the value for the XML String property of the areaChart component. To do this, click areaChart in the Component Hierarchy palette, then right-click the XML String property in the Properties Editor palette, and select Reset/Clear from the context menu. We will be supplying prices dynamically using a middle-tier component.

10. Change the XML Cache Id property of areaChart to **pricechart** and change the XML URL property to **xml/stockprice.xml**.

11. Change the LabelField property of the xAxis element to **time**. This is the name of the attribute in the CDF data that has the time values for the chart. Also change the Mn Tick Placement property of the xAxis element to **none**. This property determines whether minor ticks will be rendered in addition to the time values provided by the file.

12. Change the Label Function property of the xAxis element to the following code snippet. (This function is used to selectively display only hourly time values in the chart.)

```
function (x) { var hourmin = x.split(':');
if ( hourmin[1] == '30' ) return x; }
```

13. Change the Text property of the xTitle element to **Time**.

14. Change the Base At Zero property of the yAxis element to **FALSE**. This tells General Interface to use any reasonable base from the lowest value instead of using zero for the base.

15. Clear the Label Function property of the yAxis element by clicking the right mouse button and selecting Reset/Clear from the context menu. Removing this function will enable the default behavior for the Y Axis.

16. Change the Text property of the yTitle element to **Price**.

17. Change the Series Name property of the series1 element to `Price`, the X Field property to `time`, and Y Field property to `price`. This tells General Interface to use the value of the attribute `time` for X axis and `price` for Y axis values from the backing CDF model.

Figure 14.5 shows what the GUI will look like with the sample data provided here. In the following section, we will build the middle-tier components and put the full application together.

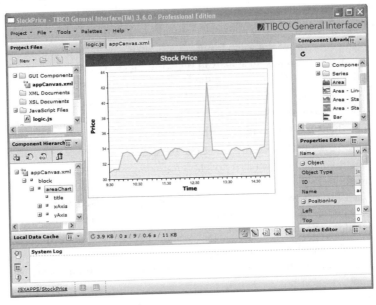

Figure 14.5   The StockPrice project in GI Builder.

Now develop the JavaScript code for the example, using the following steps:

1. Click `logic.js` and copy and paste the code from Listing 14.2.

Listing 14.2   File `logic.js` for StockPrice Project

```
function main()
{
    jsx3.require('com.tibcobooks.gi.chapter14.StockPrice');
    var sp = new com.tibcobooks.gi.chapter14.StockPrice(StockPrice);
    sp.initialize();
    com.tibcobooks.gi.chapter14.StockPrice.instance = sp;
}
```

2. Select File, Save to save the `logic.js` file.

3. Create a new JavaScript code file by selecting File, New, JavaScript File.

4. Copy and paste the code from Listing 14.3 and save it as StockPrice.js in the js/com/tibcobooks/gi/chapter14 folder, following best practices for General Interface JavaScript code. Note that you will need to create the folder hierarchy below the js folder.

Listing 14.3   File StockPrice.js for StockPrice Project

```
/*
 * This is the main controller class for StockPrice application.
 * Create a single instance of it in main by calling init only once.
 *
 * @author Anil Gurnani
 *
 */

jsx3.lang.Class.defineClass (
"com.tibcobooks.gi.chapter14.StockPrice",
null,
null,
function(StockPrice)
{
  StockPrice.instance = null;
  StockPrice.prototype.server = null;

  StockPrice.prototype.getServer = function() {
    return this.server;
  }

  StockPrice.prototype.init = function(serverobj)
  {
    this.server = serverobj;
  }

  // create exactly one instance and call this method only once
  // reason why initialize is not done in init is to avoid
  // subscribing by every instance (just in case other instances
  // are created)
  StockPrice.prototype.initialize = function()
  {
    // send subscription request
    // in this example first request
    // to get the next message
    // automatically subscribes
    // create empty doc and cache it
    var xmlDoc = new jsx3.xml.Document();
    xmlDoc.loadXML("<?xml version='1.0'?><data jsxid='jsxroot'></data>");
    this.getServer().getCache().setDocument('trades.xml',xmlDoc);
    this.getNextTick();
  }

  StockPrice.prototype.getNextTick = function()
  {
```

```
    this.sendRequest('http://localhost:8080/stockprice/GetTick');
}

StockPrice.prototype.sendRequest = function(url)
{
  var dt = new Date();
  url = url + '&requestid='+dt.getTime();

  var req = new jsx3.net.Request();
  req.subscribe(jsx3.net.Request.EVENT_ON_RESPONSE, this, 'onMessage');
  req.subscribe(jsx3.net.Request.EVENT_ON_TIMEOUT, this, 'onTimeout');
  var method = "GET";
  req.open(method, url, true);
  req.send();

}
StockPrice.prototype.onMessage = function(objEvent)
{
  var req = objEvent.target;
  var reqsponseDoc = null;
  if( req.getStatus() == 200 ) {
    responseDoc = new jsx3.xml.Document();
    var responseText = objEvent.target.getResponseText();
    jsx3.log('responseText='+responseText);
    responseDoc.loadXML( responseText );
    this.insertRecord(responseDoc);
    // post another request if not end of day
    var node = responseDoc.selectSingleNode('/data/record');
    if ( node.getAttribute('time') != '16:00' )
        this.getNextMessage();
  } else {
    this.getServer().alert('Error', 'Call failed');
  }
}

StockPrice.prototype.onTimeout = function(objEvent)
{
  // post another request
  this.getNextMessage();
}

StockPrice.prototype.insertRecord = function(responseDoc)
{
  var node = responseDoc.selectSingleNode('/data/record');
  if( node != null )
  {
    var areachart = this.getServer().getJSXByName('areaChart');
    areachart.insertRecordNode(node);
  }
}
}
);
```

5. Set the classpath for the project and set it up to call `main()` on startup. Select Project, Project Settings. Enter **main();** in the onLoad Script field in the Deployment

section of the dialog. Then click the Classpath icon in the left navigation bar and enter the values as shown in Figure 14.6. GI Builder will warn you that a restart is required for changes to take effect. Click OK to acknowledge the warning.

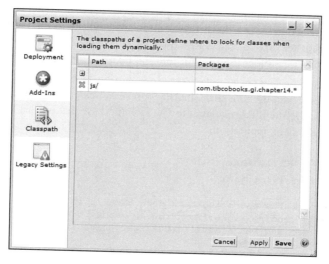

Figure 14.6   Setting the classpath for the
Chart example.

6. Close GI Builder by clicking the window Close button.

Building the Web Application

This sample uses a Java Servlet to supply the values to the client application. However, a similar component (Http Handler) as discussed in Chapter 11, "Integrating with Databases," can be used in ASP.NET to supply the data to the client built using General Interface.

Steps to build this sample web application using Eclipse are similar to the steps described in detail in Chapter 12, "Integrating with Messaging Systems," for building the rollinggrid application. High-level steps for building the stockprice application, which includes the General Interface project StockPrice, are as follows:

1. Create a new Dynamic Web Project in Eclipse named `stockprice`.

2. Import the JSX folder within the WebContent folder from the TIBCO General Interface installation folder. To do this, click the right mouse button on the WebContent folder in the Project Explorer in Eclipse, select Import from the menu, select File System, and click Next. Then click the Browse button and navigate to the TIBCO General Interface installation folder, select it, and click OK. Finally, click

the check box next to the JSX folder and `logger.xml` files to import them into the Eclipse project and click Finish.

3. Similarly, import the General Interface client application into the WebContent folder. To do this, click the right mouse button on the WebContent folder in the Project Explorer in Eclipse and select Import from the menu. Then select File System and click Next. Click the Browse button and navigate to the GI Workspace folder (`c:\GIWorkspace`), select it, and click OK. Finally, click the check box next to the StockPrice folder to import it into the Eclipse project, and click Finish.

4. Create a new Servlet `GetTickServlet.java`. Listing 14.4 shows the Java code for the sample Servlet used for this Charting sample. When creating the new Servlet in Eclipse, change the URL mapping to GetTick (because that is what was used when building the client application).

Listing 14.4   File `GetTickServlet.java`

```
/* File: GetTickServlet.java
 * Description:
 *     Servlet returns one price tick each time it is called
 *     it starts sending ticks from 9:30 on wards to every
 *     new session and sends until 4:00 after which it returns
 *     an empty data element.
 */
package com.tibcobooks.gi.chapter14;

import java.io.*;

import javax.servlet.http.*;
import javax.servlet.*;

public class GetTickServlet extends HttpServlet {
private static final long serialVersionUID = 1L;
private String[] records = {
    "<record time=\"9:30\" price=\"30.95\"/>",
    "<record time=\"9:40\" price=\"31.34\"/>",
    "<record time=\"9:50\" price=\"31.34\"/>",
    "<record time=\"10:00\" price=\"33.36\"/>",
    "<record time=\"10:10\" price=\"33.56\"/>",
    "<record time=\"10:20\" price=\"33.26\"/>",
    "<record time=\"10:30\" price=\"32.23\"/>",
    "<record time=\"10:40\" price=\"33.43\"/>",
    "<record time=\"10:50\" price=\"33.54\"/>",
    "<record time=\"11:00\" price=\"33.23\"/>",
    "<record time=\"11:10\" price=\"33.56\"/>",
    "<record time=\"11:20\" price=\"33.84\"/>",
    "<record time=\"11:30\" price=\"32.45\"/>",
    "<record time=\"11:40\" price=\"33.43\"/>",
    "<record time=\"11:50\" price=\"33.91\"/>",
    "<record time=\"12:00\" price=\"33.83\"/>",
    "<record time=\"12:10\" price=\"33.46\"/>",
```

```
    "<record time=\"12:20\" price=\"33.39\"/>",
    "<record time=\"12:30\" price=\"32.43\"/>",
    "<record time=\"12:40\" price=\"33.11\"/>",
    "<record time=\"12:50\" price=\"33.37\"/>",
    "<record time=\"13:00\" price=\"42.29\"/>",
    "<record time=\"13:00\" price=\"33.49\"/>",
    "<record time=\"13:10\" price=\"33.51\"/>",
    "<record time=\"13:20\" price=\"33.39\"/>",
    "<record time=\"13:30\" price=\"32.30\"/>",
    "<record time=\"13:40\" price=\"33.60\"/>",
    "<record time=\"13:50\" price=\"33.84\"/>",
    "<record time=\"14:00\" price=\"33.42\"/>",
    "<record time=\"14:10\" price=\"33.56\"/>",
    "<record time=\"14:20\" price=\"33.63\"/>",
    "<record time=\"14:30\" price=\"32.23\"/>",
    "<record time=\"14:40\" price=\"33.64\"/>",
    "<record time=\"14:50\" price=\"33.85\"/>",
    "<record time=\"15:00\" price=\"42.19\"/>",
    "<record time=\"15:10\" price=\"43.43\"/>",
    "<record time=\"15:20\" price=\"42.85\"/>",
    "<record time=\"15:30\" price=\"43.89\"/>",
    "<record time=\"15:40\" price=\"44.31\"/>",
    "<record time=\"15:50\" price=\"44.92\"/>",
    "<record time=\"16:00\" price=\"45.21\"/>"
};

public void doGet(HttpServletRequest req,
                  HttpServletResponse res)
    throws ServletException, IOException
{
  // give UI a chance to redraw
  try {
    Thread.sleep(100);
  } catch (InterruptedException e) {
    e.printStackTrace();
  }
  HttpSession sess = req.getSession(true);
  Integer currentTick = (Integer) sess.getAttribute("tick");
  if( currentTick == null )
    currentTick = new Integer(0);
  System.out.println("============================");
  PrintWriter out = res.getWriter();
  res.setContentType("text/xml");
  out.println("<?xml version=\"1.0\"?>");
  System.out.println("<?xml version=\"1.0\"?>");
  out.println("<data jsxid=\"jsxroot\">");
  System.out.println("<data jsxid=\"jsxroot\">");
  int intCurrentTick = currentTick.intValue();
  if( intCurrentTick >= 0 && intCurrentTick < records.length ) {
    out.println(records[intCurrentTick]);
    System.out.println(records[intCurrentTick]);
  }
  out.println("</data>");
```

```
      System.out.println("</data>");
      sess.setAttribute("tick", new Integer(intCurrentTick+1));
      out.close();
   }
}
```

5. Create an `index.html` file to launch the application using the code in Listing 14.5.

Listing 14.5   File index.html

```html
<html>
<head>
   <title>TIBCO General Interface(TM) - Professional Edition</title>
</head>

<body BGCOLOR="#9898a5" SCROLL="no"
      style="position:absolute;width:100%;height:100%;left:0px;top:0px;
             padding:0px;margin:0px;border:0px;overflow:hidden;">

<div id="jsxmain" style="position:absolute;left:0px;top:0px;
             width:100%;height:100%;">
   <script type="text/javascript" src="JSX/js/JSX30.js"
             jsxapppath="StockPrice/"
             >
   </script>
</div>

</body>
</html>
```

6. After adding all the components, click the right mouse button on the `index.html` file and select Run As, Run on Server, and then select Tomcat 5.5 from the list. You will see the application load and the area chart will render and update dynamically as the data is received from the back end. Update the 100 millisecond delay in the GetTick Servlet to adjust the motion of the graph. Figure 14.7 shows the application running in Eclipse.

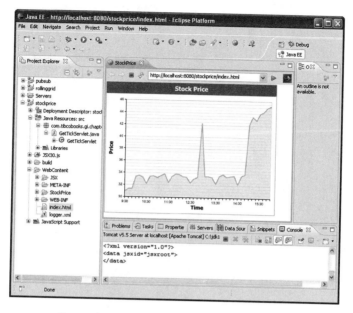

Figure 14.7   StockPrice application running in
Eclipse.

15

Using TIBCO PageBus

TIBCO PageBus, which is now OpenAJAX Hub, is a mechanism for GUI components to collaborate. This chapter explores the concepts behind TIBCO PageBus and provides a simple example that uses TIBCO PageBus.

TIBCO PageBus is a set of JavaScript functions that help client components on the same browser page communicate with each other using JavaScript.

In 2006, a group of 15 or so technology companies formed an alliance called the OpenAjax alliance (www.openajaxalliance.org). Its mission was to ensure adoption of AJAX standards and promote interoperability. TIBCO PageBus was developed as the open source reference implementation of the OpenAjax Hub specification.

Although PageBus can be used without General Interface, this chapter focuses on its use within TIBCO General Interface.

What Is PageBus?

PageBus supports one-to-many and many-to-many communications in the browser. The concept comes from a popular pattern in server-side programming known as "Pub-Sub" or "Publish and Subscribe." As the name suggests, the PageBus represents a communication "bus," which can be thought of as a channel for sending and receiving messages. Clients of the PageBus may publish messages or may subscribe to listen to the messages that are published by publishers.

A name, also known as a topic, uniquely identifies a channel or a bus. Any number of publishers may publish to one channel, and any number of subscribers may subscribe to the same channel. What's more is that a topic may be defined as a series of strings separated by a period—for example, `orders.furniture.diningroom`, `orders.furniture.livingrom`, `orders.appliances.blenders`, and `orders.appliances.refrigerators`. There are several simple rules about topic names, and they are well documented in the TIBCO PageBus developer guide.

Publishers must use a fully spelled out topic name when publishing. Clients may subscribe to topics using wildcards; so if a client wants to monitor all furniture orders, it can subscribe to the topic `orders.furniture.*` to receive messages published on any topic beginning with `orders.furniture`. The wildcard must be used for a whole segment, but it can be used anywhere in the dotted name—for example, `orders.*.lamps` or `*.*.bulbs`.

TIBCO PageBus is able to define many topics at once and manage numerous publishers and subscribers to various topics all at once. It does so with great performance. GUI applications that use PageBus will spend an order of magnitude longer when rendering to the screen than when sending or receiving messages using TIBCO PageBus.

PageBus is packaged as a single JavaScript file and can be used without using TIBCO General Interface. The JavaScript source code file `PageBus.js` can be easily included in any web page to allow components on it to communicate using PageBus. It is initialized when the file `PageBus.js` is loaded by the browser and is ready to accept publish or subscribe requests.

Obtaining PageBus

PageBus is distributed by TIBCO under the BSD license. You can download a complete package from TIBCO's website at www.tibco.com/devnet/pagebus/default.jsp. The zip file contains the `PageBus.js` file along with a comprehensive developer's guide document and several samples that show how to use the PageBus.

You only need to include the `PageBus.js` file in your HTML page to automatically create a PageBus object in the default context. JavaScript clients can then directly call methods available in PageBus to begin communicating.

Publishing Messages

The PageBus interface to publish messages is very simple. Any client who wants to publish messages can do so by invoking the `publish()` method of the PageBus object. A singleton PageBus object is automatically created when `PageBus.js` is included in the page using the `<script>` tag. Clients can invoke the methods using the singleton instance—for example, `PageBus.publish()`.

The `publish()` method takes two arguments—the topic name and the message that is to be published. The topic name must be a valid subject name as described earlier; otherwise, the method will throw a `PageBus.BadName` exception. The second argument message can be any JavaScript object.

The `publish()` method may throw another type of exception—`PageBus.StackOverflow`—which indicates that PageBus has detected a recursive loop of `publish()` and subscriber callback methods. The next section discusses this phenomena in more detail.

Subscribing to Messages

Clients who want to receive messages on a topic must subscribe to the topic using the PageBus method—`subscribe()`—which takes a total of five arguments.

The first argument is the subject name (or the topic). Subscribers are permitted to provide a subject containing wildcards. If a client subscribes to the subject `*.equity.*` it will be notified whenever a publisher publishes a message on either the `us.equity.ibm` topic or the `europe.equity.msft` topic.

The second argument to the `subscribe()` method is `scope`. which indicates whether the callback method is an instance method of an object or a static method in the default context. If your callback method belongs to a class, pass a reference to an instance of that class here. Refer to the code in Listing 15.2 for the included sample, which uses a class instance.

The third argument is the callback method. This is the function that will be called to deliver any messages on the topic of interest. This method receives three arguments from PageBus when it is called. Its first argument is the name of the exact subject where the message was published. The client may subscribe using wildcards, but this method is provided the exact subject name where the message was received. This method receives a reference to the message as the second argument, and finally it receives another argument—`subscriberData`—which is provided to PageBus by the same client in its `subscribe()` call (the next argument discussed here).

The fourth argument, `subscriberData`, is something the client can use as needed. This argument is passed back to the callback function registered by the subscribe method call. This can be used to share a single callback function among multiple subscriptions.

The fifth argument is a filter method that can be used to filter messages. The filter function is given the data first, and if it returns `False`, the callback method is not invoked, but if it returns `True`, the callback method is invoked. This filter can be used to define a fine-grained filter based on message content as the entire message is first passed to the filter function. If you do not need to filter, you can pass a null for this parameter or simply do not include it in the call to subscribe. The filter method receives all the same parameters from PageBus as the subscription callback.

It is okay to call publish from within the callback method; however, you must be careful to avoid recursive loops. A recursive loop will be caused by publishing to the same topic from the callback function of a subscriber to it. Suppose that a client subscribed to the topic `orders.songs` and registered a callback method called `songordercallback()`. Whenever a publisher publishes a message to this topic, PageBus will call this method—`songordercallback()`—with the contents of the message. Now if this method itself publishes a message on the same topic—`orders.songs`—PageBus will call it back again. Then `songordercallback()` will publish another message and PageBus will call it again. This loop will continue on and on. PageBus is designed to detect and prevent such loops. After 20 iterations, PageBus will stop publishing and instead start throwing an exception—`PageBus.StackOverflow` when you call `PageBus.publish()`.

To cancel a subscription, a client may call the `PageBus.unsubscribe()` method with the handle that was returned by the `PageBus.subscribe()` call to create that subscription.

Using the Store/Query Interface

Two new interface methods are implemented in PageBus release 1.2: `PageBus.store()` and `PageBus.query()`. Components can use the `store()` method to save some property values, which can be retrieved by other components using the `query()` method provided by PageBus.

For example, a component in the browser could save the user preference for clock type using the following code:

```
window.PageBus.store('clock.type', 'analog');
```

The clock component could then display an analog or digital clock after checking the user preference using the following code:

```
window.PageBus.store('clock.type', clock, this.drawClock(), null);
```

The preceding code snippet assumes that a JavaScript class named `clock` is defined and that it has a method called `drawClock()`, which takes as input a subject, a message, and a user data handle that can be used to correlate back to the query if the callback method is used for multiple queries.

Building the Sample Application

This sample application demonstrates the use of PageBus with TIBCO General Interface. It consists of four components:

- The first component accepts input from users and publishes a message with a new-Stock Price information.
- The second component is a subscriber that listens to all messages and displays them in a grid.
- The third component is a subscriber that filters the messages and shows only the price quotes for TIBX.
- The fourth component also filters the messages to retrieve only TIBX quotes and displays the information in a line chart.

Note that this sample does not use any middle-tier or back-end components. The entire application is contained within a single TIBCO General Interface project. Follow the next steps to build the application. All files for this application are included on the companion CD-ROM.

1. Start a new project and name it **PageBusExample**.

2. Enable charting add-in for the project in the Project Settings dialog and restart GI Builder for this change to take effect.

3. Drag and drop a Layout—Top/Over component onto the canvas.

4. Set the Rows Array property of this element to 200,200.

5. Clear the Border property for both panes of the layout component. To clear the property, select the pane in the Component Hierarchy palette, click the right mouse button on the name of the property in the Properties Editor palette, and select Reset/Clear from the menu.

6. Drag and drop a Layout—Side/Side component in each of the panes of the Layout—Top/Over component to divide the screen into four parts.

7. Set the Columns Array property to 200, 200 for each of the Layout—Side/Side components.

8. Drop form elements—two Label components, one Select Combo, one Textbox, and one Button component—and position them to create the screen for the form, as shown in Figure 15.1 in the top-left quadrant of `appCanvas.xml`.

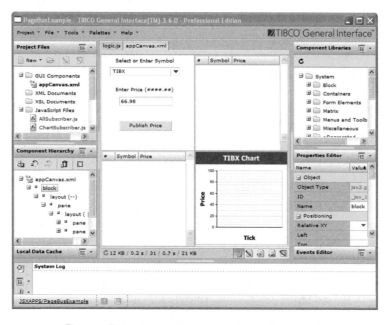

Figure 15.1   Application PageBusExample shown in
GI Builder.

9. Copy and paste the XML code from Listing 15.1 in the XML String property of the Select Combo to get the list of symbols to choose from for this application.

Listing 15.1   Content for XML String Property of the Select Combo for Symbols

```
<?xml version="1.0"?>
```

```
<data jsxid="jsxroot">
  <record jsxid="IBM" jsxtext="IBM"/>
  <record jsxid="MSFT" jsxtext="MSFT"/>
  <record jsxid="TIBX" jsxtext="TIBX"/>
  <record jsxid="ORCL" jsxtext="ORCL"/>
  <record jsxid="CNISYSTEMS" jsxtext="CNISYSTEMS"/>
  <record jsxid="ANIL" jsxtext="ANIL"/>
</data>
```

10. Drag and drop a List (Matrix) component into the top-right and bottom-left quadrants. We will display all prices published in the top-right quadrant and only TIBX prices in the bottom-left quadrant.

11. Delete default columns added in by GI Builder and add three columns to each of the List components: #, Symbol, and Price. Set the Att Name property for the three columns to be tick, symbol, and price. We will generate XML entities with these attributes to display in these grids.

    Hint: Because both List components have identical settings, you can create one component and then clone it and move it to the other quadrant as needed.

12. Clear the XML String field to remove any default values inserted by GI Builder because we will be building XML on-the-fly for these Lists.

13. Name the grid in the top-right quadrant **allquotes** (because the code refers to this component by name), and name the grid in the bottom-left quadrant **tibxquotes** (again, because the code refers to this component by name).

14. Insert a Line chart in the bottom-right quadrant. This displays the prices of TIBX in a line chart as they are published.

15. Change the title of the chart to **TIBX Chart**.

16. Change the X Axis text to Tick and the Y Axis text to Price.

17. Change the Y Field property of the **series1** element to **price** and name the chart **tibxchart**, because the source code in Listing 15.2 refers to this component.

18. To include **PageBus.js** into the project, copy the **PageBus.js** file into the **js** folder of the application and open it from GI Builder using File, Open.

19. After the file appears in the Project Files palette, make sure its Auto Load property is checked. Right-click the file and select Auto Load if it is not already checked.

20. Create a new file **AllSubscriber.js** with code as shown in Listing 15.2. Make sure to save it in a folder called **com.tibcobooks.gi.chapter15** under the **js** folder.

Listing 15.2 File **AllSubscriber.js**

```
/*
 * A class that subscribes to All quotes using PageBus.
 *
 * @author Anil Gurnani
 *
 */
```

```
jsx3.lang.Class.defineClass (
"com.tibcobooks.gi.chapter15.AllSubscriber",
null,
null,
function(AllSubscriber)
{
  AllSubscriber.prototype.server = null;

  AllSubscriber.prototype.getServer = function() {
    return this.server;
  };

  AllSubscriber.prototype.init = function(serverobj)
  {
    this.server = serverobj;
  };

  AllSubscriber.prototype.initialize = function()
  {
    PageBus.subscribe('quotes', this, this.pageBusCallback, null, null)
  };

  AllSubscriber.prototype.pageBusCallback = function(subject,
          message, subscriberData)
  {
    var tibxquotes = this.getServer().getJSXByName('allquotes');
    tibxquotes .insertRecord({jsxid: message.tick,
         tick: message.tick, symbol: message.symbol, price:
            message.price});
    tibxquotes .focusRowById(node.getAttribute("jsxid"));
  };
}
);
```

21. Create a new file named `ChartSubscriber.js` with code as shown in Listing 15.3. Make sure to save it in a folder called `com.tibcobooks.gi.chapter15` under the js folder.

Listing 15.3   File `ChartSubscriber.js`

```
/*
 * A class that subscribes to TIBX quotes using PageBus.
 *
 * @author Anil Gurnani
 *
 */

jsx3.lang.Class.defineClass (
"com.tibcobooks.gi.chapter15.ChartSubscriber",
null,
null,
function(ChartSubscriber)
{
  ChartSubscriber.prototype.server = null;
```

```
ChartSubscriber.prototype.getServer = function() {
  return this.server;
};

ChartSubscriber.prototype.init = function(serverobj)
{
  this.server = serverobj;
};

ChartSubscriber.prototype.initialize = function()
{
  PageBus.subscribe('quotes', this, this.pageBusCallback,
        null, this.pageBusFilter)
};

ChartSubscriber.prototype.pageBusFilter = function(subject,
        message, subscriberData)
{
  if( message.symbol == 'TIBX' )
    return true;
  else
    return false;
};

ChartSubscriber.prototype.pageBusCallback = function(subject,
        message, subscriberData)
{
  var tibxchart = this.getServer().getJSXByName('tibxchart');
  tibxchart.insertRecord({jsxid: message.tick, tick: message.tick,
        symbol: message.symbol, price: message.price});
};

}
);
```

22. Create a new file named **TIBXSubscriber.js** with code as shown in Listing 15.4. Make sure to save it in a folder called com.tibcobooks.gi.chapter15 under the js folder.

Listing 15.4   File TIBXSubscriber.js

```
/*
 * A class that subscribes to TIBX quotes using PageBus.
 *
 * @author Anil Gurnani
 *
 */

jsx3.lang.Class.defineClass (
"com.tibcobooks.gi.chapter15.TIBXSubscriber",
null,
null,
function(TIBXSubscriber)
{
  TIBXSubscriber.prototype.server = null;
```

```
    TIBXSubscriber.prototype.getServer = function() {
      return this.server;
    };

    TIBXSubscriber.prototype.init = function(serverobj)
    {
      this.server = serverobj;
    };

    TIBXSubscriber.prototype.initialize = function()
    {
      PageBus.subscribe('quotes', this, this.pageBusCallback,
            null, this.pageBusFilter)
    };

    TIBXSubscriber.prototype.pageBusFilter = function(subject, message,
            subscriberData)
    {
      if( message.symbol == 'TIBX' )
        return true;
      else
        return false;
    };

    TIBXSubscriber.prototype.pageBusCallback = function(subject,
      message, subscriberData)
    {
      var tibxquotes = this.getServer().getJSXByName('tibxquotes');
      tibxquotes .insertRecord({jsxid: message.tick, tick: message.tick,
            symbol: message.symbol, price: message.price});
      tibxquotes .focusRowById(node.getAttribute("jsxid"));
    };

}
);
```

23. Copy and paste the code from Listing 15.5 into the `logic.js` file.

Listing 15.5   File `logic.js`

```
function main()
{
  jsx3.require('com.tibcobooks.gi.chapter15.TIBXSubscriber');
  var s1 = new
    com.tibcobooks.gi.chapter15.TIBXSubscriber(PageBusExample);
  s1.initialize();

  jsx3.require('com.tibcobooks.gi.chapter15.AllSubscriber');
  var s2 = new com.tibcobooks.gi.chapter15.AllSubscriber(PageBusExample);
  s2.initialize();

  jsx3.require('com.tibcobooks.gi.chapter15.ChartSubscriber');
  var s3 = new
```

```
    com.tibcobooks.gi.chapter15.ChartSubscriber(PageBusExample);
  s3.initialize();
}

var tickNumber = 1;

function doPublish(serverObj)
{
  var pricefield = serverObj.getJSXByName('pricefield');
  if( !pricefield.doValidate() )
  {
    alert('Price is not in valid format');
    return;
  }

  var symbolfield = serverObj.getJSXByName('symbolfield');
  PageBus.publish('quotes', { tick: tickNumber,
          symbol: symbolfield.getValue(), price:
              pricefield.getValue() });
  tickNumber = tickNumber + 1;
}
```

24. Set the classpath in the Project Settings dialog to include path `js/` for `com.tibcobooks.gi.chapter15.*` classes.

25. Set the `onLoad` script to call the main function in `logic.js` by going to the Project Settings dialog.

26. Use the deployment utility to generate an HTML file to launch the application.

Note that the only difference between `AllSubscriber.js` and `TIBXSubscriber.js` is that `TIBXSubscriber.js` uses a filter when subscribing that is used to discard all other messages except those for the symbol TIBX. `ChartSubscriber.js` does the same thing as well, and it uses the quotes to update the chart.

Figure 15.2 shows the application running in the browser. You can click the `PageBusExample.html` file included in the Chapter 15 examples folder on the companion CD-ROM to view this application in action.

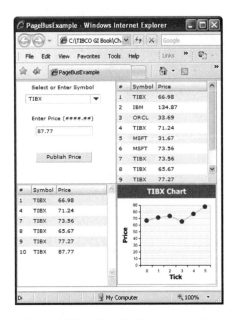

Figure 15.2   PageBusExample application running in the browser.

16

Optimizing Performance

TIBCO General Interface not only includes tools to measure performance, it also includes a wide array of features to improve the overall application performance. This chapter discusses tools and techniques available to developers to optimize the performance of General Interface applications.

Measuring Performance

It is very important to be able to measure performance before attempting to improve it. GUI performance is often measured with a stopwatch to see how long it takes for a page to load. This approach works for web applications that return plain HTML (and CSS) to the browser because there is little or no processing after the page is downloaded to the client.

However, TIBCO General Interface applications often involve several processes to render the output screens. Although it might seem that this would cause General Interface applications to be slower because they need to process data, it is not true. That's because General Interface leverages microprocesses known as threads in your browser to render multiple parts of the screen simultaneously. This improves rendering time of the overall page. It also employs other techniques, such as asynchronous loading of components and data, to further enhance the performance, as we will see in the following sections.

A GI Performance Profiler tool is available as a separate download from TIBCO's website, and it comes with lots of samples and good documentation. Complete coverage of GI Performance Profiler (or GIPP) is outside the scope of this book.

TIBCO also publishes a Debug build version of General Interface, which is a great tool by itself because it includes benchmarking logs that can be enabled easily. Live benchmark logging when General Interface components process and display data is very useful in identifying and fixing performance issues in General Interface applications.

Using the Debug Version

On the General Interface download site at www.tibco.com/devnet/gi/default.jsp, the
main download link lets you download a debug version of the product. The debug version of General Interface is a great tool for measuring performance of your application.

You can view performance characteristics of an application by enabling logging for it.
We will use the application PageBusExample from the previous chapter to see how to
measure performance of various parts of General Interface programs.

Enabling Logging in General Interface

To enable logging, the `logger.xml` file needs to be modified. By default the `<handler>`
element is commented out in `logger.xml`. Uncomment this element by moving the
comment close characters (`-->`) to a line before the beginning of the `<handler>` element
in the `logger.xml` file to make sure it is not commented out. Also make sure that the
value of the `serverNameSpace` property is set to your application name (`PageBusExample`
for our example).

The only other change needed is in the global logger element—that is, the `<logger>`
element with the attribute name equal to global. This is the global logger. You can also
configure a custom logger for smaller parts of the General Interface application by following instructions provided in General Interface's documentation. We will use the global
logger for the exercise in this chapter because that is sufficient for most purposes. Custom
loggers are a powerful feature of TIBCO General Interface for large-scale GUI development in large teams. You can also use the `activateOnHotKey` property to hide the log
monitor window by default and bring it up by pressing Ctrl+Alt+M at the same
time.

In the default `logger.xml` file the `<handler-ref>` element with the name of
`appMonitor1` is commented out. Uncomment this line to enable the monitor window.
You can use the `jsx3.log()` method to send any string to this log window. This is very
useful when debugging General Interface applications.

Viewing Benchmark Logs

The debug build of General Interface includes benchmark logging for all major components. Change the level of the logger named bench to DEBUG or INFO to enable
benchmark logging. Listing 16.1 shows the version of `logger.xml` after making all the
preceding changes to enable a monitor window that will display benchmark and any
other embedded logs from the application. The modified sections have been highlighted
using bold text.

Listing 16.1   Modified `logger.xml` to Display a Log Monitor Window and Benchmarking Logs

```
<!--
  ~ Copyright (c) 2001-2007, TIBCO Software Inc.
  ~ Use, modification, and distribution subject to terms of license.
```

```
-->

<configuration>

  <!-- Caches the most recent logging messages in memory.
       Note that Builder assumes that there is a MemoryHandler
           instance registered as 'memory',
       although it will fail quietly if a dependent operation is attempted. -->
  <handler name="memory" class="jsx3.util.Logger.MemoryHandler">
    <property name="bufferSize" eval="true" value="1000"/>
  </handler>

  <!-- Prints logging messages to Builder's system out panel.
       For logging in Builder to work there should be exactly one handler of
           type SystemLogHandler
       defined here. -->
  <handler name="ide" class="jsx3.ide.SystemLogHandler" lazy="true">
    <property name="bufferSize" eval="true" value="0"/>
    <property name="format" value="%t %n (%l) - %M"/>
    <property name="beepLevel" eval="true" value="jsx3.util.Logger.OFF"/>
  </handler>

  <!-- Sends a formatted logging message to a JavaScript alert. -->
  <handler name="alerter" class="jsx3.util.Logger.AlertHandler" level="ERROR">
    <property name="format" value="%t %n (%l) - %M"/>
  </handler>
<!-- Ensures that any fatal error is displayed in a JavaScript alert.
Fatal messages usually relate to failure to
       initialize the system or load an application and so may indicate
           that other handlers are not visible. -->
  <handler name="fatal" class="jsx3.util.Logger.AlertHandler" level="FATAL">
    <property name="format" value="%t %n (%l) - %M"/>
  </handler>

  <!-- Register an application monitor handler. When the application
           with namespace "myApp" is running outside
           of GI Builder, a separate browser window will open and receive
           logger messages. The require="true"
           attribute is required when running under as-needed class loading
           (jsxlt) because jsx3.app.Monitor is an
       optional class.

       serverNamespace - must match the namespace of the application
           to attach to. If this attribute is omitted
           completely, the monitor window is not associated with a particular
           application and the disableInIDE and
```

```
        activateOnHotKey attributes have no meaning.
     disableInIDE (default:true) - disables the application monitor
       while the IDE is running.
     activateOnHotKey (default:false) - disables the application
       monitor until the hot key ctrl+alt+m is pressed
       in the application.

-->
<handler name="appMonitor1" class="jsx3.app.Monitor" require="true">
  <property name="serverNamespace" value="PageBusExample"/>
  <property name="disableInIDE" eval="true" value="true"/>
  <property name="activateOnHotKey" eval="true" value="false"/>
  <property name="format" value="%t %n (%l) - %M"/>
</handler>

<!-- The global logger. -->
<logger name="global" level="INFO">
  <handler-ref name="memory"/>
  <handler-ref name="ide"/>
  <handler-ref name="fatal"/>
  <handler-ref name="appMonitor1"/>
</logger>

<logger name="jsx3" level="DEBUG"/>
<logger name="jsx3.ide" level="WARN"/>
<logger name="bench" level="DEBUG"/>
     <!-- "bench" and its descendants are used by GI benchmarking code -->

<!-- Since an error in the logging system may mean that other
     handlers are not working, we'll send any error to
     a JavaScript alert with the alerter handler. -->
<logger name="jsx3.util.Logger" level="WARN" useParent="false">
  <handler-ref name="alerter"/>
</logger>

</configuration>
```

Figure 16.1 shows how the logs will be displayed using the logger.xml in Listing 16.1

Identifying and Eliminating Redundant Calls to Render

The debug build includes the capability to point out redundant calls to methods that render onscreen. Browsers take a significant amount of time rendering information, and the time taken varies with browsers and the method used by the application. Therefore, it is very important to avoid redundant calls to render.

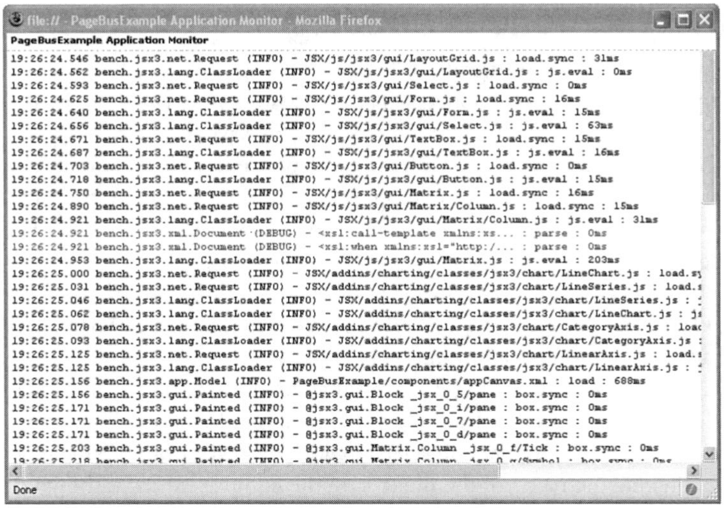

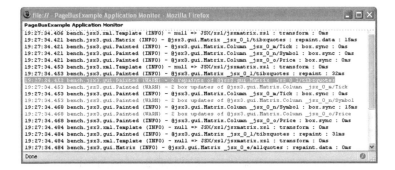

Figure 16.1   GI Application Monitor window showing
benchmark logs.

The debug build of General Interface includes logging to detect such redundant calls
to render. For example, if you make an API call that already repaints the component, there
is no need to explicitly call the `repaint()` method of the component after it. The example includes a redundant call to the `repaint()` method, which causes General Interface
to display a warning in a different color in the benchmark logs.

Figure 16.2 shows the General Interface application monitor window pointing out the
redundant call to the `repaint()` method.

Figure 16.2   General Interface Debug build points
out redundant calls to the `repaint()` method.

Using Asynchronous Loading

General Interface supports asynchronous loading of components. When a screen is made up of multiple independent components, its initial load performance can be dramatically improved by loading all components simultaneously in separate threads.

At design time, the architects must identify independent GUI components and create them as separate components. These components must then be imported using the menu option Referenced—Asynchronous into the main General Interface canvas. This tells General Interface to load these components asynchronously.

This section describes how to convert parts in the existing application of Chapter 14, "Creating Charts in General Interface," into individual components, and then import them to load asynchronously at runtime.

Individual components can also be exported as XML to be imported back in so that they are referenced asynchronously. This can be done in GI Builder. Click the right mouse button on the component and select Export, As XML from the menu as shown in Figure 16.3. Provide the name of the file to save the component in, as shown in Figure 16.4, to save the components as individual XML files.

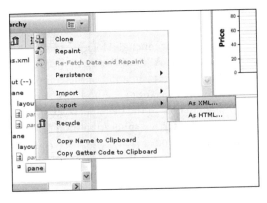

Figure 16.3   Exporting a component as XML.

To import a component, click the right mouse button in the component under which you want to import the component and select Import, Referenced—Asynchronous from the menu, as shown in Figure 16.5, and select the component to be imported in the File dialog. After the component has been imported, delete the embedded pane component by selecting it and clicking the Trash icon. Note that you will need to embed an empty block in the Layout component first and then import the referenced component into it. This is because a Layout component must contain at least one embedded pane.

After following the preceding steps for all four panes of the PageBusExample application, the Component Hierarchy palette will look like Figure 16.6. When you launch the

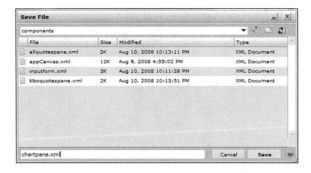

Figure 16.4   Saving as an independent component file.

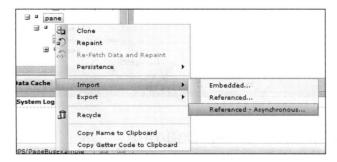

Figure 16.5   Importing an independent component from a file.

application after making these changes, you will see each quadrant painting asynchronously. For larger components or those containing data, you will see a significant difference in initial load performance of the application if the components are referenced asynchronously.

In addition to loading components asynchronously, you can load the data behind the data bound controls asynchronously. For example, a matrix that needs to load a large number of rows and columns before displaying will benefit by setting its XML Async property to Asynchronous.

Another way to achieve similar results is to set the Load Type property in the Metadata section for the component. This property controls how General Interface treats the subtree below the node. The Load Type can be set to one of Normal, Paint Async, Deserialize Async, Paint and Deserialize Async, Paint on Show, and Deserialize on Show. Each mode's name indicates the effect it has on the component (or the subtree). For example, to load and paint asynchronously, you would set the property to Paint and Deserialize Async. Paint refers to rendering of the component onscreen and Deserialize refers to the process of loading the component from the server and instantiating it in memory.

Figure 16.6   Component
Hierarchy palette showing the
layout of panes.

Using Dynamic Class Loading

TIBCO General Interface supports dynamic class loading, which means that it is capable of loading JavaScript files on demand instead of loading them all on initial load as in traditional web programming. All examples in this book make use of dynamic class loading.

There are two separate methods for loading a JavaScript class—`jsx3.require()` and `jsx3.loadInclude()`. The main difference between the two methods is that `jsx3.require()` is a synchronous method, and when it returns, the class has definitely been loaded. The method `jsx3.loadInclude()`, on the other hand, sends an asynchronous request to load the JavaScript file, and when it returns the complete file might not yet be loaded. The `jsx3.require()` method also checks to see whether the file is already loaded in the browser DOM, and does nothing if it has already been loaded.

The recommended approach is to set up a function to run in a separate thread in JavaScript in the `onLoad` script. Use `jsx3.loadInclude()` calls to load all the classes that might be needed in this thread. Then use `jsx3.require()` just before each class is used to ensure it has been loaded. This will offer the best performance. However, do not load all classes up front (even in a separate thread) if they will cause the browser to use up a big chunk of memory.

Using the Merge Tool

General Interface ships with a simple shell script `gi_merge.sh` to allow you to merge a large set of JavaScript files into a single file and obfuscate the methods and variable names to be as short as possible. This is done while making sure that all references to the variables and methods are changed properly. This process also removes all comments from JavaScript files. Obfuscating JavaScript files in this way makes them much smaller in size so they can be loaded quickly.

Another aspect of the merge tool is that it puts together all the classes into a single JavaScript file to enable loading of all classes in a single download from the server.

The functionality offered by the merge tool and that offered by dynamic class loading are opposite in nature. Architects must carefully determine the balance required to achieve the best performance for an application using both techniques.

The recommended approach is to merge all the classes that are needed for the initial screen into a single file using the merge tool and then individually obfuscate all the JavaScript files so that they can be downloaded on demand. Obfuscating them reduces the size of each individual file and enables quick loading, and keeping them as separate files enables on-demand loading.

Preferring XSLT over JavaScript

Because General Interface provides a full client-side API in JavaScript, it might be tempting to write JavaScript programs that use the API to build screens on-the-fly on the client side. Be aware that it takes almost ten times as much processing to execute a JavaScript program as it does to run an XSLT merge using the XML processor available to the browser. Therefore, use XSLT whenever possible to display components with a large data set—for example, a matrix with thousands of rows.

General Interface components consume XML in CDF format; however, all back-end applications do not produce CDF files. Use the XML Transformer property in General Interface components to tell General Interface to use an XSL style sheet to convert input XML from a back-end process into CDF format.

This technique was used in the dow30xsl example in Chapter 4, "Working with XML and XSL." Use of the XSL style sheet ensures the greatest flexibility in generating generic XML from the back end. It also ensures that the back end can be designed to work well with other clients, such as Java SWING, or Microsoft MFC-based programs.

Using Paging Models in Matrix

The Matrix component in General Interface supports two paging models that can be used to improve performance of grids as they render rows onscreen.

The first model is No-Paging, which does no paging whatsoever and simply renders the entire HTML onscreen when it is done.

The second model, 2-Pass, is the default but has poor performance for larger data sets. In this model, General Interface will first render the rows for the grid, then render data for all rows, and then display it onscreen. So if a grid has 1,000 rows, General Interface will first generate HTML for all 1,000 rows and then display them onscreen. This causes the screen to appear frozen for a while until all HTML is rendered. The table begins to appear as the data is rendered in rows. This model is good for grids with a small number of rows (fewer than 30). For a large number of rows, it is better to use one of the Paged or Chunked models described next.

The Paged model divides the set of rows to a number of pages, and each page is rendered using the 2-Pass model described previously. Each page is painted onscreen as it is rendered. Three parameters can be used to tune this mode. Panel Pool Size indicates how many panels are rendered in a single pool; Rows per Panel defines how many rows are in each panel; and Panel Queue Size determines the limit of the number of panels that can be pending to be rendered at any given time. This method uses threads very efficiently to paint table data onscreen in a highly parallel fashion.

The Chunked model is similar to the Paged model, except it assumes a fixed height for the rows and therefore is the fastest in rendering data onscreen. In the Chunked model, General Interface assumes that the height of each row is fixed and renders chunks of rows at a time.

You can see the effect of changing these models and related parameters by making changes to the sample application oilconsumption in Chapter 8, "Advanced Features of Matrix," because it has a large set of rows and columns.

Index

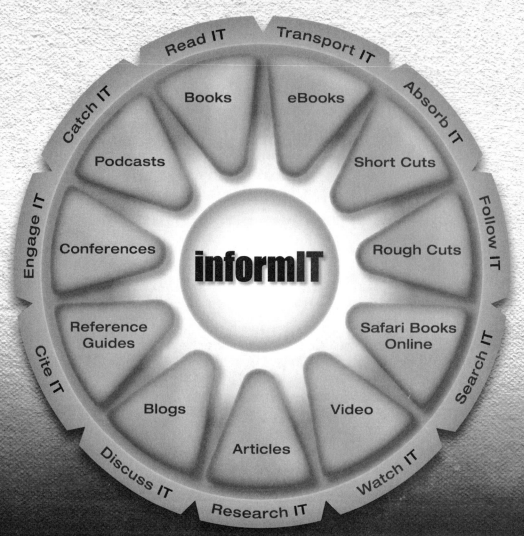

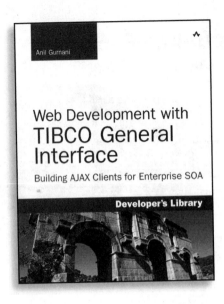

FREE Online Edition

Your purchase of **Web Development with TIBCO General Interface: Building AJAX Clients for Enterprise SOA** includes access to a free online edition for 45 days through the Safari Books Online subscription service. Nearly every Addison-Wesley Professional book is available online through Safari Books Online, along with more than 5,000 other technical books and videos from publishers such as Cisco Press, Exam Cram, IBM Press, O'Reilly, Prentice Hall, Que, and Sams.

SAFARI BOOKS ONLINE allows you to search for a specific answer, cut and paste code, download chapters, and stay current with emerging technologies.

Activate your FREE Online Edition at
www.informit.com/safarifree

> **STEP 1:** Enter the coupon code: FRYFZCB.

> **STEP 2:** New Safari users, complete the brief registration form.
> Safari subscribers, just log in.

If you have difficulty registering on Safari or accessing the online edition,
please e-mail customer-service@safaribooksonline.com